# ALCOHOL, ADDICTION AND CHRISTIAN ETHICS

Addictive disorders are characterised by a division of the will, in which the addict is attracted both by a desire to continue the addictive behaviour and also by a desire to stop it. Academic perspectives on this predicament usually come from clinical and scientific standpoints, with the 'moral model' rejected as outmoded. But Christian theology has a long history of thinking and writing on such problems and offers insights which are helpful to scientific and ethical reflection upon the nature of addiction. Christopher Cook reviews Christian theological and ethical reflection upon the problems of alcohol use and misuse, from biblical times until the present day. Drawing particularly upon the writings of St Paul the Apostle and Augustine of Hippo, a critical theological model of addiction is developed. Alcohol dependence is also viewed in the broader ethical perspective of the use and misuse of alcohol within communities.

CHRISTOPHER C. H. COOK is Professorial Research Fellow in the Department of Theology and Religion, Durham University, England and a consultant psychiatrist. He is co-author of *The Treatment of Drinking Problems*, 4th edn (2003).

NEW STUDIES IN CHRISTIAN ETHICS

*General Editor: Robin Gill*
*Editorial Board: Stephen R. L. Clark, Stanley Hauerwas, Robin W. Lovin*

Christian ethics has increasingly assumed a central place within academic theology. At the same time the growing power and ambiguity of modern science and the rising dissatisfaction within the social sciences about claims to value-neutrality have prompted renewed interest in ethics within the secular academic world. There is, therefore, a need for studies in Christian ethics which, as well as being concerned with the relevance of Christian ethics to the present-day secular debate, are well informed about parallel discussions in recent philosophy, science or social science. *New Studies in Christian Ethics* aims to provide books that do this at the highest intellectual level and demonstrate that Christian ethics can make a distinctive contribution to this debate – either in moral substance or in terms of underlying moral justifications.

**New Studies in Christian Ethics**
*Titles published in the series:*

# ALCOHOL, ADDICTION AND CHRISTIAN ETHICS

CHRISTOPHER C. H. COOK

CAMBRIDGE
UNIVERSITY PRESS

CAMBRIDGE UNIVERSITY PRESS
Cambridge, New York, Melbourne, Madrid, Cape Town, Singapore, São Paulo, Delhi

Cambridge University Press
The Edinburgh Building, Cambridge CB2 8RU, UK

Published in the United States of America by Cambridge University Press, New York

www.cambridge.org
Information on this title: www.cambridge.org/9780521851824

First published 2006
This digitally printed version 2008

A catalogue record for this publication is available from the British Library

ISBN 978-0-521-85182-4 hardback
ISBN 978-0-521-09134-3 paperback

#2184
17 MAR 2010

*This book is dedicated to*
*Ruth Elizabeth Cook*
*1955 to 1985*

*'Love is strong as death,*
*passion fierce as the grave'*
*(Song of Solomon 8:6)*

# Contents

# General editor's preface

This book is the twenty-seventh in the series *New Studies in Christian Ethics*. It is also the third in succession on a medically related issue – a subject largely unexplored in earlier books in the series. The twenty-fifth book was Celia Deane-Drummond's *Genetics and Christian Ethics*, and the twenty-sixth was my own *Health Care and Christian Ethics*. As a qualified doctor, psychiatrist and now Anglican priest, Christopher Cook has the added advantage of both clinical and pastoral experience in this area. It makes him particularly well qualified to fulfil the two key aims of the series as a whole – namely, to promote monographs in Christian ethics which engage centrally with the present secular moral debate at the highest possible intellectual level and, secondly, to encourage contributors to demonstrate that Christian ethics can make a distinctive contribution to this debate.

Christopher Cook's clinical work in the area of alcohol dependence has convinced him that there is a gap in much secular discussion. While he is critical of simplistic moralistic approaches to alcoholism (especially the nineteenth-century Christian Temperance Movement) and is deeply informed by modern biosocial studies, he argues that a careful use of Paul's and Augustine's notion of the divided self can still make a significant contribution today. The latter can suggest an important link between our experience of ourselves and that of those with a medical disorder of severe alcohol dependence. A proper sense of humility can help us to see that some experience of addiction – whether it involves alcohol, food, sex, or simply shopping – is an everyday reality in which each of us experiences a divided self. In addition, he argues that the need for grace is an essential component in any adequate response to addictive disorders – whether it is the explicit Christian concept of God's grace in Jesus Christ or the rather vaguer notion of the need for the 'Higher Power' of Alcoholics Anonymous. Indeed, at an empirical level, he suggests that spiritual or religious experience is often and unsurprisingly associated with recovery from addiction (tortuous as it often is).

This well-written book is a helpful and important contribution to *New Studies in Christian Ethics* and deserves to be read widely.

ROBIN GILL

# Preface

All sciences being connected together, and having bearings one on another, it is impossible to teach them all thoroughly, unless they all are taken into account, and Theology among them.

(John Henry Newman)[1]

It is now twenty years since I first began working as a psychiatrist with people suffering from addictive disorders. From the first, this area of work was for me both a subject of academic inquiry as well as one of clinical endeavour on behalf of those who struggle within themselves. My Christian faith preceded this work, and in many ways motivated it, but it was only much later in life that I was drawn towards the study of academic theology. I was motivated in my studies both by an extension of academic curiosity to another way of understanding human experience and also by a belief that it is only in the light of the grace of God in Christ that we can fully and truly understand our experience as human beings in this world. That belief has not fundamentally changed, but it has grown as I have attempted to explore the nature of human experience as biological, social and psychological as well as spiritual, in its relation to the incarnation of God in Christ. In theological terms, it seems to me that the grace of God in Christ is the hermeneutical key to understanding human being.

The hermeneutical task in theology is often, although by no means always, concerned with texts. My interest in hermeneutics is concerned both with the text of Christian scripture and also with the metaphorical text of human experience. In particular, in the context of the present work, it seems to me that interpretation of the 'text' of the experience of addiction is better achieved when the natural and social sciences are brought together with theology as tools to assist in undertaking the hermeneutical task. As Newman argued in *The Idea of a University* ([1852] 1996),

[1] Newman, [1852] 1996, p. 75.

xi

all areas of learning are interconnected. The exclusion of theology from
the process of interpreting human experience can therefore be seen only
to impoverish our understanding of that experience, unless, of course, one
begins with prior atheistic assumptions concerning the human 'text' and
its context.

With a few notable exceptions, under the influence of the Enlightenment, the vast interdisciplinary literature that surrounds addiction and
alcohol studies has come to exclude theology. It is my conviction that we
are much poorer as a result, and I offer this book as a small contribution
towards correcting the deficiency. However, I could not have written it
without the help of many friends and colleagues, towards whom I am glad
to acknowledge my debt of gratitude here.

Many of the debts that I owe are explicitly acknowledged in the text,
where I have quoted other authors, living and dead. I am especially grateful
to Paul of Tarsus and Augustine of Hippo, whom I have obviously never met
face to face, but whom I have come to know through the texts that they left
behind them, and with whom I share in the communion of saints. Among
those living friends and colleagues who have helped me in ways that are not
explicitly acknowledged elsewhere in the text of this book, I would like to
thank Professor John Barclay, Professor Virginia Berridge, Dr John Court,
Professor Griffith Edwards, and three anonymous reviewers, each of whom
read one or more of the draft chapters of this book and kindly provided
helpful comments having done so. Griffith has also been an author, mentor
and friend from whom I have learned much about addiction over the years,
and my debt to him in these respects is especially great.

Numerous other colleagues and students have recommended reading,
posed important questions, discussed ideas and generally encouraged me
during the course of my writing this book. I cannot mention them all
by name, but I would particularly like to thank Dr Carol Harrison, with
whom I much enjoyed discussing the section on Augustine of Hippo, and
Derek Rutherford and other colleagues at the Institute for Alcohol Studies
in London. I am also grateful to the latter, and especially to Judith Crowe,
for allowing me to use, and assisting me with access to, the almost unique
collection of temperance publications that is held in their library.

I am greatly indebted to Dr Katharina Brett, Senior Commissioning
Editor, Religious Studies, at Cambridge University Press, and to Canon
Professor Robin Gill, Series Editor. They have both offered much encouragement and constructive advice on numerous occasions. Robin has also
taught me much of what I know about applied theology, and has been a

valued friend. This book would not have been written but for his patient, unfailing and wise support.

Finally, my thanks go, as always, to my wife Joy, and to Andrew, Beth, Rachel and Jonathan, for the countless loving ways in which they have provided such an important part of the context within which this text was written.

# THE
# TEMPERANCE EXAMINER.

" Prove all things; hold fast that which is good."—*St. Paul.*

No. 11.]  NOVEMBER 1, 1839.  [PRICE 1*d.*

**"WHICH WAY SHALL I TURN ME?"**  *or, Ruin and Salvation.*

OLD FUDDLER.—Come along, Charley my boy; come along! *Only just one glass!* A short life and a merry one! that's my ticket.

CHARLES.—Well, your'e a good-natured fellow, tho' you've ruined yourself by drinking. I was thinking about abstaining; but surely *one glass* won't hurt me!

TEE-TOTALLER.—Don't listen to him, my dear Charles. You see what drinking has done for him. If you take *one glass* you won't know when to stop. You promised to go to our meeting. Come, and learn the blessings of Total Abstinence.

PRINTED AND PUBLISHED BY J. PASCO, 90, BARTHOLOMEW CLOSE, LONDON.

From *The Temperance Examiner*, no. 11, 1 November 1839

# CHAPTER I

# Alcohol, addiction and Christian ethics: introduction

Alcohol has many and contrasting associations. A glass of wine with a meal can symbolise love, friendship, relaxation and enjoyment of a special occasion. It can represent romance, coming of age, success, beginnings and endings, good news and good company. At a Christian Eucharist or Jewish Passover, where wine is also shared, thanks are given to God for divine salvation from all that enslaves, restricts and condemns. In drinking the wine, Christians participate with the first disciples in their last supper with Christ, and Jews participate with the ancient Hebrews in their exodus from enslavement in Egypt. But sadly, the sacredness and redemptiveness of these occasions contrasts with the associations of alcohol with drunken violence in our towns and cities, cirrhosis of the liver on our medical wards, debt in families, and death on our roads. It contrasts also, and more especially, with the enslavement that is alcoholism, or alcohol addiction.

In more purely statistical and objective terms, alcohol misuse is a contemporary social problem of enormous economic significance, which exacts a high toll of human suffering as a result of the social, psychological and medical harms to which it gives rise. Alcohol-related morbidity and mortality are high in most parts of the world, and in many developing nations alcohol consumption and its concomitant harms are on the increase.[1] Yet, moderate alcohol consumption is tolerated, enjoyed and encouraged in most countries around the world, with the majority of the adult population being drinkers of alcohol, in almost all countries other than those with an Islamic culture.[2]

What are we to make of these observations? It is easy to project blame to a safe distance by arguing that they are the responsibility of other people or forces beyond our control. Governments, industries and

---

[1] World Health Organization, 1999.

[2] This is not to suggest that problems of alcohol misuse are not significant in Islamic countries. Although a minority of people drink alcohol, often contrary to the law and therefore in secrecy, some of the alcohol-related problems experienced by these people are extremely serious.

moderate drinkers can blame a minority of irresponsible citizens for their excesses. The beverage alcohol industry can easily be blamed for promoting a product which causes so much harm. Or else, the product itself can be blamed and made the subject of prohibition, on the basis that everyone would be better off if it were not consumed at all in civilised society.

But perhaps no-one needs to be 'to blame' at all? Rather than blaming people for being irresponsible – whether in their own drinking behaviour or their promotion of alcohol in society so as to cause harm indirectly – and rather than blaming alcohol itself, as though it had some demonic and ubiquitous power to bring innocent people to ruin, perhaps the problem is better understood more in terms of disease? Perhaps some people are exceptionally vulnerable, because of a disease of some kind, in such a way that (although they are not really to blame for it themselves) alcohol causes them harm, and through them harms other people too. This disease might be understood simply as that of having a liver, or brain, or other organ system, which is peculiarly sensitive to the toxic effects of alcohol. Or, in a more complex fashion, it might be understood as a disease affecting the moral and spiritual nature of human beings in such a way as to impair their judgement, self-control and integrity in a far more fundamental way. And, at risk of over-simplifying things and jumping ahead of the argument, this disease might be called 'alcoholism' or 'addiction'. If this model is valid, then most people can drink without harm or guilt, but some – the addicts or alcoholics – must abstain for their own good and that of others. No-one is responsible for such a disease, although sufferers have a responsibility to seek help and society has a responsibility to provide them with treatment.

It might be argued that such a disease model is simply another way of projecting blame – so that most people can continue drinking without any sense of guilt, and so that the alcoholic is responsible only for engaging in a programme of recovery and not for the root of the problem. However, that would be to prejudge the case. If alcoholism is a disease, it surely is a most malignant and destructive one, and those who suffer from it, and their families, certainly deserve sympathy and understanding rather than blame. But another argument arises which makes it difficult to leave the matter here. Extensive research, on alcohol consumption and on a variety of addictive behaviours, suggests that there is in fact no completely separate group of people who can easily be distinguished as 'addicts', in contrast to the 'normal' population. It is true that addiction, in its more severe forms, is easily perceived as alien to the statistical normal range of human experience. But the many shades of grey between addictive and normal drinking, for example, make it difficult to know where to draw the line.

The concept of addiction, in its more clearly distinguishable and severe manifestations, also presents another challenge to ethical analysis. If individuals can suffer from a disease which impairs their own self-control over certain behaviours, to what extent are they responsible for these behaviours? Contemporary ethical analysis tends to assume a central importance of human autonomy in choosing freely between available arbitrary options. But what if some people cannot freely make certain choices in such a fashion? Where then does the responsibility lie if their choices cause others harm? Can blame be projected on to a disease, the causes of which lie outside an individual person's control?

But do any of these projections of blame, attractive to the extent that they make someone or something else responsible for the problem, actually do anything in practice to address the problem effectively? And does that problem lie outside of us – in the community, in industry, in other people, in a disease, or in alcohol itself – or does it lie within each of us? Whatever our response to that question may be, there is a series of important and immediate practical and ethical questions which we face as individuals and as a society if we are to respond adequately to so pervasive and destructive a problem as that of alcohol misuse.

For the individual drinker, there is the important ethical question as to what criteria should be adopted in order to ensure that personal alcohol 'use' does not become alcohol 'misuse' (or, worse still, addiction). Whatever criteria are adopted, they may come into conflict with other influences upon drinking behaviour and they will be likely to increase or reduce the risk of a variety of threats to personal well-being. What should individuals do when they discover that what they had thought to be responsible drinking actually causes harm? In what way, and to what extent, should they modify their drinking? How great a risk to health is justified by the pleasures and benefits of moderate alcohol consumption? Or else, what should total abstainers do when told that they might acquire benefits to health from moderate drinking?

For society as a whole, for governments, industries, health professionals and academics, important ethical questions are raised in respect of social policy, health promotion, and planning of medical services which will have important consequences for economic and social stability, as well as for public health and the well-being of individuals. An enormous body of scientific literature and research has attempted to inform the governments, authorities and individuals who seek answers to such questions.[3] However, this is not merely a question of science or social policy. Governments and industries gain economic benefit from the production, sale and taxation of alcoholic beverages. The enormous popularity of alcohol – our 'favourite drug'[4] – can at times make wise evidence-based policies politically unattractive. And if alcohol is both a profitable commodity and also a cause of social and medical harm, or disease, then shareholders in the alcohol industry might, at least conceivably, face a choice between a sales policy which provides maximum achievable sales and one which minimises harm.

The matters of production, distribution, and consumption of alcohol therefore present a variety of important ethical questions to both individuals and societies. And yet, the debate about the proper answers to these questions is often now conducted primarily as though it were not an ethical debate, but rather simply one of scientific opinion, political expediency and consumer choice. Against this trend, it is argued here that, while science, politics and personal preference are all important and legitimate considerations, alcohol is also an important ethical issue which concerns us all. The debate about its proper production and use should therefore include, not only scientific and political and commercial considerations, but also explicitly ethical considerations. Alcohol policy should be based, not only upon sound and carefully considered scientific evidence, but also upon soundly reasoned ethical principles.

Before embarking upon construction of an ethical framework for response to the problems of alcohol misuse and addiction in our society, however, it must be noted that there is a remarkable dearth of ethical debate at many levels. It is true that some religious groups continue to eschew the use of alcohol.[5] It is also true that academics and others have expressed concern about the influence of the alcohol industry upon research and policy formation.[6] However, for many young and not so young people, drunkenness is at best socially unacceptable, and at worst is understood as being a very good objective for an evening out with friends.[7] As an example of governmental discourse, the 2004 Alcohol Harm Reduction Strategy for England, published by the British Prime Minister's Strategy

---

[3] For an authoritative and recent account of this literature as applied to social policy considerations, see Babor et al., 2003.

[4] Royal College of Psychiatrists, 1986.

[5] See, for example, the detailed defence of total abstinence (based mainly upon scripture) by Samuele Bacchiocchi, a Seventh Day Adventist (Bacchiocchi, 1989).

[6] See Chapter 2.     [7] Prime Minister's Strategy Unit, 2004, p. 23.

Unit, nowhere gives explicit consideration to ethical issues.[8] Rather, it talks about the 'pleasures' of 'drinking responsibly', as opposed to 'harmful patterns of drinking', and of strong encouragement of the drinks industry towards 'social responsibility'.[9]

Some encouragement may be derived from the 'Ethical principles and goals' of the European Charter on Alcohol published by the World Health Organization (WHO).[10] These are undoubtedly a welcome reminder that ethics as well as research should underlie social policy at the national and international level, and no issue is taken here with their fundamental merit. However, perhaps they raise more questions than they answer. Their prime concerns are with freedom from harm, access to information, access to care, and freedom to choose abstinence. But, does freedom to choose abstinence also imply freedom to drink? If so, is it possible to exercise complete freedom of choice in relation to alcohol consumption? If it is, then what happens when this freedom conflicts with the right to freedom from harm? More fundamentally, the language used is that of human rights, and yet there is no legal status to these rights. Human rights are social realities only insofar as they are a product of human agreement,[11] and it is not clear to what extent these human rights might be agreed upon outside of the 1995 conference from which they originated. Whether or not they might also be considered in some sense natural rights is not discussed, but would inevitably require a theological position to be adopted, and would in any case be very debatable.

Where the ethics of alcohol are discussed in more detail, conflicts emerge between different sets of ethical principles. For example, Robin Room has argued that the responsibility that modern societies place upon individuals for rational and responsible behaviour conflicts with the 'ethic of free trade', which sees alcohol as just another commodity which should be made freely available.[12] For Pekka Sulkunen, the conflict is between the consequentialist ethics of rationally based public rules and the ethics of individually conceived notions of 'the good life'.[13] Further ethical analysis is required in

---

[8] Prime Minister's Strategy Unit, 2004.    [9] Ibid., pp. 2–3, 6.
[10] World Health Organization Regional Office for Europe, 1995.
[11] Vardy and Grosch, 1994, pp. 191–193.
[12] Room, 1997. As a result, control of consumption and alcohol related harm becomes the responsibility of the individual consumer rather than of society. Those who fail to manage this responsibility, according to Room, are defined as alcoholics. Room concludes that, historically, alcohol problems have usually been best addressed by strong popular moral movements.
[13] Sulkunen, 1997. Sulkunen writes as an employee of ALKO, what was then the Finnish state monopoloy on alcohol. His solution to the conflict that he identifies is in the form of a social understanding of ethical decision-making whereby groups with shared moral values might be encouraged to adopt lifestyles in which alcohol features less prominently, or not at all. He seems to be optimistic that this might in time influence national policy on pricing and availability of alcohol.

order to provide a non-conflicted ethical framework for understanding the place of alcohol in our society.

To attempt a comprehensive ethical analysis of this field would be an enormous project. It raises questions concerning the social, developmental, psychological, genetic and other biological influences upon human behaviour and, assuming that radical determinism is not accepted, the ways in which people exercise 'free will' in the face of these influences. It would be a multidisciplinary project, requiring an understanding of a range of social, biological and health sciences as well as theology and ethics. It would be concerned both with the factors which generate a range of social, psychological and medical alcohol-related problems, and also with the human responses and solutions which are offered in an attempt to address these problems. A comprehensive ethical analysis of all of these facets of the problem would be a very valuable, but complex, lengthy and time-consuming undertaking. Necessarily this book will therefore be able only to allude to some of these facets, and in many cases references alone will have to suffice to direct the reader towards the relevant wider literature.

However, this book will also be limited in scope to a specifically Christian ethical and theological perspective, and I imagine that some readers will feel that this requires a little further justification. Christian ethical thinking has had an enduring influence upon the now largely secular ethical values of the developed world, not least Europe and North America, as well as on much of the developing world. Even if many of these nations and continents might now be considered largely post-Christian (not to mention postmodern), yet their Christian history has affected their commonly accepted ethical values in ways that are often not apparent. An analysis of this history and its relevance to the present is therefore of importance to all people, regardless of their religious faith or lack of it.

A specifically Christian perspective is obviously also of importance to the worldwide Christian Church. This might seem self-evident, and yet it is apparently not a matter about which the Church is currently greatly concerned; at least insofar as that concern may be judged by heatedness of public debate and content of published works. Whereas in the nineteenth century the matter of temperance or, more correctly, total abstinence from alcohol consumption was a major topic of debate and disagreement among Christians, now the popular ethical concern is apparently with matters such as human sexuality. Whereas in the nineteenth century a large proportion of Christians in all denominations (and all Christians in some denominations) in Europe and North America concluded that they should remain abstinent from alcohol, now the majority conclude that moderate

alcohol consumption is ethically uncontroversial and generally unremark-
able. And this, despite the fact that we are more aware than ever of the
toll that alcohol exacts. According to WHO estimates, 1.1 million people
worldwide died of alcohol-related causes in 1990, and by 2004 this had
risen to 1.8 million per annum.[14] Doubtless nineteenth century Temperance campaigners would be left completely aghast at the sanguine stance
of twenty-first-century Christians in the face of this massive toll of human
life. And indeed twenty-first-century Christians continue to be concerned
about morbidity and mortality on a much lesser scale when it is due to
other causes or when it is encountered in other contexts.

Furthermore, the Christian ethics of alcohol misuse tell some interesting
stories of how scripture, tradition and reason variously interact and assume
greater or lesser importance from one generation to the next in terms of
their importance as a basis for ethical argument. Perhaps some lessons may
be learned here which are of relevance to contemporary Christian debates
about human sexuality, and other matters which we perversely consider
more important subjects for argument than the lives of 1.8 million people
every year.

It might, however, be argued that God is best kept out of the argument
and that the ethics of alcohol are best analysed by human reason alone.
Richard Holloway, for example, has argued that the ethical analysis of
alcohol and other drugs in society is a matter of 'moral calculus', which
is concerned with the tension between freedom and personal morality on
the one hand, and the public good on the other.[15] Among his arguments
against involving God in the debate appears to be his concern about the
influence of what he considers to be a fundamentalist superstition that
alcohol and drugs are inherently evil.[16] He rightly recognises that the ethical
arguments concerning alcohol and drug use are more complex than this,
and draws attention to the failures of prohibition, and to the plurality
within society which makes it unlikely that such negative absolute views
will ever again achieve widespread consensus. But this seems to imply that
the only contribution that theology has to make to such debate is one of
offering unpopular and naïve moral absolutes.

A Christian theological perspective is offered here on the basis of a belief
that theology should not be excluded from secular discourse and, indeed,

---

[14] World Health Organization, 1999, p. 46; World Health Organization, 2004, p. 1. This is partly
offset by estimated deaths averted as a result of the cardio-protective benefit of light to moderate
alcohol consumption. The net worldwide mortality due to alcohol for 1990 was thus estimated by
the WHO to be 773,594.
[15] Holloway, 2000, pp. 87–107. Reference to 'moral calculus' is to be found on pp. 96, 105.
[16] Ibid., p. 94.

that it has a useful contribution to make to such discourse on the important topics of our time. Alistair McFadyen has argued that 'consciously relating the world to God . . . holds explanatory and symbolic power in relation to reality'.[17] While the present work does not primarily attempt to prove this, it proceeds on the basis that it is true, and the reader must judge whether or not the perspective that is offered has gained in explanatory or symbolic power as a result. While the truth of this assertion is accepted by the present author, however, it is accepted from a position of theological realism,[18] acknowledging that there are many and important continuities between theological and secular discourse. This is made clear, not to deny that there are also certain discontinuities, but rather to indicate that it is not necessarily expected that theological and secular discourse will be in radical conflict with each other. Theology has been brought into this conversation, not with the purpose of creating an argument, but because it has something of value to say.

Finally, however, a Christian perspective is offered because this author is a Christian. I cannot write from any other perspective. I write from a personal conviction that in Christ there is grace for those who suffer, and that this includes those who are poor, addicted, ill and abused as a result of alcohol misuse. I hope that this will not distract from the fact that I also write with due respect for those who come from other faith traditions, as well as those who are agnostic or avowedly atheist. I hope that they will also write about the ethics of alcohol misuse from their standpoints. With those from other faith traditions I especially share a concern that too much ethical, social and scientific discourse now takes place from a standpoint of pragmatic atheism. As a result of the Enlightenment, faith and religion have become private matters which are not usually addressed in public debate in the so-called developed world. A Christian perspective is therefore offered here in the hope that it can be seen that theology *does* have something to say which is of value to wider contemporary debate about an important social problem of our time.

[17] McFadyen, 2000, p. 12.     [18] Gill, 2004.

# CHAPTER 2

# An addiction in context: the use, misuse and harmful use of alcohol

The use of terminology in ethical and theological discourse about alcohol is complicated by the fact that history and Christian scripture have tended to employ a variety of different terms, most of which do not correspond readily with contemporary popular or scientific usage. Thus, terms such as 'intemperance' and 'chronic inebriety' are either unfamiliar or potentially misleading to the modern reader, whereas terms such as 'addiction' or 'dependence' are conceptually anachronistic to scripture and the Church Fathers. On the other hand, a historical and scriptural term such as 'drunkenness', which still seems familiar and unambiguous today, does not necessarily encompass all that contemporary ethical discourse must engage with. But drunkenness is important, since ethical concerns about drunkenness appear in Judeo-Christian scripture, and recur throughout Christian history up to and including the present day.

Contemporary terminology in the field of the use and misuse of alcohol is also contentious and confusing. The term 'alcohol misuse' is nowhere tightly defined. Whereas the terminology of the World Health Organization (WHO) prefers to refer to 'harmful use' of alcohol, the American Psychiatric Association (APA) refers to 'abuse' of alcohol. Similarly, although the term 'addiction' is still widely used, it is without consistent definition. In scientific circles, the term 'dependence' is therefore preferred, and is now employed by both the WHO and APA. The scientific context for discussion of these matters is, however, that of alcohol as a psycho-active drug, and thus all the preceding terms can be, and are, also used in reference to drugs other than alcohol.

What is clear today, despite all the confusions of terminology, and the various interests of the alcohol industry, researchers, clinicians and policy-makers, is that the matter for concern is located in the various forms of harm that arise from the consumption of alcohol as a beverage. It is actual or potential alcohol-related *harm* that is the cause for scientific, political and clinical concern. Harm may be biological, social or psychological, and

:nds importantly (but not exclusively) upon the pharmacological properties of alcohol. This harm is generally mediated by the effects of alcohol
intoxication, or drunkenness, by the toxicity of alcohol, and by the phenomenon of addiction or dependence.[1] The remainder of this chapter will
therefore be concerned with providing a brief contemporary (and therefore
largely scientific) account of drunkenness, and various kinds of alcohol-
related harm. Especial attention will be paid to the concepts of addiction
and dependence. But first, it will be well to consider in a little more detail
what is meant by the 'use' and 'misuse' of alcohol.

### THE USE AND MISUSE OF ALCOHOL

To 'use' alcohol generally means to consume it in beverage form. Reference
to alcohol use and misuse parallels the terminology of drug use and misuse,
where use can involve injection, inhalation and forms of administration
other than merely swallowing. However, alcohol is rarely 'used' in these
other senses today, unless one allows, perhaps, its use on swabs to clean
the skin prior to medical and surgical procedures.[2] To use alcohol, in the
contemporary context, almost always means to consume it by mouth –
usually as a drink, and sometimes in food.

To refer to the 'use' of alcohol carries also a connotation of (beneficial) purpose and function. This might be understood as merely that in
common with any other beverage that is consumed to relieve thirst and
for enjoyment of taste. However, alcohol is not simply any other beverage;
alcoholic beverages contain ethyl alcohol, a psycho-active drug with important intoxicant properties. There are also important religious, cultural and
social connotations of alcohol use, such that the purposes and functions of
its use are often complex, diverse and subtle. Alcohol is 'used' for celebration, in thanksgiving, to facilitate social intercourse, to relieve anxiety, as a
medicine, as a poison, to produce a state of drunkenness, to please others,
to escape reality, and for a variety of other good or bad, or good and bad,
purposes.

What, then, distinguishes the 'misuse' of alcohol, with its concomitant economic and human costs, from the proper 'use' of alcohol, with
its concomitant benefits? One possible answer to this question might be
to take the physical, social and psychological costs of alcohol-misuse as
themselves definitive. Thus, the term 'alcohol misuse' might be taken as

[1] Babor et al., 2003, pp. 19–26.
[2] In the past, alcohol has also been administered intravenously in the course of medical procedures
including, notably, the management of acute alcohol withdrawal.

broadly synonymous with the concept of 'drinking problems', or 'alcohol-related problems'. However, although relatively non-judgemental, the word 'misuse' seems to suggest 'improper' or 'incorrect' use of alcohol, as though it should be possible to know in advance whether or not its use on any particular occasion, or in any particular way, might be likely to lead to problems. In other words, the word 'misuse' seems to suggest that it is not the resulting problems which are definitive of the concept of alcohol misuse, so much as the potentially harmful way in which alcohol has been used. Thus, it might well be possible to consume alcohol in such a way that actual harm by chance did not arise at all, but which still constituted alcohol 'misuse' because of the risk that was entailed in the manner of use.

Of course, it might be argued that this inference is invalid. Perhaps it is not possible to predict the outcome of particular patterns or occasions of drinking at all. Or, if it is possible to offer a degree of prediction, in a statistical kind of way, perhaps the reliability of such predictions might be considered too poor to be worth taking the risks involved in any given set of circumstances. In this case, given the possible seriousness of the consequences of drinking, perhaps any responsible person should not drink alcohol at all. If we accept this view, then any human consumption of alcohol at all would constitute misuse of alcohol. But the widespread consumption and enjoyment of alcohol in western society imply that most people believe that this is not the case.[3]

Of course, in other parts of the world an entirely different state of affairs pertains. In Islamic countries, total abstinence from alcohol is the norm, and it might well be argued on a statistical and/or religious basis that drinking alcohol as a beverage, in itself, constitutes 'misuse', whether or not harm arises and whether or not there is even any risk of harm. The basis for this is to be found, not so much in an understanding of misuse as use associated with harm or risk, as in an understanding of use that is contrary to divine command. Thus, for example, in the Qur'ān, we find this injunction:

---

[3] I am, of course, not wishing to prejudge matters here, nor am I suggesting that total abstinence might not reasonably be justified on this basis. It could be the case that the drinking majority are simply ignorant of, or wrong in their assessment of the risk of, the dangers to which they expose themselves and others. Furthermore, it might be argued that some drinkers of alcohol are simply fooling themselves, and one another, and that they well know, at some level which is consciously or unconsciously denied, that their drinking might be harmful. However, it seems to me that the collective and publicly acknowledged understanding of the majority, in societies in which the drinking of alcohol is generally affirmed, must be that drinking is at least 'predictable enough'. That is, that the general understanding of things is that alcohol may properly be consumed in such a fashion as to pose only an acceptable minimal risk of harm. In other words, there is a category of proper 'use' which contrasts with the category of 'misuse'.

O ye who believe!
Intoxicants and gambling,
(Dedication of) stones,
And (divination by) arrows,
Are an abomination –
Of Satan's handiwork;
Eschew such (abomination),
That ye may prosper.

Satan's plan is (but)
To excite enmity and hatred
Between you, with intoxicants
And gambling, and hinder you
From the remembrance
Of Allah, and from prayer:
Will ye not then abstain?[4]

If misuse is here to be understood as use associated with harm, it would appear to be specifically the harms of social disharmony, forgetfulness of God, and neglect of prayer which are singled out. However, the fundamental consideration would appear to be more that alcohol, as an intoxicant, is an 'abomination' to God and thus to be eschewed for that reason alone. Not that God is understood to be arbitrary in his pronouncements. Elsewhere in the Qur'ān it is stated in respect of wine and gambling that

In them is great sin,
And some profit, for men;
But the sin is greater
Than the profit.[5]

It is thus in the best interests of humankind that God is understood to prohibit the drinking of alcohol. The harm that it causes is understood to be greater than the profit. Very similar considerations were characteristic of the thinking of the Christian temperance movement of the nineteenth century, and these will be considered more carefully in Chapter 5. However, Christian scripture and tradition are (all things considered) much less unambiguous about the drinking of alcohol, and in general Christians have been loath to describe as 'misuse' that which Christ himself engaged in. Even Christians convinced of the divine imperative of total abstinence have therefore tended to argue on the basis of the risk of harm. The only question has been whether misuse should be construed as any use at all, or

---

[4] Sūrah 5:90, 91; Ali, 2000.    [5] From sūrah 2:219; Ali, 2000.

only as use which quantitatively or contextually is associated with greater risk of harm.

Drunkenness is usually taken to refer to alcohol intoxication, and in particular can be understood to refer to 'habitual' intoxication.[6] Drunkenness and intoxication are both capable of manifestation in varying degrees. The degree of intoxication is directly related to the amount of alcohol consumed, and is directly proportional to the degree of harm which is likely to arise. The crucial factor is the actual dose of alcohol in grams. The type of beverage (beer, wine, spirits, etc.) does not in itself influence the degree of intoxication at all.

Intoxication[7] is a transient state, arising as a biological result of consumption of alcohol. Alcohol is traditionally described as a Central Nervous System depressant. In fact, not only does its depressant effect on inhibitory neurones lead to initial disinhibition, but it also has important stimulant as well as depressant effects, and its depressant action is in any case not global.[8] Intoxication is thus characterised initially by excitement, gregariousness and loquacity. As the level of intoxication increases the effects are more likely to include depression and irritability, but the effects on mood vary according to context and from one individual to another, as well as according to the degree of intoxication. Importantly, the stimulant effects of alcohol include euphoria, and its depressant effects include reduction of anxiety. Consumption of alcohol is thus rewarding and desirable. However, consciousness is progressively impaired, as are coordination and cognition. Speech is slurred and physiological functioning is altered in various ways.[9] Subjects may experience fragmentary or complete amnesia for periods of heavy intoxication. Importantly, judgement, attention and memory are all impaired, performance at psychomotor tasks such as driving is degraded, and social behaviour is disinhibited and maladaptive. These manifestations have diverse implications and consequences in terms of personal behaviour, ability to fulfil social obligations, and risk of accidents.[10] Intoxication may also, in extreme cases, lead to coma and death.

---

[6] Macdonald, 1982, p. 398.

[7] World Health Organization, 1992, pp. 73–74; American Psychiatric Association, 1994, pp. 196–197; Victor and Adams, 1977, pp. 709–710; G. Edwards, Marshall and Cook, 2003, pp. 101–103.

[8] See Little, 2000.    [9] Notably, a diuresis and an increase in pulse and blood pressure.

[10] G. Edwards, Marshall and Cook, 2003, pp. 70–93.

Drunkenness is as much dependent upon culturally determined expectations as it is the physical properties of alcohol, and should be distinguished from intoxication. Drunkenness refers to 'behaviour displayed by people who have consumed, believe that they have consumed, or want others to believe that they have consumed, alcohol'.[11] Importantly, drunkenness may be more associated with aggression than is intoxication. Cultural attitudes towards drunkenness importantly influence the nature and prevalence of harms experienced as a result of drinking.[12] In some cases, as in contemporary youth culture, drunkenness may be perceived as a very positive state, which even becomes the objective of drinking.[13]

Where intoxication and drunkenness become chronic or frequent states, a range of other problems may also be experienced, including dependence and other medical, social and psychological complications. Research has shown that frequency of drunkenness is a predictor of both social harms and dependence.[14] While drunken behaviour is determined by social and cultural expectations as well as by the biological effects of alcohol, it is clear that drunkenness has presented a significant social problem of an essentially similar nature across a variety of different cultures[15] and over a longer period than the two millennia of Christian history.[16]

### HARMFUL USE AND ABUSE

While drunkenness may remain an important social concern today, it is not the main concern of modern medicine. In the tenth revision of the International Classification of Diseases (ICD-10) of the WHO, we find a variety of 'Mental and behavioural disorders due to use of alcohol', including, notably, 'Acute intoxication', 'Harmful use' and 'Dependence syndrome'.[17] However, the category of acute intoxication in ICD-10 is provided only to cover cases where persistent and recurrent alcohol-related problems do not occur. Where there are such problems, precedence is explicitly given to making a diagnosis under other categories, notably 'harmful use'[18] or 'dependence

---

[11] Rix, 1989.    [12] G. Edwards, Marshall and Cook, 2003, pp. 19–20.
[13] Prime Minister's Strategy Unit, 2004, p. 23.    [14] Dawson and Archer, 1993; Midanik, 1999.
[15] G. Edwards, Marshall and Cook, 2003, pp. 19–20.
[16] See, for example, Sullivan, 1965, pp. 45–88, for an example taken from first-century Roman culture.
[17] World Health Organization, 1992, pp. 70–83; ICD-10 also provides classifications for withdrawal states, and various psychotic disorders due to use of alcohol. The separation of amnesic syndrome and other psychotic disorders from other harmful consequences of alcohol use would seem to be fairly arbitrary, except insofar as these disorders, although caused by alcohol, persist after alcohol consumption is discontinued. For sake of simplicity, the distinction will not be laboured here.
[18] For the sake of simplicity, the term will be taken here to include psychotic disorders arising from alcohol use.

syndrome'. The primary concern of ICD-10 is thus with alcohol use that either damages health (i.e. 'harmful use') or else leads to dependence. Harmful use in ICD-10 is explicitly defined in a very medical way, restricted to damage to mental and physical health, and specifically excludes negative social consequences of drinking. The definition further requires that 'actual damage' to physical or mental health should have been 'caused' by alcohol.

In the fourth edition of the *Diagnostic and Statistical Manual of Mental Disorders* of the APA (DSM-IV), 'Alcohol use disorders' include 'Alcohol abuse' and 'Alcohol dependence'.[19] The term 'alcohol abuse' is somewhat unfortunate, as the word 'abuse' has connotations of injustice, corruption and ill-treatment. It is very often used in reference to the ill-treatment of other people (e.g. child abuse). However, alcohol abuse is defined here as 'a maladaptive pattern of [alcohol] use leading to clinically significant impairment or distress', and emphasises social harms such as impairment of work, legal problems and interpersonal problems. Alcohol abuse, according to this definition, is therefore another variation on the theme of harmful use. Whereas ICD-10 emphasises medical harm, DSM-IV emphasises social harm. In both cases, however, the concern is with use of alcohol that leads to, or causes, harm.

The notion that alcohol 'leads to' or 'causes' harm is an important one, but it easily obfuscates the complexity of the relationship between alcohol and the various harms with which it is associated. In individual cases, it may not be at all clear whether alcohol was a cause of a particular harm or not. Causation is often multifactorial, and alcohol may be only one of a number of contributory causes. In other cases it may be more of a predisposing or risk factor rather than a direct cause of harm. Sometimes, the association of alcohol with harm may not be causal at all, as for example in the case of lung cancer, where it is the higher prevalence of smoking which causes the increased incidence of the disease among drinkers and where other factors in turn probably lead to both drinking and smoking.[20] The relationship of alcohol to social harms is often especially difficult to determine with confidence. Furthermore, it is sometimes the average level of consumption of alcohol which is the cause of harm, and sometimes the pattern of drinking. When speaking in general terms it is therefore usually better to refer to 'alcohol-related' harm, as a reminder that the

---

[19] American Psychiatric Association, 1994, pp. 194–196. Alcohol intoxication is classified separately, along with alcohol withdrawal and various psychoses, under the heading of 'Alcohol induced disorders'.

[20] A useful analysis of the relationship between alcohol and the various harms with which it is associated is to be found in Babor et al., 2003, pp. 57–92.

relationship between alcohol and harm is complex, multiform and often uncertain.

A detailed review of the nature and characterisation of the diverse and multitudinous medical and social harms that are related to the use, abuse or misuse of alcohol is beyond the scope of this book.[21] Alcohol may lead to, exacerbate, or increase the risk of liver disease, and other gastro-intestinal disorders, musculo-skeletal disorders such as gout and osteoporosis, hypertension and haemorrhagic stroke, enlargement of red blood cells, damage to the central and peripheral nervous systems, foetal damage (as a result of drinking during pregnancy), and a variety of other problems due to toxicity, as well as the traumatic consequences of accidents caused by the effects of intoxication. Generally speaking, the risk of these complications of alcohol consumption is increased according to the amount of alcohol that is regularly consumed, and guidance is therefore offered by various medical authorities as to what might constitute 'safe' or 'sensible' levels of consumption.[22] There is also debate about the cardio-protective effect of light to moderate alcohol consumption, which may reduce the risk of coronary heart disease in men over the age of forty years, and in post-menopausal women.[23]

Similarly, heavy drinking and binge drinking may be associated with diverse social problems, including marital disharmony, an adverse family environment for children, problems at work, financial hardship, violent crime, drink-driving offences, and homelessness. Such drinking is also associated with psychological problems, including depression, anxiety and jealousy, and antisocial personality traits.

In general, acute episodes of drinking associated with intoxication, due to rapid elevation in blood alcohol concentration, are more likely to be associated with physical and social trauma as a result of accidents and violence. Chronic heavy alcohol consumption is more characteristically associated with physical organ damage due to alcohol toxicity (e.g. cirrhosis) and psychological problems such as anxiety and depression.[24]

## ADDICTION

The concept of addiction is concerned with the way in which people behave. Traditionally, this behaviour was understood specifically as being

---

[21] For a more detailed introduction, see G. Edwards, Marshall and Cook, 2003.
[22] Ibid., pp. 26–27.     [23] Ibid., p. 159.
[24] Babor et al., 2003, p. 7; G. Edwards, Marshall and Cook, 2003, pp. 19–20.

related to habitual use of psychoactive drugs, including alcohol.[25] More recently however, the concept has been broadened in general usage to include other repeated behaviours of diverse kinds, with the defining focus being more upon impaired voluntary control of the behaviour, or its continuance despite harmful consequences, than upon the immediate object of the behaviour itself.[26] It may thus be defined as 'behaviour over which an individual has impaired control with harmful consequences'.[27]

Addiction has thus become concerned with the subjective human experience of continuing in a habitual behaviour which is recognised at some level, by the subject or others, as being undesirable.[28] It is a concern with behaviour in which motivation appears to be disordered, or in which the usual human experience of free choice appears to be violated.[29] It is one possible kind of answer to a question as to why people repeatedly engage in behaviour which is harmful to themselves or others. But what kind of answer is it? And, given that Christian theology concerns itself with not dissimilar questions about human behaviour, how is addiction understood by theologians?

Gerry May has suggested that there are three popular models of the nature of addiction.[30] The *moral model* proposes that addiction is the result of sin, evil, or moral weakness and that the addict is personally culpable. The *disease model* sees addiction as being the result of pathology for which the addict is not culpable, but nonetheless still ascribes responsibility for the behaviours that result from this disorder. This is, generally speaking, the model employed by the addiction treatment centres following the Twelve Step programme of Alcoholics Anonymous (AA) and its various sister organisations. The *scientific model* is concerned with neurological, physiological and psychological processes, but does not address issues of culpability. However, there are many other models which are employed in academic

---

[25] Thus, for example, in 1957 the World Health Organization defined addiction as 'a state of periodic or chronic intoxication produced by the repeated consumption of a drug' (Seevers, 1962).

[26] Thus, for example, it has been defined as 'habitual psychological and physiological dependence on a substance or practice that is beyond voluntary control' (Felscher and Koenigsberg, 1993, p. 7) or as the 'habitual use of any chemical substance . . . which can harm the spiritual, emotional, mental, physical or social well-being of users and/or those around them' (Carr et al., 2002, p. 7).

[27] West, 2001, p. 3. But this approach does not receive universal acceptance. For some, addiction is the exact antithesis of this, a matter of deliberate choice. For example, it has been described as 'a fondness for, or orientation toward, some thing or activity' (Schaler, 2002, p. xiv).

[28] Although Schaler would argue that addiction need not be harmful, and that virtues are merely addictions which are approved of (Schaler, 2002, p. xiv).

[29] West, 2001, p. 3.    [30] May, 1988.

discourse.[31] For example, John Booth Davies,[32] a social psychologist, in his book *The Myth of Addiction*, considers addiction to be an explanation that people offer for their behaviour which attributes causality to external sources. Again, Jim Orford,[33] another psychologist, proposes an *excessive appetite model* of addiction, in which the addict is understood to have developed a strong attachment to a risky behaviour. A common concern of all these models, except perhaps for the scientific model as defined by May, is with asserting and explaining the ability or lack of ability, as the case may be, of the subject to exert free control over his or her own behaviour. Thus, all these models are generally viewed as having implications (one way or the other) for understanding the moral responsibility of the addict for his or her behaviour.

There has been some theological interest in the concept of addiction, although the total number of publications offering serious theological reflection is smaller than one might expect. Most of what has been published, with only a few exceptions,[34] arises from the Christian tradition. Thus, for example, William Lenters, an addictions counsellor and ordained minister, understands addiction as the universal human condition.[35] For Lenters, addiction is a response to the stresses of life by means of a sinful pursuit of an absolute freedom which refuses to recognise contingency upon God. Similarly, although with differing emphases, Patrick McCormick, a Roman Catholic professor of moral theology, argues that there are various biblical models for sin, one of the more useful of which (in his view) is sin as sickness or disease. According to this model, McCormick argues, sin can best be understood as the disease of addiction, which he construes as being 'concerned with both human freedom and the moral dimension' or a 'pathological relationship with a (normally) mood altering substance or process'.[36] In contrast, William Playfair, a physician writing from an apparently strong biblicist position, understands addiction as the result of the sinful use or misuse of drugs.[37] For Playfair, biblical injunctions against drunkenness[38] are interpreted as being firmly in support of the moral model of addiction, and the disease model is presented as both unscientific and unbiblical. For Playfair, addiction is sin.

---

[31] See also Siegler et al., 1968, who identify eight models: the impaired model, the 'dry' moral model, the 'wet' moral model, the Alcoholics Anonymous model, the psychoanalytic model, the family interaction model, the 'old' medical model, and the 'new' medical model.
[32] J. B. Davies, 2000.
[33] Orford, 2001.     [34] E.g. Suliman, 1983; Groves and Farmer, 1994.     [35] Lenters, 1985.
[36] McCormick, 1989, pp. 146, 150.     [37] Playfair, 1991.
[38] E.g. 1 Corinthians 6:9–10; Galatians 5:19. See Playfair, 1991, pp. 29–32.

On the one hand, the approach of Lenter and McCormick seems to make sin a form of universal human addiction, such that all human beings are in some sense 'addicted'. On the other hand, the approach of Playfair understands addiction as the sinful result of just one form of human sinfulness, which people have in some sense chosen to follow. Whereas, for McCormick, addiction is both sin and disease, for Playfair, addiction is sin but definitely not disease. Lenter also expresses serious reservations about the disease concept, but is less overtly antagonistic towards it.

Yet another approach to sin and addiction is provided by Cornelius Plantinga.[39] Eschewing both the moral model and the disease model as inadequate and simplistic, Plantinga prefers to understand addiction as a tragedy, in which sin is only one of a number of factors involved. Sin and addiction, according to Plantinga, are overlapping domains. Sin is not always addiction, and addiction is not always sin, although the two often overlap. The overlap occurs where sin reveals the dynamics of addiction – primarily in the case of appetitive sins (avarice, gluttony and lust). Unfortunately, Plantinga's defining 'dynamics of addiction' are presented without reference to the scientific literature and are therefore somewhat idiosyncratic.

A much more nuanced theological understanding of addiction is to be found in Linda Mercadante's book *Victims and Sinners*.[40] Mercadante, a Methodist professor of theology, recognises both that addiction is an attractive analogy for sin, and also that its usefulness in this role is limited. According to Mercadante, the association of the contemporary concept of addiction with the scientific paradigm leads to the danger that sin conceptualised as addiction will veer towards determinism or Manichaeism. On the other hand, she points out that the association of the concept with the 'Twelve Step' recovery movement of AA and its sister organisations carries a danger of over-emphasising the place of free will and thus Pelagianism. For Mercadante, neither behaviour nor will alone defines sin. Sin is concerned with orientation towards (or rather, away from) God. Addiction, according to her view, is primarily a therapeutic concept which groups together diverse problematic behaviours. Sin and addiction are not opposed, nor are they purely analogous. The addict may be understood as a victim of harms inflicted in life, to which addiction is a response, but addiction may also result from a sinful turning away from God. However addiction begins, it

[39] Plantinga, 1996, pp. 129–149.   [40] Mercadante, 1996.

exerts an influence which is likely to bring about an increasing orientation away from God.

In scientific usage, the ill-defined term 'addiction' has now largely been replaced by, or at least is interpreted by, the concept of the dependence syndrome. Thus, both of the major psychiatric diagnostic systems in current international usage, ICD-10 and DSM-IV, employ dependence terminology.[41] The authors of the WHO report in which the alcohol dependence syndrome was first described clearly saw dependence and addiction as being closely related.[42] However, the dependence syndrome concept was understood as offering an advance on previous medical and scientific conceptions of addiction. It recognises, for example, that dependence is a continuously variable phenomenon which exists in varying degrees of severity, that alcohol-related problems may occur in the absence of dependence, and that the dependence syndrome has multifactorial aetiology and may present differently in different cultures and in different individuals.[43] Furthermore, the employment of the medical concept of syndrome as the basis for understanding dependence moved the discussion firmly towards a reliance on empirical evidence, and made the debate as to whether or not it was a disease largely semantic. It also recognised that there were both psychological and physiological aspects to the disorder of alcohol dependence, thus providing a more holistic perspective. The concept thus promised, and was later confirmed actually to have, a utility for both clinical work and research.[44]

Although the dependence syndrome was described initially in relation to alcohol, it has subsequently been applied to virtually all other 'addictive' drugs and a variety of other behaviours which are understood as having an addictive quality.[45]

---

[41] The fourth revision of the *Diagnostic and Statistical Manual* of the American Psychiatric Association (DSM-IV; American Psychiatric Association, 1994), and the tenth revision of the *International Classification of Diseases* (ICD-10; World Health Organization, 1992). In contrast, the Twelve Step self-help and treatment movement generally continues to employ addiction terminology, often without reference to the dependence syndrome. The Twelve Step movement is especially strong in North America, and it is of note that May, Lenters, McCormick, Playfair, Plantinga and Mercadante are all from the United States of America. Playfair is strongly antagonistic to the Twelve Step movement, and Mercadante provides a theological critique of it, whereas May, Lenters and McCormick are all more or less sympathetic towards it and draw to varying degrees upon its insights. Plantinga appears to take a fairly neutral position. However, all have clearly been influenced by the Twelve Step movement, and write from a context in which it has been dominant for half a century or more.

[42] G. Edwards et al., 1977, p. 7.     [43] Ibid., pp. 7–8.

[44] Ibid.; Hasin and Paykin, 1999; G. Edwards, Marshall and Cook, 2003, pp. 47–50.

[45] The concept has been applied to other psychoactive drugs in both DSM-IV and ICD-10. Other behaviours to which it has been applied include, for example, exercise dependence (de Coverley Veale, 1987).

### THE ALCOHOL DEPENDENCE SYNDROME

The concept of the alcohol dependence syndrome was introduced initially by way of a 'provisional description' in a paper in the *British Medical Journal* in 1976.[46] In the following year, a WHO report adopted the same concept in its task of identifying and classifying 'disabilities related to alcohol consumption'.[47] The 'essential elements' of the syndrome comprised

> narrowing of the drinking repertoire
> salience of drink-seeking behaviour
> increased tolerance to alcohol
> repeated withdrawal symptoms
> relief or avoidance of withdrawal symptoms by further drinking
> subjective awareness of compulsion to drink
> reinstatement after abstinence

Each element was considered to be potentially present in varying degrees of severity, and it was recognised by the authors that not all elements would always be present. It was recognised that the natural history (the evolution of the pathological process) would be affected by social and cultural factors. Other alcohol-related problems (e.g. cirrhosis, problems at work, marital disharmony, etc.) might occur in the absence of alcohol dependence but, all things being equal, would be more likely to be observed the greater the severity of alcohol dependence.[48] The scientific basis of the syndrome was then a matter for speculation, but has since been greatly elaborated in terms of neurobiological and psychological processes, although a comprehensive account is still lacking.[49]

The alcohol dependence syndrome represents a characteristic constellation of signs and symptoms which are observed together. Initially, this constellation was described on the basis of empirical clinical experience. Subsequently, it has been verified by research.[50]

The essential elements of the syndrome were characterised as follows.

### Narrowing of the drinking repertoire

The type, quantity, context and pattern of drinking vary for most people from day to day and over the longer term. In alcohol dependence, the usual variety of drinking patterns tends to become restricted, with each day

---

[46] G. Edwards and Gross, 1976.   [47] G. Edwards et al., 1977.   [48] Drummond, 1990.
[49] G. Edwards, Marshall and Cook, 2003, pp. 49–50.   [50] Ibid., pp. 48–50.

following an increasingly standard pattern in terms of the quantity, context and type of drinking.

### Salience of drink-seeking behaviour

In alcohol dependence, drinking assumes increasing priority in life, at the expense of other activities, responsibilities and commitments. Marriage, work, health, morality and finances thus tend to suffer in direct proportion to the degree of dependence.

### Increased tolerance to alcohol

As tolerance develops, increasing amounts of alcohol must be consumed in order to obtain the same subjective experience or objective effects of intoxication. Thus, impairment of performance in various activities will be less than for other drinkers consuming similar amounts of alcohol. Various forms of tolerance have been identified and the mechanisms are somewhat obscure. However, they almost certainly involve both pharmacological and psychological components, with the former involving various changes in neurotransmitter functioning in the Central Nervous System.[51]

### Repeated withdrawal symptoms

After a period of habitual drinking, cessation of drinking leads to character-istic alcohol 'withdrawal symptoms', including tremor, nausea, vomiting, sweating and anxiety. With increasing severity of dependence, the frequency and severity of these symptoms are likely to increase so that they may occur on waking each morning, or even during the night. The withdrawal syn-drome is probably the result of adaptive biochemical changes in the brain which accommodate the continued presence of alcohol. When alcohol is removed suddenly from the system, the neuroadaptational changes oppos-ing the effects of alcohol are left unopposed, and the signs and symptoms of alcohol withdrawal are the result.[52]

### Relief or avoidance of withdrawal symptoms by further drinking

As dependence develops, the drinker learns that alcohol prevents and relieves symptoms of alcohol withdrawal. Increasingly, drinking is engaged

---

[51] Ibid., pp. 42–43.    [52] Ibid., pp. 42–44.

in with the purpose of relieving or avoiding these unpleasant consequences of abstinence.

## Subjective awareness of compulsion to drink

The dependent drinker recognises that he or she subjectively experiences a desire to continue drinking. This element was understood to include various subjective phenomena that had previously been described and debated, including 'craving' and 'loss of control'. As the theological texts considered in Chapter 6 have been chosen on the basis of the parallels that they offer with the subjective experience of addiction, more needs to be said here about this element of the alcohol dependence syndrome.

Craving is a more or less greatly increased desire for alcohol, which has in the past been understood as providing an explanation of the basis of addiction. Although this fundamental role is now challenged, it nonetheless provides a theoretical focus of a number of new pharmacological and psychological approaches to treatment.[53] The phrase 'loss of control' is almost certainly a misnomer, as it is more strictly a question of impairment of control of drinking, or a decision not to exercise control, rather than *loss* of control *per se* that is involved. It is also vague and ill defined. Nonetheless, dependent drinkers are aware of drinking more than they in some sense 'intended' to. Along with 'inability to abstain', recent research has suggested that this is part of a unitary dimension of impaired control of drinking as a part of the alcohol dependence syndrome.[54] Subjective measures of dependence may collectively form better predictors of relapse to harmful drinking than do so-called objective measures.[55]

Edwards and Gross initially suggested that the subjective experience of the drinker was close to that of people with compulsive disorders.[56] In particular, they noted that drinkers know that the desire to drink is irrational, and they resist that desire, but yet they still continue to drink. Raul Caetano, while also recognising the internal struggle of the drinker with the desire to drink, has subsequently challenged this position.[57] First, he noted a difference in the relationship between the obsessional thought

[53] Drummond, 2001.    [54] Kahler, Epstein and McCrady, 1995.

[55] Heather, Rollnick and Winton, 1983.

[56] G. Edwards and Gross, 1976, p. 1060; Obsessive-compulsive disorder is characterised by obsessional thoughts or compulsive acts. Obsessional thoughts are recurrent, intrusive ideas, images or impulses, which are usually distressing (or at least recognised as senseless), and which are unsuccessfully resisted. Compulsive behaviour is also repetitive, is neither rewarding nor constructive, and is recognised as senseless and is also usually resisted. (See World Health Organization, 1992, pp. 142–145.)

[57] Caetano, 1985.

and compulsive action. In obsessive-compulsive neurosis, the compulsive act serves to counter the obsessive thought, whereas, in alcohol dependence, drinking serves to indulge the subjective 'obsession' with alcohol. Secondly, he argued that the presumed biological nature of the compulsion to drink renders it an involuntary action, more akin to signs and symptoms of other biological brain diseases than to other neurotic disorders. Thirdly, drinking is not senseless or irrational in the same way that compulsive rituals are; it is completely understandable as the expression of a 'need' of someone with a long history of drinking. While these arguments are all cogent and important, they are somewhat flawed by Caetano's apparent failure to recognise the conflict between his understanding of drinking as the purposive indulgence of a subjective obsession with alcohol on the one hand, and his characterisation of it as the involuntary sequel of biological brain disease on the other.

### *Reinstatement after abstinence*

Once alcohol dependence has been established, it appears to be readily reinstated, even sometimes after prolonged periods of abstinence. Thus, a man who began drinking in his teens may take a decade or more to establish alcohol dependence. However, after a period of abstinence it does not take another decade to redevelop the dependence syndrome. Rather, the dependent pattern of drinking may be reinstated after a few months, weeks, days, or even hours.

It may now be seen that the alcohol dependence syndrome offers a coherent psycho-biological model of addiction. It reflects an 'altered relationship between a person and their drinking'.[58] Whatever the initial reasons for drinking, dependence provides a reason for continued drinking. However, research is generating an increasingly clear picture of what the underlying aetiological factors for alcohol dependence might be.[59]

#### THE AETIOLOGY OF ALCOHOL-RELATED HARM

On the one hand, individual vulnerability to alcohol dependence is now understood scientifically as being determined by various genetic and other constitutional factors in a fashion not dissimilar to many other complex behaviours and psychiatric disorders. In particular, it would seem likely that a vulnerability to alcohol dependence is mediated, at least in part, by

[58]  G. Edwards, Marshall and Cook, 2003, p. 47.     [59]  Ibid., pp. 16–29; Cook, 1994.

genetic factors.[60] On the other hand, population level research is held to have demonstrated that drunkenness and alcohol dependence, and most other alcohol-related problems, are in fact closely correlated with overall *per capita* consumption for the population as a whole.[61] These different areas of research need not be seen as incompatible with each other, and do not require a strongly deterministic interpretation. Rather, a variety of individual, biological, psychological and social factors may be seen to increase or moderate the risk or probability that any given individual might experience problems with his or her drinking at any given time. Within any given population, certain individuals will be at greater risk of developing alcohol dependence than others, on the basis of genetic vulnerability, occupational risk, life events or numerous other factors. On the other hand, increasing the availability and acceptability of alcohol within a population is almost certain to increase consumption across the board. In such circumstances, more people are likely to drink more alcohol more often, and more people are more likely to become dependent or to sustain other alcohol-related harms.

The more each individual drinks, the greater his or her risk of becoming dependent upon alcohol, or of experiencing other alcohol-related harms. The more a population drinks, the more alcohol-related harm it will sustain, and the higher the prevalence of alcohol dependence will be within it. It may thus be seen that alcohol use and misuse are not categorically separate entities, but that they are closely related. Similarly, harmful use and dependence are interrelated and each in turn is closely related to alcohol use at the population and individual levels.

Within this overall analysis of the aetiology of alcohol-related harm lays the crucial issue of personal choice. At one level, it is clear that everyone has the choice as to whether or not they will drink alcohol at all. A minority of people in most western nations choose complete abstinence from alcohol for a variety of reasons, varying from religious faith to concerns about health, or simply not liking the taste.[62] In the Middle East, owing to the

---

[60] Reich et al., 1998; Cook and Gurling, 2001.    [61] G. Edwards, Marshall and Cook, 2003, pp. 16–18.

[62] For example, in a survey undertaken for the Department of Health, in Great Britain in 2002, 9% of men and 14% of women reported that they had not drunk alcohol at all in the preceding year (Lader and Meltzer, 2002, p. 12). In England, in 1999, another survey undertaken on behalf of the Department of Health revealed that the proportion of men and women who had never drunk alcohol was higher among most ethnic minority groups, and especially among those that are predominantly Muslim (Erens and Laiho, 2001). In this survey, 86% of Pakistani men, and 92% of Bangladeshi men, indicated that they had never drunk alcohol. However, research involving Christian abstainers has suggested that, even where religious factors apparently provide the main reason for abstinence, motivation may be based upon diverse factors, including family history of alcoholism (Goodwin et al., 1969).

be drink aware

position adopted by Islam, the great majority of Muslims choose not to drink alcohol at all. It is self-evident that none of these people, so long as they remain completely abstinent from alcohol, will ever develop alcohol dependence. However, for any person who does choose to drink, further important choices do remain. The literature clearly shows an increasing risk of alcohol dependence in direct proportion to the amount of alcohol consumed.[63] Advice is offered concerning 'sensible' or 'safe' levels of drinking, and individuals are free to make a choice as to whether or not they adhere to such advice.[64] In times of stress, alcohol may seem to offer relief[65] and is available as one option for coping, among a variety of others. It has even been argued that addiction itself is ultimately a choice.[66] However, in other ways, choice is in practice restricted. Society, family, colleagues and friends may 'expect' drinking in certain contexts, and may exert social pressure to conform. Psychological patterns of behaviour, including alcohol consumption, are reinforced at a largely unconscious level. As dependence develops, and even before it develops, biological factors may also influence the subjective experience of drinking and decision-making capacity, thus making continued drinking more or less likely.[67]

For the individual drinker, alcohol dependence may be seen as a condition in which alcohol is an increasingly important focus in life. The central focus upon, or priority of, alcohol is reflected in altered physiological, psychological and social functioning. In the advanced stages, or in severe dependence, life is dominated physiologically, psychologically and socially by the presence of alcohol. As the severity of dependence increases, the barriers to reducing or discontinuing alcohol consumption increase. Social and psychological functioning becomes dependent upon the presence of alcohol, and any significant reduction in the level of consumption is likely to trigger unpleasant withdrawal symptoms, which become a cue for further drinking. On the other hand, social and psychological functioning and health are also all grossly impaired by heavy alcohol consumption. To the extent that drinkers are able to recognise this, they will find themselves

[63] G. Edwards et al., 1994, pp. 63–65.
[64] G. Edwards, Marshall and Cook, 2003, pp. 26–27. The evidence suggests that, when this advice is offered through mass media educational campaigns, it is generally not heeded (G. Edwards et al., 1994, pp. 172–175). On the other hand, individually directed interventions, aimed at modifying excessive drinking, or the early stages of problem drinking, are apparently effective (G. Edwards et al., 1994).
[65] G. Edwards, Marshall and Cook, 2003, pp. 20–21.     [66] Schaler, 2002.
[67] G. Edwards, Marshall and Cook, 2003, pp. 21–23. See also Kalivas, 2004, for an example of the kinds of ways in which neurobiological research might approach the issue of choice in addiction; and Paulus, 2005, pp. 7–8, for a brief review of the ways in which decision-making processes might be dysfunctional in drug-using and addicted patients.

trapped between the consequences of drinking and the consequences of reducing or discontinuing their drinking.

### ⋏ HARM REDUCTION ⋌

The explicit language of harm reduction is heard more often in the clinical and policy arena concerned with illicit drug use than in the arena concerned with alcohol. However, harm reduction techniques may be employed for all forms of substance use, and for other behaviours, including social and prescribed drug use as well as illicit drug misuse. Thus, for example, harm reduction programmes for alcohol misuse might include the provision of 'wet accommodation', within which actively drinking and alcohol dependent people will be, to some extent, sheltered from the harms associated with drinking on the streets. Treatment approaches orientated towards a goal of 'normal drinking' would also fall under this heading.[68] Less controversially, a range of policies designed to modify the drinking context have attempted to reduce alcohol-related harm in the community.[69]

Harm reduction is defined with different emphasis and varying perspective in different publications. However, in general, definitions include the following elements:

1. A focus on all types of harm (although the spiritual is often not specifically mentioned, and harm is usually construed in terms of social, psychological and physical harm).
2. An evidence-based approach.
3. Harm reduction is generally understood as a strategy used in support of achieving an overall goal of harm minimisation. Harm reduction methods or approaches to treatment are thus implemented as objectives in support of the aim of achieving the minimum possible drug-related harm.
4. Harm reduction strategies are addressed in practice to a hierarchy of short-term, achievable and pragmatic treatment goals.
5. A non-judgemental stance, which neither condones nor condemns drug or alcohol use.

Harm reduction is often understood as being polarised with abstinence-based approaches to drug rehabilitation. This polarisation is unnecessary, and in most cases appears to be very unhelpful. Abstinence may or may not be considered an achievable goal of harm reduction. However, harm reduction may provide a step (or a series of steps) towards abstinence (although it

---

[68] G. Edwards, Marshall and Cook, 2003, pp. 343–355.   [69] Babor et al., 2003, pp. 141–156.

does not require abstinence as an immediate goal), and in turn abstinence provides an excellent harm reduction goal in itself. In general, complete abstinence from drug use will not only minimise but will actually eliminate drug-related harm.[70]

Harm reduction operates on at least two levels, and it is important to distinguish these. At the *individual* level, harm reduction may be employed as a strategy to achieve harm minimisation for an individual drinker or drug user. In this case, harm reduction provides a hierarchy of possible treatment goals for an individual who may or may not wish to discontinue alcohol or drug use. At the *population* level, harm reduction programmes seek to minimise the sum total of alcohol or drug-related harm experienced within a community. In general terms, it is difficult to see how there could be any objection to such a goal. In essence it simply indicates that the aim of policy and service provision should be to reduce drug- or alcohol-related harm to the minimum possible and achievable level for the community as a whole. Clearly, in theory, this would be a total elimination of alcohol and drug-related harm from the community. However, given that in practice it is always likely that some members of a community will continue to use drugs, and even more are likely to continue drinking alcohol, total elimination of alcohol and drug-related harm in a community is considered to be an unrealistic, if worthy, aspiration. Harm reduction can therefore be controversial, and raises important ethical questions, as it engages with those who continue to drink or use drugs in a harmful fashion. It raises the question of what is the minimum *achievable* level of harm for an individual or community, and we shall return to this in Chapter 7.

Harm reduction techniques are applied across the full spectrum of alcohol-related problems, from the counselling of those who are at risk but who have not yet experienced actual alcohol-related problems, or who have experienced only minor problems, through to those who are severely dependent and those who have suffered serious social, medical and psychological problems as a result of their drinking. At the milder end of the spectrum, so-called 'brief' or 'early' interventions have been found to be extremely effective. Consisting simply of a brief assessment followed by provision of information and advice, usually by a doctor or a nurse, such interventions have been shown to be highly effective in reducing alcohol

---

[70] It is recognised that this statement is not strictly true. For example, there is evidence that moderate alcohol use for some groups of people may be associated with lower cardiovascular morbidity and mortality. Furthermore, abstinent individuals may continue to experience harm resulting from the drug use of non-abstinent members of the population. However, in general, abstinence is likely to be associated with harm minimisation.

consumption, and thus risk of harm.[71] However, for the dependent drinker, more than this will usually be required.

## TREATMENT OF ALCOHOL DEPENDENCE

Just as the development of alcohol dependence involves biological, psychological and social processes, so treatment is a multi-modal concern. Patients may initially resist recognition of the nature of their problem, perhaps owing mainly to shame at the implications, and fear of the consequences of doing so.[72] The initial management of the alcohol withdrawal syndrome, however, is a relatively simple medical procedure, albeit with potentially serious complications, and can usually be accomplished within the space of a few days or, at the most, two or three weeks.[73] The work of preventing relapse to a dependent pattern of drinking is likely to continue for a considerably longer period, and involves psychological and social, as well as biological, processes. Attention must be paid to the relationship between therapist and patient, the family setting, and psychological problems which may have resulted in heavier drinking.[74] For some patients, special psychological techniques may be appropriate, and others benefit from pharmacological treatments, such as the newer so-called 'anti-craving' agents.[75] AA, the mutual-help approach based upon a distinctive Twelve Step programme, and with historical roots in the Christian tradition, is helpful for some patients. It emphasises a secular form of spirituality, which involves a need to recognise personal powerlessness over alcohol, and dependence upon a 'Higher Power' as vital to recovery.[76] In AA, life-long abstinence from alcohol is seen as essential to recovery. Even where professionally based treatments are orientated towards restoration of 'social' or 'moderate' drinking for some people with drinking problems, it is generally recognised that (owing to the phenomenon of reinstatement) complete abstinence from alcohol is almost always required once alcohol dependence is fully established.[77]

It has long been recognised that some patients spontaneously recover from patterns of addictive or dependent drinking, without the help of either professional treatment or self-help programmes. For some of these people, religious or spiritual experience seems to have played an important role in bringing about such a sudden change.[78]

---

[71] Babor et al., 2003, pp. 212–213.    [72] G. Edwards, Marshall and Cook, 2003, pp. 220, 361–363.
[73] Ibid., pp. 263–279.    [74] Ibid., pp. 280–299.    [75] Ibid., pp. 313–342.
[76] Ibid., pp. 300–312.    [77] Ibid., pp. 345–346.
[78] Ibid., pp. 208–209; Vaillant, 1983, pp. 190, 193; Miller and C'de Baca, 2001, p. 133.

## ALCOHOL POLICY

Alcohol policies have been defined as 'authoritative decisions made by governments through laws, rules and regulations [which] pertain to the relation between alcohol, health, and social welfare'.[79] It has been proposed that such policies should serve the prime purpose of improving public health and social well-being,[80] and they are thus generally concerned with harm reduction at the population level. The scientific literature providing the evidence base for such policies is enormous, and the diversity of policy options includes such measures as taxation, licensing laws and restrictions on sale, measures to create safer drinking environments, drink-driving legislation, regulation of advertising, education in support of 'safe' or 'sensible' drinking, and provision of treatment facilities for those who do develop alcohol-related problems. Again, a full review is beyond the scope of this book. The interested reader is referred to an excellent recent report sponsored by the WHO: *Alcohol: No Ordinary Commodity*.[81]

Alcohol policy has proved to be an increasingly controversial domain. Over the last thirty years, a series of three influential WHO-sponsored reports, having drawn extensively upon the scientific evidence available, have concluded that alcohol policy must address the consumption of the entire population, and not only that of the heavy drinker, the drinker experiencing alcohol-related problems or the alcohol addict.[82] This approach is premised upon the strong correlation between the average level of consumption of alcohol and the incidence of alcohol-related problems, at the population level. It notes also that there is a 'prevention paradox' whereby, although heavy drinkers are at greater risk of harm, yet, in respect of at least some alcohol-related problems, they contribute only a minority of the total number of cases of harm. This is because, although light and moderate drinkers are at much less risk of harm, they are much more numerous. According to this approach, alcohol policy therefore cannot afford to focus only on the heavy drinker, but must address the alcohol consumption of the whole population.[83] The arguable implications of this are various, but more significantly might require moderate drinkers as well as heavy drinkers to reduce consumption, and implies a need for consumption across whole populations (and not just subsections of populations) to be reduced. The former threatens the freedom of choice of individuals, and the latter threatens the profits of the

---

[79] Babor et al., 2003, p. 6.     [80] Ibid., p. 7.     [81] Ibid., 2003.
[82] Ibid., p. 5. See also Beauchamp, 1976.     [83] Kreitman, 1986.

alcohol industry. Thus, although the population approach to alcohol policy receives overwhelming academic support, it has generated heated debate.

It would appear to be the perceived threat to the beverage alcohol industry, or perhaps rather the industry's response to this threat, which has generated most of the heat. An editorial in the journal *Addiction* in 2000 suggested that the drinks industry has objectives other than those of improving public health and social well-being:

Alcohol producers are engaged in a campaign to capture the hearts and minds of alcohol researchers and public health people, as part of a major effort to win the war of ideas that shapes alcohol policy at national and international level. They are driven by the imperative for sales and profits, which is often in fundamental conflict with the public health goal of reducing hazardous drinking and alcohol-related harm.[84]

This particular editorial arose in relation to a concern about the activities of the International Center for Alcohol Policy (ICAP). ICAP, which is funded by a number of international beverage alcohol companies, describes itself as being 'dedicated to helping reduce the abuse of alcohol worldwide and to promoting understanding of the role of alcohol in society through dialogue and partnerships involving the beverage alcohol industry, the public health community and others interested in alcohol policy'.[85] Based upon a review of the publications and funding of ICAP, the *Addiction* editorial argues that ICAP is actually engaged in promoting an industry-favourable ideology, and that partnerships with ICAP could lead alcohol research away from effective policy strategies, towards a greater focus on individual choice, ineffective interventions and consumption of alcohol for 'beneficial' reasons. One commentator, although partly sympathetic to ICAP, suggested that developing countries might be especially vulnerable to such an influence on debate about alcohol and public health.[86]

ICAP is but one of a number of 'social aspects organisations' (SAOs) established at national and international level by the alcohol industry. Peter Anderson, in an important paper on SAOs,[87] has argued that each of the main viewpoints espoused by SAOs betrays an overall aim to benefit the alcohol industry rather than public health or the public good. Thus, for example, an emphasis on patterns of drinking as the best basis for alcohol policy ignores the evidence that volume of alcohol consumed is also important. Similarly, an emphasis on learning responsible drinking ignores

[84] McCreanor, Casswell and Hill, 2000, p. 179.    [85] International Center for Alcohol Policies, 2000b.
[86] Parry, 2000.    [87] Anderson, 2002.

both the importance of social environment and also the research evidence that policies based upon individual responsibility are ineffective. In fact, in a review of alcohol policy options, which he undertakes in this paper, Anderson shows that those options demonstrated by research to be effective in reducing alcohol-related harm are generally not supported by SAOs, whereas those unsupported by research, or shown by research to be ineffective, are generally supported by them.

Unfortunately, there is also evidence to support the contention that the alcohol industry is capable of exerting an effective and adverse influence upon national alcohol policy. Thus, Professor Robin Room, a sociologist who is the Director of the Centre for Social Research on Alcohol and Drugs at Stockholm University, has noted that the 2004 *Alcohol Harm Reduction Strategy for England (AHRSE)*, introduced by the British Government, proposes policy options which correspond almost entirely with those ranked (on the basis of research evidence) as 'ineffective' in the WHO-sponsored report *Alcohol: No Ordinary Commodity*.[88] Similarly, the strategy eschews almost all the 'effective' strategies, but gives a significant place to 'working with the alcohol industry'. Professor Room suggests that, in the *AHRSE* and in the European Union, the UK Government has 'generally sided . . . with British alcohol industry interests at the expense of public health and safety'.[89] He notes with even greater concern the highly restricted powers of licensing authorities proposed in the draft guidance issued under Section 182 of the Licensing Act 2003. Behind these ineffective policy measures he sees a strong alcohol industry lobby influencing the British Parliament, as well as a tendency for New Labour to define social problems in terms of individual responsibility rather than social context.

Other examples of allegations of the industry exerting an adverse influence upon alcohol policy and debate are not difficult to find. For example, in Australia, a partnership between industry and the Alcohol and Drug Foundation – Queensland (ADFQ) led to the creation of Alcohol Education Australia Ltd (AEA), an organisation whose mission and objectives allegedly subordinated public health to industry interests. ADFQ also soon began to support a manufacturer wishing to obtain a licence for an alcoholic milk drink, *Moo Joose*. This support for the industry appears to have been somewhat in contrast to its previous opposition to the introduction of alcoholic drinks aimed at children.[90]

A further example, this time involving the academic community more directly, is to be found in allegations which were widely reported in 1994

---

[88] Room, 2004.    [89] Ibid., p. 1083.    [90] Room, 2004.

to the effect that the drinks industry sought to discredit the WHO report, *Alcohol Policy and the Public Good,* by offering payment to academics who were willing to write critical reviews which would 'rubbish' its findings.[91] Further allegations of 'rubbishing' WHO policy appeared at about the same time in the academic journal *Addiction,* in relation to a drinks industry commentary on the WHO's European Alcohol Action Plan.[92]

The industry response to these allegations appears to be that, on the one hand, the need for population level reduction of alcohol consumption is flawed[93] (even though this is supported by the WHO and the findings of extensive research) and that, on the other hand, there is no inherent conflict between public health goals and the industry's interests.[94] The 'ethics of cooperation' are presented as supportive of the 'common good of society'.[95] But to assert that there is no inherent conflict between the common good and the industry's interests is at the very least highly debatable, and more arguably completely untenable. Perhaps if the level of sales of alcohol which maximises profit coincided with the level of consumption of alcohol which minimises harm to the population, such an argument could be persuasive. In other words, if alcohol-related harm always harmed the profits of the industry, there might be no inherent conflict. However, if anything would seem to be inherent, given the well-documented direct correlation between consumption and harm, it would seem to be the unlikelihood that this will actually be the case. To argue that there is no inherent conflict therefore appears to presume that shareholders and executives could never be tempted to persuade themselves, against good evidence, of the harmlessness of the extra profit that might come with increased sales, and thus increased consumption of their product. Given human nature, this presumption would not appear to be well founded. Furthermore, it might be argued that the reported activities of ICAP, and allegations of the 'rubbishing' of WHO reports, suggest that evidence against the presumption already exists.

If we assume that the beverage alcohol industry does, as it claims, have a genuine concern for public health and the common good of society, it

---

[91] Smith, 1994; Anonymous, 1995.    [92] Raw, 1994.    [93] Winstanley, 1995, p. 583.

[94] Indeed, the Board members of ICAP took 'strong exception' to the assertion that there was a 'fundamental conflict' between commercial interests and the public health goal of 'reducing alcohol-related harm and hazardous drinking' (Leverton et al., 2000, p. 1430); Broadly speaking, the industry approach emphasises co-operation between industry, government and others in the formation of policy. Responsibility, education and promotion of responsible drinking behaviour are offered as effective policies, in preference to taxation and other measures directed at reducing the consumption of all drinkers (International Center for Alcohol Policies, 2000a) even though there is a lack of evidence that the former policies are effective and a wealth of evidence that the latter policies are effective (Babor et al., 2003, pp. 189–207, 263–272).

[95] Hannum, 1997a, b.

must in fact be caught in a serious conflict of interests, which pits this concern against corporate profit. Its denial of such a conflict therefore might represent dissimulation or else, more generously, a self-deluding defence against corporate cognitive dissonance. However, the argument that they do not have any conflict of interest cannot stand upon their non-acceptance of the population level approach, for it is in the evaluation of this well-researched and widely accepted approach to alcohol policy that the conflict of interest exists. Given that governments benefit from beverage alcohol industry profit through taxation, this conflict of interest potentially afflicts them too. Indeed, Robin Room's account would suggest that it has already adversely affected the *AHRSE*.

## ALCOHOL, ADDICTION AND CHRISTIAN ETHICS

The foregoing overview of alcohol, its effects and harms, and the nature and understandings of alcohol addiction and dependence, immediately draws attention to a number of important concerns that require the attention of the Christian ethicist.

1. The use of alcohol is associated with many and varied harms, which may be biological, social or psychological. Collectively, their toll on populations is enormously expensive – both financially and in terms of human suffering. The reduction of these harms has properly become a major concern of alcohol policy formation and is also a goal of treatment programmes for those with alcohol-related problems.

2. Alcohol use and alcohol misuse are not completely separate categories. Risk of alcohol-related harm is directly correlated with level of consumption at the individual and population levels, but there is no clear threshold beyond which harm begins and below which it is never encountered.

3. The use of alcohol is nonetheless very popular in many western nations and in many developing countries of the world today, and the benefits of light to moderate consumption may include a protection against coronary heart disease in men over the age of forty years and in post-menopausal women.

4. The proper goal of alcohol policy, as proposed in the most recent WHO report on the subject, is that of improved public health and social well-being.

5. In debate about alcohol policy, a conflict of interest would appear to exist on the part of the alcohol industry, between the benefits accrued to shareholders by increased sales of beverage alcohol and the harms accrued to any given population by increased consumption of alcohol.

Because governments benefit from beverage alcohol industry profits, through taxation, they are also potentially caught in the same conflict of interest.

6. For the individual drinker, there are questions to be faced concerning the effects of acute intoxication which vary, in direct proportion to the dose of alcohol, from trivial through to lethal. The nature of intoxication is such as to impair good judgement and cognitive function, alter mood, and impair co-ordinated action. Drunkenness, which is a cultural as well as a biological phenomenon, is associated with an enhanced risk of violence, and yet may be a goal of drinking for many young people.

7. The phenomenon of addiction to alcohol, or alcohol dependence, is a bio-psycho-social state which includes as one of its features a subjectively strong desire to continue drinking or to resume drinking. The motivation of the dependent drinker is therefore divided between the desire to continue drinking and the need to avoid the harms associated with drinking.

We shall return to further consideration of these concerns in Chapter 7. However, they need now to be considered in the context of the history of Christian theological reflection on what scripture and experience have to teach us. Accordingly, Chapter 3 will give consideration to drunkenness as understood in scripture, and especially in the New Testament. Chapter 4 will review the various ways in which the teaching of scripture was interpreted by Augustine of Hippo, Aquinas and the Church Reformers. In Chapter 5, the nineteenth-century reinterpretation of the virtue of temperance will be considered in the context of changing perceptions of drunkenness, or 'inebriety', and the emergence of the concept of addiction.

In Chapter 6, the concept of the alcohol dependence syndrome, and especially its element of 'subjective compulsion', will be brought into dialogue with two theological texts: one from the apostle Paul, and one from Augustine of Hippo.

In Chapter 7, we shall return to the lessons of the earlier chapters as a basis for constructing a theological and ethical understanding of alcohol misuse and addiction.

# CHAPTER 3

# Drunkenness as vice in the New Testament

The history of the Christian ethics of alcohol use and misuse has roots in Hebrew and Christian scripture, and especially in the Christian New Testament references to drunkenness as a vice. A careful tracing of these roots is foundational to a complete analysis of the Christian ethics of alcohol misuse and addiction.

In the New Testament literature, drunkenness finds a place within the so-called 'catalogues' of vices and virtues. These catalogues, or lists, provide an especially helpful key to understanding the historical, cultural and theological context of the Christian ethics of alcohol misuse. First, they enable an estimation of the relative seriousness of the problem of drunkenness alongside a number of other vices, as understood by the New Testament authors and communities. Secondly, they enable consideration of the ways in which the problem of drunkenness was related to these other vices. Thirdly, since the practice of compiling such catalogues was adopted from the wider classical world, they enable an assessment of the way in which early Christian ethics in this field drew upon, or reacted to, other philosophical and religious systems of thought.

Before proceeding to a detailed consideration of the New Testament texts in question, it is necessary to consider what is known about the background and context of the New Testament literature, in terms of both drunkenness and alcohol misuse in New Testament times, and the literary and ethical device of compiling 'catalogues' of virtues and vices.

## THE HISTORICAL, PHILOSOPHICAL AND LITERARY CONTEXT OF THE CONCEPT OF DRUNKENNESS AS USED IN THE NEW TESTAMENT

What was the contemporary understanding of problems of drunkenness and alcohol misuse in the Greco-Roman and Jewish world of the first century CE? Fee[1] suggests that the 'pagan world' had little of a negative nature to say about drunkenness, except insofar as it led to other vices such as 'violence, public scolding of servants [and] unseemly sexuality'.[2] However, Reicke,[3] describing the context in Asia Minor in the mid-first century CE, refers to social 'clubs', which were prohibited by the Roman emperors on the grounds that the excessive drinking which they encouraged easily led to revolutionary sentiment. Such clubs were understood as being under the 'protection' of an oriental or Greek deity, often Dionysos. The activities of these clubs were marked by violence, dissipation, unlawful cultic practice and anti-Roman sympathies.

The association of drunkenness as a problem specifically associated with the worship of Dionysos (in Greek mythology) or Bacchus (in Roman mythology) is perhaps easily susceptible to over-statement.[4] Wine was understood as a gift of this god and perhaps as an aid to communion with him, but he was primarily a god of abundant life and liberation, and the ecstatic frenzies of devotees of the cult were not necessarily alcohol-induced. That said, the cult was outlawed by the Roman Senate in 186 BCE because of concerns about its effect on social order and evidence of its association with immorality and human sacrifice.[5] There is also evidence that it was influential in Corinth, and that Paul's correspondence with the Corinthian church was influenced by his concerns at its adverse effect on the congregation there.[6] The association of drunkenness with the Dionysiac cult must therefore have been a negative social consideration in the Greco-Roman world.

Petronius' *Satyricon* was written at a date sometime before 66 CE, probably within ten years of Paul's letter to the Romans.[7] Petronius was a courtier of Nero. Although there is debate about the literary genre of this work, with some seeing it as satire, and others as the first realistic novel in European literature,[8] it portrays a vivid account of a Roman banquet at which excessive drinking is very much in evidence, alongside other excesses of numerous and diverse kinds.[9] The guests are given wine in which to wash their hands,

---

[1]  Fee, 1987, pp. 225–226.

[2]  His primary sources are somewhat unclear. His only reference is to the work of Lucian (see below), who was writing a century later than Paul.

[3]  Reicke, 1980, pp. 117–119.

[4]  See, for example, the comments on the Dionysiac cult offered by Kalivas, 2004, pp. xi–xx, and Vellacott, 1971, pp. 24–32, in their introductions to Euripides' play *The Bacchae*. This play, written in the late fifth century BCE, provides a vivid picture of the practices of the cult in the fictional context of a play in which a mother possessed by a Dionysiac frenzy murders her own son.

[5]  Vellacott, 1971, pp. 401–415.

[6]  Kroeger and Kroeger, 1978a, b. Note in particular his concern at drunkenness in the context of eucharistic practice in 1 Corinthians 11:21.

[7]  Sullivan, 1965, pp. 7–10; Dunn, 1988, p. 789.     [8]  Sullivan, 1965, pp. 13–20.     [9]  Ibid., pp. 45–88.

are offered an amusingly ostentatious wine of impossible vintage, and are treated to recitals of the host's works by a youth acting the part of Bacchus, the god of the vine and of ecstasy. The serving of wine is associated with the bringing in of statues of household deities, which the guests are expected to kiss. Enormous quantities of wine and food are consumed by all concerned, and the banquet continues until at least the middle of the night. Even the servants are offered wine to drink, and the host issues instructions that it is to be poured over their heads if they will not drink it. A guest arrives already drunk, and immediately asks for wine. The host, delighted at this, demands an even larger cup for himself. The effect of alcohol on the narrator of the tale is such that 'there seemed to be more lights burning and the whole dining room seemed different'.[10] The effect on the host's wife is such that she wishes to dance – a public display of bad manners.[11] For Petronius, drunkenness is associated with pagan ritual, altered perceptions of one's surroundings and poor manners. However, the greatest emphasis by far is on a pattern of behaviour which is governed by excessive indulgence in pleasures of all kinds. It is not at all clear that drunkenness is any more the cause than it is the result of these excesses.

Lucian, a Greek rhetorician writing in the second century CE, provides an interesting, albeit slightly later, account of drunkenness in his book *Timon, or the Misanthrope*.[12] Through the words of the character Timon, he describes the effects of drinking on Thrasycles, a character who, when sober, is gentlemanly, correct in demeanour and profuse in praise of virtue, albeit somewhat superior in attitude, covetous, dishonest and sycophantic. When drinking, Thrasycles becomes overtly gluttonous, insatiable and riotous. He abuses others and 'flies into a passion'. His drinking is apparently brought to an end only when he vomits and has to be carried out of the dining room. Even then, he tries to assault a girl playing the flute as he is taken away. For Lucian, it would seem that drinking reduces inhibitions and brings to the surface the evil of the drinker's true character; evil which otherwise lays hidden by decorum and a concern about public appearances.

In a similar vein, the Roman philosopher Seneca, writing in the first century CE, is quoted as saying, 'Drunkenness does not create vices, but it brings them to the fore.'[13] Pittacus, one of the seven sages of ancient Greece, is attributed with having understood wine as being a 'mirror of the soul', which reveals what a man is really like.[14] Rolleston, in his survey of

---

[10] Ibid., p. 75.   [11] Ibid., p81; see n. 63.
[12] Harmon, 1960, pp. 387–389.   [13] Skehan and Di Lella, 1987, p. 390.
[14] Rolleston, 1927, p. 104.

alcoholism in classical antiquity, quotes a variety of other similar Greek and Roman sayings to the same effect.[15]

It would therefore appear that the Greco-Roman world of the first century CE saw drunkenness as a form of excess, sometimes associated with pagan cults, which led to, or brought to the surface, immoral or antisocial behaviour. As Fee has suggested, there would appear to be little evidence that it was seen as being wrong in itself. However, it was clearly seen as a risky activity, which could easily lead to embarrassment or worse.

Fee similarly argues that Judaism of this period was more concerned with the behaviour to which drunkenness leads than with drunkenness itself.[16]

A comprehensive and detailed survey of all references to drunkenness in the Jewish scriptures is beyond the scope of this chapter. However, some consideration must be given to the ways in which drunkenness is portrayed in the Old Testament and in the Apocrypha.[17] For example, in the book of the Wisdom of Ben Sira[18] (31:25–31), there is an interesting passage relating to the drinking of wine at banquets. On the one hand, wine is seen as being a good part of creation:

Wine is very life to human beings if taken in moderation. What is life to one who is without wine? It has been created to make people happy. Wine drunk at the proper time and in moderation is rejoicing of heart and gladness of soul. (31:27–28)[19]

On the other hand, wine drunk to excess is understood as the cause of 'bitterness of spirit', quarrels, anger, and loss of strength (31:29–30). But the Greek text may also be translated in such a way as to bring out a

---

[15] Ibid., p. 105. He further documents the recognition by Greco-Roman writers of the adverse effects of 'alcoholism', including impairment of sexual performance, insanity, crime, poverty and the adverse effects upon the child conceived in drunkenness (pp. 112–116). However, his use of the term 'alcoholism' in reference to a historical period two millennia before that term had been coined is obviously anachronistic.

[16] Fee, 1987, p. 225.

[17] These are, of course, Christian terms, the latter reflecting the Protestant terminology for Roman Catholic 'deuterocanonical' writings. The Jewish canon was in fact not clearly defined until the end of the first century CE, but the Christian Church separated from Judaism before the First Jewish Revolt (66–70 CE). It is therefore difficult to speak meaningfully of what was or was not Jewish 'scripture' prior to approximately 90 CE. Most of the Christian, 'New Testament', scriptures containing the vice lists which are the subject of this chapter were written prior to this date. For the sake of precision and convenience, the terms 'Old Testament' and 'Apocrypha' will therefore be used here, albeit with full awareness that they are somewhat anachronistic as far as the historical context is concerned. (See Skehan and Di Lella, 1987, pp. 17–19, for a helpful discussion of the canonicity of Jewish scriptures, the Old Testament and the Apocrypha.)

[18] Probably written in the early second century BCE (Skehan and Di Lella, 1987, pp. 8–16).

[19] All quotations of scripture are from the New Revised Standard Version (Anglicized Edition), unless stated otherwise.

different emphasis. Where verse 28 refers to the drinking of wine 'at the proper time', verse 29 can be understood as referring to the drinking of wine 'amid anger and strife' as a contrast to this.[20] In other words, the harmful effects of alcohol are not simply a result of excessive drinking, but also of drinking at the wrong time or, more specifically, in the wrong emotional frame of mind. Similarly (v. 31), a time of drunkenness is not the time to engage in argument or dispute – especially at a banquet or in 'the presence of others'.[21]

Verse 30 of this passage describes the effects of wine on 'the fool'. The fool in the Wisdom of Ben Sira, and elsewhere in the Hebrew wisdom literature, is generally taken as referring to the sinner who rejects the path of wisdom.[22] The effect of drunkenness upon the fool is again harmful:

Drunkenness increases the anger of a fool to his own hurt, reducing his strength and adding wounds. (31:30)

This is apparently a very similar view to that later espoused by Seneca (see above), to the effect that wine is not the cause of vice, but rather brings it to the fore.[23] However, it is not so much vice that is emphasised here as the harm that the fool brings upon his own head.

There are other references to drunkenness in the Hebrew wisdom literature, which further emphasise the themes of the dangers of excess,[24] and the unmasking of vice.[25] Elsewhere, related themes emerge. In the Pentateuch, the only references[26] are to be found in the book of Genesis, where Noah plants the first vineyard, produces the first wine from its grapes, and then becomes drunk on it.[27] As a result, Noah's son Ham sees him laying naked in his tent and is cursed by his father.[28] In Hebrew prophetic literature, drunkenness is often used in a metaphorical sense, usually to emphasise incapacity, shame and desolation,[29] or satiation.[30] A similar usage is found in Hebrew poetry, perhaps most beautifully in the reference to being 'drunk with love' which is to be found in the Song of Songs.[31] In the historical literature of the Old Testament and Apocrypha, drunkenness appears as a

---

[20] Skehan and Di Lella, 1987, pp. 385, 390.     [21] Ibid., pp. 385, 390–391.     [22] Ibid., p. 310.
[23] Ibid., p. 390.     [24] Proverbs 23:20–21; 23:29–35.     [25] Proverbs 20:1.
[26] Apart from metaphorical 'drunkenness' in Deuteronomy 32:34.
[27] See also Genesis 43:34, where Joseph and his brothers drink and 'become merry'.
[28] Genesis 9:20–25. It has been suggested that this provides a parallel with the story of 'the fall' in Genesis 3. In Genesis 3 Adam and Eve eat the fruit and become aware of their nakedness. In Genesis 9 Noah takes the fruit of the vine and, losing his senses, exposes his nakedness (Tomasino, 1992).
[29] Isaiah 19:14; 24:20; 28:7; 29:9; Jeremiah 25:27; 48:26; 51:39, 57; Ezekiel 23:33; Joel 1:5.
[30] Isaiah 28:1; 34:5; 49:26; 51:21–22; Ezekiel 39:19; Habakkuk 2:15–16.
[31] Song of Solomon 5:1; see also Lamentations 4:21; Psalm 107:27.

successful or attempted means of taking advantage of another person, as for example in the stories of Judith and Holofernes, and David and Uriah.[32]

Mounce, offering a brief contemporary overview of drunkenness and drinking in the Old Testament, argues that the drinking of wine is sometimes viewed as good, but that elsewhere it is viewed as evil, and that drunkenness is always seen as evil.[33] This would appear to be a somewhat simplistic view. As the above survey of Old Testament and Apocryphal references shows, it is invariably the consequences of drunkenness that these authors condemn. Drunkenness itself, insofar as it is seen as undesirable, is more to be understood as a form of 'excess' associated with the risk of possible harm.[34] It is perhaps 'unwise', rather than strictly 'evil'.

But how did Jewish commentators and non-canonical Jewish authors understand drunkenness at the time when the New Testament texts were being written?

The *Testaments of the Twelve Patriarchs* form a pseudepigraphical work of uncertain date, probably written somewhere between the second century BCE and the second century CE. Depending upon the view taken on their date, they may either be originally Jewish writings, with later Christian interpolation, or else primarily from Christian authorship.[35] The *Testament of Judah* contains an interesting comment on drunkenness, which draws attention to its evil consequences.[36] Among these are lust, fornication, filthy talk, wrath, riot, war and confusion. The writer encourages his readers to drink in moderation: 'If ye drink wine in gladness, with shamefacedness, with the fear of God, ye shall live.' He advises them that they should exercise discretion, and that a man should drink only 'as long as he keepeth decency'.

A more extended treatment of drunkenness is provided by Philo, an Alexandrian Jew writing during the first half of the first century CE. In *De Plantatione*, he considers what the philosophical schools have to say about drunkenness. In *De Ebrietate*, he proceeds to consider what he believes the views of Moses to have been on the subject. In *De Plantatione*, he raises the question: 'Will the wise man get drunk?' The term used for 'get drunk' is the verb μεθυειν. This term may be used in two senses. On the one hand it may mean simply 'hard drinking' (οινουσθαι), and on

---

[32] Judith 13:15 and 2 Samuel 11:13 respectively. See also 1 Maccabees 16:16; 1 Kings 16:9–10; 20:14–21.

[33] Mounce, 2000, p. 175.

[34] For a cataloguing of harms attributed to alcohol in the Old Testament, see Seller, 1985.

[35] Cross and Livingstone, 1997, p. 1593.

[36] Paragraphs 14–16; Christian Classics Ethereal Library website, <http://www.ccel.org/fathers2/ANF-08/anf0808.htm>.

the other hand it may mean drinking to the point of foolish behaviour (λερειν). Philo asserts that all believe that heavy drinking carried to the point of 'foolish behaviour' is wrong. The question is really whether or not the wise man may engage in 'hard drinking' that does not lead to foolish behaviour. It seems fairly clear that Philo concludes that 'the wise man will get drunk', although the manuscript is incomplete, its conclusion having been lost.[37] In *De Ebrietate* he asserts that Moses uses wine as a symbol for five things: foolishness or foolish talking, complete insensibility, greediness, cheerfulness and gladness, and nakedness. Clearly the first three of these are evil, while the fourth is good. The manuscript is again incomplete, and the discussion of the last two has been lost.[38] However, the general sense here is again that drunkenness is wrong where it leads to wrong behaviour. This impression is further reinforced in *De Somnii*, where Philo describes the differing effects of wine on different people. Some are 'bettered' by it, and others 'worsened'.

## CATALOGUES OF VIRTUES AND VICES

There are various accounts of the 'catalogues' of vices and virtues which were a common feature of the literature of the first century CE in the Greco-Roman world, including Hellenistic Judaism.[39] There is no clear or agreed definition of what constitutes such a list. Longenecker refers to 'systematic lists, often with descriptions of the items listed',[40] but this hardly clarifies things. Their origins appear to date back to Plato, Aristotle and Zeno.[41] They usually encompassed the conventions of the period and included abstract and concrete terms, and mental dispositions as well as overt behaviour. They were used for diverse purposes, including 'characterisation, description, exemplification, instruction, exhortation, apology and polemic'.[42] Greco-Roman philosophers would frequently commence a speech with a list of vices as an illustration of the 'wretched moral condition of the masses'.[43]

There are said to be no examples of catalogues of vices and virtues in the Old Testament, although lack of a clear definition makes it difficult

---

[37] Colson and Whitaker, 1968, pp. 209–211.    [38] Ibid., pp. 308–317.

[39] See, in particular, Longenecker, 1990, pp. 249–252; Conzelmann, 1981, pp. 100–101; Betz, 1979, pp. 281–283, and Freedman, 1997 (entry on 'virtue/vice lists') upon which the following account is largely based.

[40] Longenecker, 1990, p. 249.    [41] Ibid., pp. 249–250.

[42] Freedman, 1997 (entry on 'virtue/vice lists').    [43] Ibid.

to understand why some passages[44] should not be seen as 'catalogues' of a kind. However, these lists did not constitute a distinctive literary form, and neither did they serve as models for later Jewish or Christian usage. Hellenistic Judaism, however, did adopt this device, and Philo of Alexandria (30 BCE–50 CE) is perhaps the best example of a Jewish writer who made extensive use of them. One of his lists contains almost 150 items![45] Catalogues of virtues and vices are also to be found in the Apocrypha.[46] In Hellenistic Jewish usage, the virtues tend to be seen as commandments of God, and the vices as 'pagan trademarks'.[47]

The catalogues of vices and virtues were taken up by the writers of the New Testament, as well as by later Christian writers, and were probably also used in catechetical teaching prior to baptism.[48] There is no agreement as to specific sources from which particular New Testament lists might have been taken.[49] Their content was not intended to convey a new system of ethics, but was a continuation of Jewish ethical teaching.[50] The functions of the New Testament lists were apparently largely analogous to those of the lists of the surrounding culture. There is generally no particular system to their compilation, or any attempt at comprehensiveness, but there may be a rhetorical method in their order.[51] The traditional form of the lists is said by some scholars to forbid any contextual links with local circumstances.[52] However, this does not seem to prevent others from making direct links between the content of the lists and the local context.[53]

There are numerous catalogues of vices and virtues in the New Testament, and they are diverse in length and content. There is also some divergence of opinion as to which texts should be understood as constituting 'catalogues' and which should not. Some texts, such as Matthew 11:19 (and its synoptic parallel, Luke 7:34), which might be considered as fairly clear examples, seem not to appear in many (or any) such listings.[54]

---

[44] Lists of virtues may be found in Exodus 31:3; 34:6–7; 35:31; Numbers 14:18; Job 1:1, 8; 2:3; Psalms 15:1–5; 86:15; 103:8; Ecclesiastes 2:26; Jeremiah 7:5–6; Ezekiel 18:5–9, 14–17; Jonah 4:2. Lists of vices may be found in Proverbs 6:16–19; 8:13–14; Jeremiah 7:9; Ezekiel 18:10–13, 18; Hosea 4:1–2.

[45] Colson and Whitaker, 1958, pp. 116–119.

[46] Wisdom of Solomon 8:7; 14:22–27; 4 Maccabees 1:2–4, 18–28, 32a; 2:15; 5:23–24; 8:3.

[47] Conzelmann, 1981, p. 100.     [48] Longenecker, 1990, p. 251.

[49] Freedman, 1997 (entry on 'virtue/vice lists').     [50] Conzelmann, 1981, p. 101.

[51] Conzelmann, 1981, p. 101; Betz, 1979, p. 282.     [52] Conzelmann, 1981, p. 101.

[53] See, for example, Reicke, 1980, p. 118, in relation to the list in James 4:3; and Mounce, 2000, pp. 166, 175, in relation to the lists in 1 Timothy 3:2–7, 8ff.; Titus 1:7–8.

[54] See, for example, the listings provided by Freedman, 1997 (entry on 'virtue/vice lists'); Betz, 1979, p. 281; Conzelmann, 1981, p. 100; Fee, 1987, p. 225; Longenecker, 1990, p. 250; Francis and Sampley, 1984, pp. xxiii, 98.

The use of catalogues of vices and virtues continued, in non-canonical Christian literature, into the second and third centuries CE.[55]

## DRUNKENNESS IN THE NEW TESTAMENT CATALOGUES OF VICES AND VIRTUES

Nine of the New Testament vice and virtue lists make reference to drunkenness. Four occurrences are in epistles of Pauline authorship,[56] four are in the pastoral epistles,[57] and one is in 1 Peter (4:3). Three of these lists are among those usually considered as 'virtue' lists, and in these lists the reference is to *not* being a drunkard, *not* indulging in much wine, or *not* being a slave to drink.[58] However, in the so-called 'vice' lists, there are also references to *not* living in drunkenness,[59] and *not* being addicted to wine.[60] The distinction between vice lists and virtue lists, at least so far as drunkenness is concerned, may therefore not be quite so clear-cut as some commentators appear to assume.[61]

Six different Greek words or phrases are used in these lists in reference to 'drunkenness' or related concepts:

1. μεθη (meaning[62] 'drunkenness' or 'debauchery')
2. μεθυσος (meaning 'drunkard' or 'drunken')
3. οινοφλυγια (meaning 'drunkenness')
4. παροινος (meaning 'drunkard' or 'given to strong drink')
5. οινω πολλω προσεχω (meaning 'to be addicted to wine', 'be fond of much wine')
6. οινω πολλω δουλοω (meaning 'to enslave to drink' or 'to make [someone] a slave to drink')

Four other Greek words are used elsewhere in the New Testament in reference to 'drunkenness' or related concepts:

1. οινοποτης (meaning 'drinker' or 'drunkard')
2. κραιπαλη (meaning 'drunken dissipation', 'drunken nausea', or 'surfeiting')
3. μεθυσκομαι (meaning 'to get drunk' or 'to intoxicate')
4. μεθυω (meaning 'to be drunk' or 'to drink freely')

---

55 Longenecker, 1990, p. 251; Freedman, 1997 (entry on 'virtue/vice lists').
56 Romans 13:13; 1 Corinthians 5:10–11; 6:9–10; Galatians 5:19–21.
57 1 Timothy 3:2–4; 3:8–10; Titus 1:7; 2:2–10.
58 1 Timothy 3:2–4, 8–10; Titus 2:2–10, respectively.     59 Romans 13:13.     60 Titus 1:7.
61 A 'virtue' is usually considered to be 'a quality of living in particular moral excellence' (Carr et al., 2002, p. 388) and therefore the negatives of drunkenness ('not being a drunkard', 'not indulging in much wine', etc.) would hardly qualify as virtues in the strict sense.
62 Meanings of the Greek are taken from Bibleworks for Windows version 4.0; CD-ROM, 1998.

There is debate as to the relative strength of these terms. It is suggested by some that πάροινος is to be understood as a stronger term than φίλοινος[63] or οινω πολλω προσεχω.[64] However, it would seem unwise to place too much significance upon these apparently fairly speculative differences.

In total, there are twenty-two occurrences of these words and phrases in the New Testament, of which nine are in a context usually understood as being a vice or virtue list. However, a further six (all in the gospels) occur in the context of some kind of 'list' of vices, albeit not one which is usually considered to be a 'vice list'. Table 3.1 provides a full listing of the occurrence of all these words and phrases in the New Testament.

References to drunkenness in the gospels occur in the context of accusations made against Jesus, where drunkenness is associated with gluttony;[65] in the context of eschatological parables, where drunkenness is associated with not being ready for the coming of the Son of Man;[66] and in the context of the miracle at the wedding at Cana, where drunken guests are provided with vast quantities of additional wine.[67] A reference in Acts is concerned with the possibility that the effects of the Holy Spirit on the day of Pentecost might be confused with drunkenness.[68] Two references occur in the book of Revelation, and both exemplify metaphorical usage of the word – in the one case to drunkenness with the 'wine of fornication', and in the other to drunkenness with the 'blood of the saints'.[69]

The remaining twelve occurrences, in the New Testament epistles, are all Pauline[70] except for 1 Peter 4:3. Only three of these references are not in the context of a vice or virtue list. Of these, one is concerned with a contrast between drunkenness and being filled with the Holy Spirit,[71] one is in the context of contrasting the activities of the day and night,[72] and one is in the context of an admonition about inappropriate behaviour at the Eucharist, where some were going hungry and others becoming drunk.[73]

---

[63] Meaning 'fond of wine'. The word is not found in the New Testament.

[64] Mounce, 2000, p. 175.     [65] Matthew 11:19; Luke 7:34.

[66] Matthew 24:49; Luke 12:45; 21:34.

[67] John 2:10. An eschatological theme may also be inferred here: Barrett, 1978, p. 193; Brown, 1966, pp. 104–105.

[68] Acts 2:15.

[69] Revelation 17:2 and 17:6 respectively.

[70] That is, they are all in the Pauline tradition. At least six of these occur in epistles of 'indisputably' Pauline authorship, four are in the pastoral epistles, and one is to be found in Ephesians.

[71] Ephesians 5:18.

[72] 1 Thessalonians 5:7; cf. Romans 13:13 – the contrast of activities appropriate to the day and the night has Old Testament and Apocryphal precedents, and is to be found elsewhere in the New Testament. In Roman society it was believed that 'during the night everything was permitted' (Dunn, 1988, pp. 788–789).

[73] 1 Corinthians 11:21.

Table 3.1 *New Testament Greek words for drunkenness and related concepts.*

| Greek | Part of speech | Meaning[a] | Occurrence in vice and virtue lists | Occurrence elsewhere in the New Testament |
|---|---|---|---|---|
| μεθη | noun | 'drunkenness' or 'debauchery' | Romans 13:13 Galatians 5:21 | Luke 21:34[b] |
| μεθυσος | noun | 'drunkard' or 'drunken' | 1 Corinthians 5:11 1 Corinthians 6:10 | |
| οινοφλυγια | noun | 'drunkenness' | 1 Peter 4:3 | |
| παροινος | adjective | 'drunkard' or 'given to strong drink' | 1 Timothy 3:3 Titus 1:7 | |
| οινω πολλω προσεχω | noun, adjective and verb | 'to be addicted to wine', 'be fond of much wine' | 1 Timothy 3:8 | |
| οινω πολλω δουλοω | noun, adjective and verb | 'to enslave to drink' or 'to make [someone] a slave to drink' | Titus 2:3 | |
| οινοποτης | noun | 'drinker' or 'drunkard' | | Matthew 11:19[b] Luke 7:34[b] |
| κραιπαλη | noun | 'drunken dissipation', 'drunken nausea', or 'surfeiting' | | Luke 21:34[b] |
| μεθυσκομαι | verb | 'get drunk' or 'intoxicate' | | Luke 12:45[b] John 2:10 Ephesians 5:18 1 Thessalonians 5:7 Revelation 17:2 |
| μεθυω | verb | 'be drunk' or 'drink freely' | | Matthew 24:49 Acts 2:15 1 Corinthians 11:21 Revelation 17:6 |

[a]Meanings of the Greek are taken from Bibleworks for Windows version 4.0; CD-ROM, 1998.
[b]References which provide 'lists' of vices, but which are not usually quoted as being 'vice lists'.

References to drunkenness in the New Testament therefore generally appear to assume that drunkenness is a vice. However, the miracle at Cana, where Jesus turns an enormous volume of water into wine for wedding guests who are already drunk, suggests that drunkenness is not an entirely negative concept.[74] Similar themes to those in Greco-Roman society, the Old Testament, Apocrypha and Jewish literature may be detected. In particular, the sense of drunkenness as 'excess', satiation or over-indulgence is

---

[74] *Pace* Mounce, who argues that drunkenness is always seen as evil in the New Testament, and that drinking wine is at best 'neutral' (Mounce, 2000, p. 175).

apparent, including (in Revelation) a metaphorical application. However, new themes also emerge. Similarities and contrasts between the effects of drunkenness and the effects of the Holy Spirit are apparent in Acts and in Ephesians, and an eschatological context is also found in the gospels, in which drunkenness is seen as impairing readiness for the coming of the Son of Man.

The references to drunkenness within the vice and virtue lists raise a number of issues which reinforce and extend the general impressions that have been outlined, based upon the Old and New Testament context.

First, for those who believe that the content of the lists reflected local concerns, the references to drunkenness imply that there were problems with drunkenness in the various communities to which the epistles relate. Thus Mounce, commenting on the pastoral epistles, sees evidence of such problems in the Ephesian church and in Crete, and makes reference to contemporary epitaphs which listed heavy drinking as a virtue.[75] Similarly Kelly, although he believes that the list in 1 Peter 4:3 has probably been taken from elsewhere, sees its use there as reflecting the contemporary problems of first-century CE Asia Minor.[76]

Secondly, there is evidence that at least some of the drunkenness referred to may have occurred in the context of festivals in honour of the god Dionysos (or Bacchus).[77] Kelly notes that the lists in 1 Peter 4:3 and Galatians 5:20 both refer to idolatry as well as drunkenness.[78] However, the evidence for a cultic association appears to be largely based upon the use of the word κωμος, which occurs in association with μεθη in Romans 13:13 and Galatians 5:21, and in association with οινοφλυγια in 1 Peter 4:3. Κωμος was originally a festal procession in honour of Dionysos, and carried a sense of 'uninhibited revelry to excess'. When used in conjunction with μεθη, the meaning may be 'drinking bout' or 'drunken revelry'.[79] Dunn suggests that Trimalchio's banquet may give a fair idea of what Paul had in mind when using these words in Romans 13:13.[80] Bruce sees a somewhat more positive connotation, such as might be associated with a celebration of victory at the games, but also recognises that 'insobriety' at the conclusion of such celebrations might have invited moral censure.[81] Reicke, on the other hand, refers to evidence that these celebrations were of a more

[75] Mounce, 2000, pp. 174–175, 390, 410.     [76] Kelly, 1990, p. 170.
[77] Longenecker, 1990, p. 257; Reicke, 1980, pp. 117–118; Best, 1982, p. 153.
[78] Kelly, 1990, p. 170.     [79] Dunn, 1988, p. 789.
[80] Ibid., p. 789.     [81] Bruce, 1998, p. 250.

seditious nature, being associated with revolutionary sentiment, rioting and violence.[82]

Thirdly, the association of drunkenness with other items in some of the lists may be taken as suggesting that the author (usually Paul) was concerned with the problems and vices to which drunkenness leads. For example, Cranfield suggests that the drunken revels of Romans 13:13 can be seen as the cause of the debauchery, strife and jealousy mentioned in the same list. He also quotes Chrysostom as seeing a link between drunkenness and fornication in this list.[83] Similarly, Bruce sees drunkenness as the cause of the behaviours of the reviler and the robber, who appear alongside the 'drunkard' in the lists in 1 Corinthians 5:11 and 6:10.[84] Fee also draws attention to the connection between drunkenness and reviling, and the association of drunkenness with carousing, in 1 Corinthian 5:11.[85]

Fourthly, the theme of drunkenness as excess is again apparent in these lists. In 1 Corinthians 5:11 and 6:10, the 'drunkard' is mentioned in close proximity to the 'greedy'. Bruce suggests that μεθη represents the vice of excessive indulgence in wine, just as gluttony is the vice of excessive indulgence in food.[86] Similarly, Best suggests that the vices of drunkenness, revels and carousing in 1 Peter 4:3 are all 'sins of intemperance'.[87] Again, Kelly sees sexual and alcoholic excess as prominent in 1 Peter 4:3, Romans 13:13 and Galatians 5:19–21.[88]

Fifthly, three of the lists are presented in terms of a contrast in which drunkenness is understood as in some sense being a desire of 'the flesh'. In Romans 13, drunkenness is seen as among those vices which are making 'provision for the flesh, to gratify its desires' (v. 14). In contrast, the reader is urged to 'put on the Lord Jesus Christ'. In Galatians 5, drunkenness is among the 'works of the flesh' (v. 19) which are contrasted with the 'fruit of the Spirit' (vv. 22–23). Drunkenness and the other vices listed are ways of gratifying the 'desires of the flesh' (v. 16) and are 'opposed to the Spirit' (v. 17). In 1 Peter 4, the reader is urged to live 'no longer by human desires but by the will of God' (v. 2). Drunkenness is clearly among these 'human desires'.[89] In Pauline usage, 'desire' has a negative connotation, and is a key concept in his analysis of human sinfulness.[90] While it might have a connotation of 'natural/animal appetites'[91] which could be understood as including the physical craving for alcohol, its usage is clearly broader

[82] Reicke, 1980, pp. 117–118.  [83] Cranfield, 1995, p. 334.
[84] Bruce, 1998, p. 250.  [85] Fee, 1987, pp. 225 n. 29, 225–226.
[86] Bruce, 1998, pp. 249–250.  [87] Best, 1982, p. 153.  [88] Kelly, 1990, p. 170.
[89] In v. 6, which is somewhat difficult to interpret, it would appear that drunkenness is among those works for which people will be judged 'in the flesh', in order that they might live 'in the Spirit'. (See Best, 1982, pp. 155–158).
[90] Dunn, 1993, p. 297.  [91] Ibid., p. 791.

than this.[92] Although it would be wrong to attribute to 1 Peter a Pauline understanding of 'the flesh',[93] it would seem that the use of the word 'desire' in this epistle is similarly concerned with those appetites which keep a person away from God.[94] In this sense, drunkenness is not simply excessive indulgence of an appetite, it is indulgence of a wrong appetite.

Sixthly, four of the references occur in the Pastoral Epistles, in lists concerned with the qualities expected of church leaders. While these lists do not vary in any significant way from what might be expected of all Christians,[95] it does suggest the possibility that the author understood drunkenness as offering an example which is potentially unhelpful to others. In each case, it is also possible to understand drunkenness as prejudicial to the qualities which are expected of leadership. Bishops are expected to be 'above reproach' and 'blameless',[96] deacons must be 'serious',[97] and the older women should be 'reverent in behaviour'.[98] Drunkenness is clearly likely to undermine or jeopardise these qualities.

Finally, in the case of three of the lists, there is an eschatological context. In Romans 13, this serves particularly to contrast the activities appropriate to the coming age with those appropriate to the present time.[99] Drunkenness is among those activities characteristic of the 'night', or of the present age, in contrast to those which belong to the 'day' of God's coming kingdom. In 1 Corinthians 5, the contrast is between those who will, and those who will not, inherit the 'kingdom of God'. In 1 Peter 4, the contrast is between living according to human desires and living according to the will of God (v. 2). In each case, it would seem that drunkenness is understood as being inappropriate to the coming kingdom, or at least likely to make a person unprepared for its coming.[100]

## A BIBLICAL BASIS FOR A CHRISTIAN ETHICAL UNDERSTANDING OF CONTEMPORARY ALCOHOL MISUSE

On the basis of the above review, it is argued here that a comprehensive biblical basis for a Christian theology and ethics of drunkenness should take account of

---

[92] Ziesler, 1989, p. 321.
[93] It would, however, be interesting to develop further a Pauline understanding of drunkenness as a desire of the 'flesh'. The concept of the flesh in Pauline theology is an interesting one. To live by the flesh is to live by a power which is not God (Ziesler, 1990, pp. 77–80), and Romans 13 and Galatians 5 show that Paul understood drunkenness as an example of such a power.
[94] Kelly, 1990, pp. 68, 104.    [95] Houlden, 1989, p. 77.    [96] 1 Timothy 3:2; Titus 1:7.
[97] 1 Timothy 3:8.    [98] Titus 2:3.    [99] Cranfield, 1995, p. 331.
[100] Cf. Matthew 24:49; Luke 12:45; 21:34; 1 Thessalonians 5:7.

1. the nature and extent of the alcohol-related problems that arise in a given community
2. the consequences of drunkenness
3. the religious and spiritual context of drinking
4. a concept of drunkenness as a vice of 'excess' indulgence
5. the subjective individual experience of 'desire' to drink
6. the example that drunkenness sets to others
7. the appropriateness of drinking in an eschatological context

Problems of alcohol misuse were not unknown to the Old or New Testament authors. In particular, drunkenness was recognised as a problem which led to a range of other vices, including 'sins of speech', sexual immorality, violence, strife and jealousy. It appears to have been understood as a problem of excess indulgence of an appetite, rather similar to gluttony as excess indulgence in food. It appears to be this excessive self-indulgence, and the problems to which it led, which were considered to be the root of the problem that it constituted. Although in many places drunkenness is apparently portrayed as being a vice in and of itself, it would appear that it is seen in this light both because of the excessive self-indulgence from which it arises, and because of the other vices to which it leads. This would appear also to have been the view of the Jewish and Greco-Roman cultures from within which the New Testament authors wrote. As such, it represented the kind of behaviour which leaders of the early Christian community were encouraged to avoid, and which was not considered to be a good example to others.

However, within the New Testament, there are also more specifically Christian reasons offered for avoiding drunkenness. Some of the New Testament catalogues of vices suggest that Christians were concerned about the association of drunkenness with the worship of pagan deities in a context which represented an especially extravagant, and possibly seditious, form of revelling and dissipation. As a 'desire of the flesh', drunkenness represented life under a power which is 'not God'. There was also an eschatological understanding of drunkenness as being inappropriate to life in the kingdom of God. Drunkenness was understood as putting the believer at risk of not being 'ready' for the coming Son of Man.

The problems of alcohol misuse faced by contemporary western society are in many ways similar to those found in the New Testament context. A direct relationship between quantity of alcohol consumed, and the prevalence of alcohol-related problems within a population, has been demonstrated by numerous research studies. Similarly, recommendations are made concerning the 'sensible' or 'safe' limits of alcohol consumption for individuals, above which drinking is likely to lead to harm.[101] Alcohol misuse is, perhaps more than ever, seen as a vice which represents excessive indulgence of an appetite that is otherwise accepted as good by the majority of the population.

Heavy drinking leads to a variety of other problems of a social, psychological and medical nature. Among these, drunkenness is a problem primarily because of the other behaviours to which it leads, and because of the contexts in which it occurs. Among these are family disharmony, drinking and driving, violence and problems in the workplace. Some of the contexts of concern are even perhaps not entirely dissimilar to the κωμος of New Testament times. Although stripped of the pagan religious connotations,[102] contemporary experience of football violence is similarly fuelled by alcohol, contrary to law and order in society, and representative of the kind of dissipation which most members of society would condemn.

The similarity of New Testament and contemporary ethics of alcohol misuse might also be seen in the apparent agreement between the Christian community and wider society as to the nature of the vice of drunkenness. Both then and now, it would appear that there was widespread consensus between Christian communities and wider society that drunkenness is a potential source of vice which the wise will eschew. Then as now, the wisdom of this was also flouted by many.

A distinctively Christian theology or ethic of drunkenness should go beyond this common ground with the surrounding culture. Where drunkenness is the result of a desire which exerts over an individual a power which competes with the call of God, and where it results in a life which is inappropriate to, or unready for, the kingdom of God, it is something which Christians have additional and especial reasons to eschew.

---

[101] See G. Edwards, Marshall and Cook, 2003, pp. 16–18, 26–27.

[102] However, sport is viewed by some as being a form of 'secular' spirituality (Thomas, 1996). It may, therefore, potentially be understood by Christians as offering a focus of idolatry of a kind arguably equivalent to the Dionysian focus of the κωμος of New Testament times.

# CHAPTER 4

# *Drunkenness as intemperance: Augustine, Aquinas, Luther and Whitefield*

The history of the Christian ethics of alcohol use and misuse is instructive as an example of the ways in which Christians with various experiences and theological positions may variously argue from the premises of scripture, tradition and reason in order to reach their ethical conclusions. In respect of alcohol, at least up until the nineteenth century, these ethical conclusions were actually remarkably uniform. All agreed that drunkenness was a sin. Insofar as moderate drinking was generally understood as good, or at least morally neutral, drunkenness was generally conceived of as a sin of intemperance. However, these conclusions were reached in various ways, and the ethical analysis of individual cases was not always as consistent as the overall uniformity might promise. The history of Christian ethical discourse on drunkenness is thus important to understanding both the context and the analysis of contemporary Christian ethics in this field.

In this chapter, a review of the history of the Christian ethics of drunkenness will be limited to post-New Testament works published prior to the nineteenth century. In the nineteenth century the debate took a new turn, and this deserves more detailed and separate analysis, which will be undertaken in the following chapter.

The task to be undertaken in the present chapter will be attempted by means of a focus on the works of Augustine of Hippo (354–430), Thomas Aquinas (c. 1225–1274), Martin Luther (1483–1546) and George Whitefield (1714–1770). Augustine, Aquinas and Luther represent three of the most influential Christian thinkers in the period in question, and their work has had an enduring influence upon Christian ethics. They further represent the contrasting perspectives of the undivided Catholic Church, the medieval Roman Catholic Church, and the Reformed/Protestant Church.[1] Whitefield has been included in this list in addition to Luther, partly because of

---

[1] Gill, 1997, p. 2.

the limited references to the subject in the works of Luther, and also in order to add a later (early modern) Reformed perspective on the problem.

## AUGUSTINE OF HIPPO

Augustine was born in Thagaste, in North Africa, in 354 and was brought up as a Christian by his mother Monica. However, he lost this early faith, became a Manichee, and then converted back to Christianity in 386. He was ordained a priest in 391 and was ordained a bishop of Hippo in 395. He wrote extensively, and his works include refutations of the beliefs of the Manichees, the Donatists and the Pelagians, as well as an account of his own conversion to Christianity, and a defence of Christianity against its Roman pagan critics. His influence on subsequent Christian theology has been enormous.[2]

For Augustine, ethics was concerned with the *summum bonum*: the supreme good.[3] He believed that this supreme good is to be found in God. It is ultimately that alone which can make us happy. In this, eudaimonistic, aspect to his ethics he closely followed contemporary classical philosophers. However, he also took very seriously the dominical commands to love God above all, and to love our neighbours as ourselves. God is to be loved for his own sake, and we are to love ourselves and our neighbours in relation to God. For Augustine, virtue was defined as 'rightly ordered love'[4] and was itself a gift from God. He criticised the self-love which placed self as a higher concern than God or neighbour, and he saw this as being the pride which is at the root of all sin. He also saw fear as being a less worthy motivation than love.

For Augustine, the will was a central concept in ethics – he understood the will rather than the action as being the primary focus of ethical concern.[5] The will, in Augustinian thinking, is a characteristically human power which is the first cause of sin. It is the freedom of the will which makes human beings responsible for sin. But Augustine also importantly introduced the concept of the divided will. In his *Confessions*, he wrote about two wills being at war with each other within himself, and of his willingness to do what he viewed as right being only partial because of its association with a degree of unwillingness to do the same.[6] The division of the will results from the struggle within oneself between competing habits,

---

[2] Cross and Livingstone, 1997, pp. 128–129; Gill, 1997, pp. 31–32.
[3] The following account of Augustine's ethics is based upon the summary provided by Kent, 2002.
[4] Kent, 2002, p. 215.  [5] Bernasconi, 1992, p. 58.
[6] Book 8, Chapters 9 and 10; this is discussed further, with quotations from *Confessions*, in Chapter 6.

emotions and motivations. Furthermore, our desires are disordered as a result of concupiscence, which Augustine saw as being an aspect of the punishment for the original sin of Adam, in which we all share. We can be good at all only by virtue of the gift of God's grace.

Classical philosophers had argued for the inseparability of virtues. The Pelagians argued that human beings were capable of perfection and that virtue was thus worthy of merit. Augustine argued, contrary to both, that virtue depended upon love. The more love one revealed, the more virtuous one would be. Complete or perfect virtue was impossible in this life, but equally virtues could exist alongside vices. Virtue, he argued, was not necessarily completely perfect or completely absent. However, we can acquire virtue only through God's grace, and thus it does not constitute a basis for pride. This position leaves something of a tension in Augustine's thought between his concept of free will, on the one hand, and his understanding of virtue as attributable to God's grace alone, on the other.[7]

A survey of specific references to the subject of drunkenness within Augustine's published works reveals a large number of minor references which are not of great significance, and a smaller number in which the manner of application of his general ethical principles to this subject becomes more clear. Two of his published letters to his bishop,[8] while he was still a presbyter, specifically addressed the problems of drunkenness experienced in his congregation in North Africa. A number of other works[9] address the subject in passing. Four of his works[10] offer an exposition in passing on Galatians 5:19–21, in which drunkenness is referred to as a 'work of the flesh'. Two other works[11] deal in passing with the matter of the relationship between drunkenness and the will and, in one of these,[12] reference is also made to God's grace as the basis of freedom from drunkenness.

In the year 392, Augustine wrote to Bishop Aurelius:

For rioting and drunkenness are so tolerated and allowed by public opinion, that even in services designed to honour the memory of the blessed martyrs, and this not only on the annual festivals (which itself must be regarded as deplorable by every one who looks with a spiritual eye upon these things), but every day, they are openly practised.[13]

---

[7] Stump, 2002, p. 139.     [8] *Letter 22* and *Letter 29*.
[9] Mostly, or entirely, written after his ordination to the episcopate.
[10] *The City of God*, *Letter 29*, *Our Lord's Sermon on the Mount*, and *On Baptism, against the Donatists*.
[11] *Confessions*, and *Our Lord's Sermon on the Mount*.     [12] *Confessions*.
[13] *Letter 22*, chapter 1, para. 3. The texts from Augustine, Aquinas, Luther and Whitefield cited and quoted in this chapter are those contained in version 4 of the Christian Classics Ethereal Library CD-ROM produced by Calvin College, Grand Rapids, USA.

Augustine's response to this problem was initially to refer to Romans 13:13–14 as providing a scriptural basis for censure of this behaviour.[14] This was reinforced by an allusion to 1 Corinthians 5:2 as a basis for excluding offenders from communion.[15] He then proceeded to cite the example of churches elsewhere:

Both throughout the greater part of Italy and in all or almost all the churches beyond the sea, these practices either, as in some places, never existed, or, as in other places where they did exist, have been, whether they were recent or of long standing, rooted out and put down by the diligence and the censures of bishops who were holy men, entertaining true views concerning the life to come; when this, I say, is the case, do we hesitate as to the possibility of removing this monstrous defect in our morals, after an example has been set before us in so many lands?[16]

This section of his letter concluded with a tactful recommendation to his bishop that the problem should be dealt with in the main by proper scriptural teaching, and by gentle advice. Only in relatively few cases did he consider that 'exemplary severity' was necessary, and then only with sorrow.[17] He concluded with a positive proposal, in terms of suggesting that the feasts commemorating the dead should be more moderate and less ostentatious, and that monetary offerings should be given to the poor. In this way, he hoped that 'that which is a pious and honourable act of religious service shall be celebrated as it should be in the Church'.[18]

Writing three years later to Bishop Alypius, Augustine addressed similar problems in relation to the feast of Laetitia. Here, it seems, there were problems of 'immoderate indulgence in wine', 'drunken revels', 'drinking to excess' and 'drunkenness'.[19] On this occasion, Augustine provided a longer account of his attempts to address this problem. Again, his immediate reference was to scripture. In the course of his teaching, he made reference to Matthew 21:12; Exodus 32:6; 1 Corinthians 5:9–11; 11:20–22; and Galatians 5:19–21 as authority for condemning drunkenness.[20] Evidently his sermon moved his congregation to tears.[21] Despite this, some of those who were there present were, the following morning, persisting in the same behaviour, and were justifying it on the basis that their practice was supported by Christian tradition.[22] On this occasion, he was able to deal with the problem by means of a personal meeting with those concerned. His response to the question 'Wherefore *now* prohibit this custom?' was apparently, 'Let us now at last put down what ought to have been earlier

---

[14] *Letter 22*, chapter 1, para. 2.    [15] *Letter 22*, chapter 1, para. 3.    [16] *Letter 22*, chapter 1, para. 4.
[17] *Letter 22*, chapter 1, para. 5.    [18] *Letter 22*, chapter 1, para. 6.    [19] *Letter 29*, paras. 3 and 5.
[20] *Letter 29*, paras. 3–6.    [21] *Letter 29*, para. 7.    [22] *Letter 29*, para. 8.

prohibited.'[23] He further proceeded to a historical analysis of how earlier examples of drunkenness had been tolerated, but not condoned, in certain churches, and then quoted 1 Peter 4:1–3 as apostolic authority for condemning 'excess of wine'.[24]

Augustine quoted Galatians 5:19–21 in full in at least six places in his published works.[25] In this passage, Paul refers to drunkenness, alongside a list of other vices, as being a 'work of the flesh'. Augustine saw drunkenness as being a 'pleasure of the flesh',[26] or a 'desire of the body',[27] but concluded that Paul's use of the term 'flesh' cannot simply refer to such vices, since the listed 'works of the flesh' also include 'vices of the soul' such as 'idolatries, witchcrafts, hatreds, variance, emulations', etc.[28] The devil cannot be called a drunkard, he argued, since the devil has no body. However, the devil is 'exceedingly proud and envious', and it is pride which Augustine understood as being the root of all other works of the flesh. The 'flesh' is therefore not the cause of sin, but rather the corruptibility of the flesh is the result of the sin of Adam.[29] The flesh, in Augustine's interpretation of Galatians 5:19–21, is 'the man himself',[30] and the 'works of the flesh' are the works of man living self-centredly and not for God.[31] Drunkenness is thus one of the 'fruits' by which it will be known that someone is living according to the flesh, rather than according to the Spirit of God.[32] Furthermore, drunkenness is, in Augustine's view, rarely found alone. Rather, it tends to lead to other works of the flesh:

Take the case of drunkenness, which people have now become accustomed to talk of not only without horror, but with some degree of merriment, can it possibly exist alone in any one in whom it is found? For what drunkard is not also contentious, and hot-tempered, and jealous, and at variance with all soundness of counsel, and at grievous enmity with those who rebuke him? Further, it is not easy for him to avoid being a fornicator and adulterer.[33]

---

[23] *Letter 29*, para. 8.  [24] *Letter 29*, para. 9.

[25] *The City of God*, book 14, chapter 2; *Letter 29*, para. 6; *Our Lord's Sermon on the Mount*, book 2, chapter 24, para. 81; *On Continence*, para. 9; *On Baptism, against the Donatists*, book 4, chapter 18, para. 26; *In Answer to Petilian*, book 2, chapter 105, para. 239.

[26] *The City of God*, book 14, chapter 2.   [27] *On Continence*, para. 28.

[28] *The City of God*, book 14, chapter 2.   [29] *The City of God*, book 14, chapter 3.

[30] *The City of God*, book 14, chapter 2; *On Continence*, para. 28.

[31] *On Continence*, para. 28.

[32] *Letter 29*, para. 6; and *Our Lord's Sermon on the Mount*, book 2, chapter 24, paras. 78–81. In both places, Augustine quotes the text of Matthew 7:20 ('Ye shall know them by their fruits') and then uses the text of Galatians 5:19–21 as an interpretative key. Whereas Paul refers to 'works of the flesh' in contrast to the 'fruit of the Spirit', Augustine sees the works of the flesh as being just as much 'fruit' as are the 'fruit' of the Spirit. In the former case, Augustine would argue, the fruit ('works of the flesh') is that of a life lived in pride and self-centredness, and in the latter case, the fruit ('fruit of the Spirit') is that of a life lived in the Spirit, with God at its centre.

[33] *On Baptism, against the Donatists*, book 4, chapter 20, para. 28.

It is interesting, given the difficulties that Augustine experienced with drunkenness in his own congregations, that he also used Galatians 5:19–21 in his arguments against the Donatists, where he listed drunkenness among the vices of which he considered that they were guilty.[34] It is easy to conclude that he was critical of his opponents for faults which were equally to be found in his own church. However, he went on to criticise them for apparently tolerating or even condoning these vices. Assuming that this was a valid judgement,[35] perhaps he was drawing a contrast between works of the flesh which were accepted without qualms by the Donatists, and those which were at least a source of concern to him where found to be present in his own church?[36]

In *Our Lord's Sermon on the Mount*, Augustine addressed the matter of the intention related to drunkenness. Here, drunkenness was classed along with debaucheries, blasphemies and thefts as something which 'manifestly cannot be done with a good intention'.[37] This must be understood in the context of the whole book, in which Augustine's theme is one of singleness of heart:

No one therefore has a single, *i.e.* a pure heart, except the man who rises above the praises of men; and when he lives well, looks at Him only, and strives to please Him who is the only Searcher of the conscience. And whatever proceeds from the purity of that conscience is so much the more praiseworthy, the less it desires the praises of men.[38]

---

[34] *In Answer to Petilian*, book 2, chapter 105, para. 239.

[35] Of course, it is difficult to know whether or not it was valid. Perhaps the Donatists would simply have suggested that he was being hypocritical? It certainly sounds as though drunkenness was a problem both inside and outside the Christian Church.

[36] In *Letter* 29, at the end of his account of his attempts to address the problems of drunkenness in his own congregation, he relates an interesting contrast: 'And as we heard the noise of the feasting, which was going on as usual in the church of the heretics, who still prolonged their revelry while we were so differently engaged, I remarked that the beauty of day is enhanced by contrast with the night, and that when anything black is near, the purity of white is the more pleasing; and that, in like manner, our meeting for a spiritual feast might perhaps have been somewhat less sweet to us, but for the contrast of the carnal excesses in which the others indulged; and I exhorted them to desire eagerly such feasts as we then enjoyed, if they had tasted the goodness of the Lord. At the same time, I said that those may well be afraid who seek anything which shall one day be destroyed as the chief object of their desire, seeing that every one shares the portion of that which he worships; a warning expressly given by the apostle to such, when he says of them their "god is their belly," inasmuch as he has elsewhere said, "Meats for the belly, and the belly for meats; but God shall destroy both it and them." I added that it is our duty to seek that which is imperishable, which, far removed from carnal affections, is obtained through sanctification of the spirit.' It would appear, then, that Augustine was personally convinced that he was taking his Christian congregation in a direction different from that in which the 'heretics' were moving. In his writings against the Manichaeans he explicitly recognises the potential for criticism of the Church in relation to the drunkenness of 'bad Christians' and 'worshippers of tombs' (*Of the Morals of the Catholic Church*, chapter 34, paras. 74–75), and here appears to refute it on the grounds of even greater scope for criticism of his opponents.

[37] *Our Lord's Sermon on the Mount*, book 2, chapter 18, para. 59.

[38] Ibid., book 2, chapter 1, para. 1.

Drunkenness, Augustine implies, cannot be seen as a striving to please God. As we have already noted, it was understood by Augustine as a fruit of living to please self. Even in the case of Lot, who was made drunk by his daughters, Augustine imputed guilt on the basis that he must have consented 'to receive from his daughters all the cups of wine which they went on mixing for him'.[39] In contrast, Augustine considered Lot to have been innocent of the incest that his daughters committed with him while he was drunk, since 'he was unaware of what happened'.[40]

Augustine was keen that the offender should have opportunity to amend his ways, and emphasised that any reproof of such a person should be offered without 'despair of a return to a right state of mind'.[41] Elsewhere he emphasised that freedom from drunkenness, and redemption from drunkenness, are both matters of the grace of God:

I hear the voice of my God commanding: 'Let not your heart be overcharged with surfeiting and drunkenness.' Drunkenness is far from me. Thou wilt have mercy that it does not come near me. But 'surfeiting' sometimes creeps upon thy servant. Thou wilt have mercy that it may be put far from me. For no man can be continent unless thou give it. Many things that we pray for thou givest us, and whatever good we receive before we prayed for it, we receive it from thee, so that we might afterward know that we did receive it from thee. I never was a drunkard, but I have known drunkards made into sober men by thee. It was also thy doing that those who never were drunkards have not been – and likewise, it was from thee that those who have been might not remain so always. And it was likewise from thee that both might know from whom all this came.[42]

Freedom from drunkenness may be a matter of the grace of God, but it is the responsibility of drunkards to pray for their own deliverance:

For then exhorting them to prayer He ended thus; 'this kind is not cast out but by prayer and fasting.' If a man must pray, to cast out devils from another, how much more to cast out his own covetousness? how much more to cast out his own drunkenness?[43]

In summary, we may see that drunkenness illustrates many of the general themes of Augustine's approach to ethics. The *summum bonum* is to be found in pleasing God. Drunkenness patently cannot be pleasing to God. Augustine never fully justifies this assumption, but rather bases it

---

[39] *Reply to Faustus the Manichaean*, book 22, para. 44.
[40] Ibid. Augustine does not make explicit his views concerning the matter of Lot's lack of intention to commit incest. However, it would seem consistent with his argument that Lot would not simply have had to be 'unaware' in order to be innocent in Augustine's eyes, but would have had to be unable to form the intention to commit incest.
[41] *Our Lord's Sermon on the Mount*, book 2, chapter 18, para. 61.
[42] *Confessions*, book 10, chapter 31, para. 45.
[43] *Sermons on Selected Lessons of the New Testament*, Sermon 30, para. 3.

upon quotation of scripture. The tradition of the Church also appears as a subsidiary basis of argument employed by his opponents and accepted in principle by Augustine. However, he is quick to point out that custom and practice in parts of the Church cannot be taken as evidence of a tradition endorsed by the Church.

For Augustine, whose perspective relies heavily upon Pauline theology, drunkenness is a 'work of the flesh'. It is evidence of the wrong intention of a life which is focussed on pride in self rather than on God. It leads in turn to other vices. Yet, in tension with this view of sinful human responsibility for drunkenness, we find that Augustine still perceives it to be a matter of God's grace as to whether or not someone avoids drunkenness, or is rescued from drunkenness. The only hint of a solution to this apparent contradiction is to be found in his assertion that individuals have a responsibility to pray that they might be delivered from drunkenness.

Augustine did not explicitly relate the full implications of his understanding of a divided will to the matter of drunkenness. He made clear that drunkenness is a result of a disordered will, consequent upon the sin of Adam. However, he did not proceed to an account of the way in which the decision to drink must result from the inner struggle of a will divided against itself. The modern concepts of subjective compulsion, craving and addiction might be greatly illuminated by an application of this aspect of Augustine's thought.[44]

### THOMAS AQUINAS

Aquinas was born in Roccasecca in Naples in about 1225. He joined the Dominican order and studied at the University of Paris, and in Cologne, before becoming a Master of Theology in 1256. From 1268 to 1272 he held a chair in theology at the University of Paris. In 1274 he apparently underwent some kind of mystical experience, which led to his famous assertion, 'Everything I have written seems like straw by comparison with what I have seen and what has been revealed to me.'[45] Only three months later, he died as a result of a head injury.[46]

Aquinas published a number of important works, including *Summa contra Gentiles*, a work which was intended for the use of Dominican missionaries in their work with non-Christians, and the *Catena Aurea*, which

---

[44] Eleonore Stump has presented a helpful account of the way in which Augustine's understanding of the divided will might be applied to a craving for cigarettes (Stump, 2002). The principles of this account could equally well be applied to craving for alcohol. However, Stump does not follow through the full implications of her thinking in terms of the light that it sheds upon the concept of the dependence syndrome or recent treatments for alcohol/nicotine dependence.

[45] Cross and Livingstone, 1997, p. 1615.     [46] Ibid., pp. 1614–1616.

offered a commentary on the gospels assembled from patristic sources. His best-known work, the *Summa Theologica*, was designed as a basic text in theology for friars not intending university studies.[47] Although he saw revelation as the primary source for knowledge of God, he also saw a rational basis to Christian faith, and viewed philosophy and theology as complementary to each other. The main philosophical influence upon his work was from Aristotle.[48] His work has been hugely influential, particularly in Roman Catholic moral and systematic theology.[49]

The ethical thinking of Aquinas derives from his analysis of human action.[50] For Aquinas, human acts have their basis in reason and the will, faculties which are distinctive of, and peculiar to, human beings. Using the reason and the will, human beings are able to direct their actions towards an end. Aristotle, and Aquinas after him, saw the concern of moral philosophy as being 'to consider human operations insofar as they are ordered to one another and to the end'.[51] Aristotle further saw an ultimate end of human happiness, towards which all other human ends were eventually directed. For Aquinas, the ultimate human end was the perfect good, the *ratio boni*. Human actions, for Aquinas, are all undertaken (mistakenly or otherwise) on the assumption that they tend towards this end.

Aquinas believed that, in order to determine whether or not something is actually good, it is necessary to know what its function is. The 'virtue' of something is to be found in the extent to which it performs its proper or natural function well. For human beings, it is activity in accordance with reason and will which is their distinctive function, and virtue is thus to be found in the extent to which they use these faculties well. However, he saw virtues of the faculty of reason as being merely intellectual virtues. Moral virtues, in contrast, are concerned with an appetitive faculty:

The appetitive faculty obeys the reason, not blindly, but with a certain power of opposition . . . the habits or passions of the appetitive faculty cause the use of reason to be impeded in some particular action . . . Accordingly for a man to do a good deed, it is requisite not only that his reason be well disposed by means of a habit of intellectual virtue; but also that his appetite be well disposed by means of a habit of moral virtue. And so moral differs from intellectual virtue, even as the appetite differs from the reason. Hence just as the appetite is the principle of human acts, in so far as it partakes of reason, so are moral habits to be considered virtues in so far as they are in conformity with reason.[52]

---

[47] Ibid., p. 1614.    [48] Ibid., p. 1615; Gill, 1997, pp. 32–33.    [49] Gill, 1997, p. 33.
[50] See McInerny, 1993, upon which this summary of Aquinas' ethical thinking is based.
[51] Quoted by McInerny, 1993, p. 197.
[52] *Summa Theologica*, First Part of the Second Part, Q58.2.

Following Aristotle, Aquinas considered virtues to be habits.[53] The moral virtues thus confer an acquired tendency towards the good. However, following a definition of virtue which he took from Augustine, Aquinas also appears to have understood virtues as being conferred, or infused, by the grace of God.[54] There is clearly a tension between the definitions.[55]

Aquinas adopted from Aristotle the concept of the mean of virtues. The mean of virtues, according to Aquinas, is conformity with reason in relation to the area of life which is the concern of the virtue in question, and it is the virtue of prudence which enables a judgement to be made concerning the nature of the mean in any given case.[56]

For temperance intends that man should not stray from reason for the sake of his concupiscences; fortitude, that he should not stray from the right judgment of reason through fear or daring . . . But it belongs to the ruling of prudence to decide in what manner and by what means man shall obtain the mean of reason in his deeds.[57]

Aquinas' ethics were also influenced by his concept of natural law. He asserted that 'law is nothing but a dictate of practical reason issued by a sovereign who governs a complete community'.[58] He then identified four types of law: eternal, natural, human and divine. The eternal law is that 'the whole community of the universe is governed by God's mind', and the natural law is then to be understood as 'nothing other than the sharing in the eternal law by intelligent creatures'.[59] Natural law, according to Aquinas, thus provides an underlying set of general principles of moral discourse which are the same for all people.[60] The actual value of this law for moral discourse is limited by the extent to which it is understood to have been corrupted by human sin. However, Aquinas believed that nature was not wholly destroyed by sin, and that God's grace was 'more efficacious' than nature.[61]

Aquinas did not mention drunkenness in the *Summa Contra Gentiles*, but made a series of references to the subject in the second part of the *Summa*

[53] Jordan, 1993 pp. 236–237; *Summa Theologica*, First Part of the Second Part, Q55.1.
[54] *Summa Theologica*, First Part of the Second Part, Q55.4.
[55] Jordan, 1993, pp. 236–238.    [56] Porter, 2002, p. 153.
[57] *Summa Theologica*, Second Part of the Second Part, Q47.7.
[58] Quoted by Gill, 1997, p. 76.
[59] Both quotations taken from Gill, 1997, pp. 76 and 77 respectively. Human law is then seen as being derived from natural law, and divine law is understood as necessary for salvation (p. 77).
[60] McInerny, 1993, pp. 208–212; Gill, 1997, p. 77. The actual existence of such universal principles is debatable in the light of modern anthropology, and the use to which Aquinas put them (as in his defence of slavery) is questionable (Gill, 1997, pp. 86–87).
[61] *Summa Theologica*, First Part of the Second Part, Q94.6; McInerny, 1993, p. 213.

*Theologica.*[62] In particular, in the Second Part of the Second Part, Question 150 deals specifically with drunkenness. Four questions are addressed specifically:

1. whether drunkenness is a sin
2. whether drunkenness is a mortal sin
3. whether drunkenness is the gravest of sins
4. whether drunkenness excuses from sin

Aquinas distinguished two ways of understanding drunkenness. On the one hand it is 'a penal defect resulting from a fault', which is especially manifest in terms of loss of the use of reason.[63] On the other hand, it is 'the act by which a man incurs this defect'.[64] He concluded that drunkenness in the second sense may be without sin, it may be a venial sin, or it may be a mortal sin, according to the degree of cognisance of the likely intoxicating effects of the amount and type of wine consumed.[65] Where drunkenness is sinful, it was understood by Aquinas as being a form of gluttony. In support of this conclusion he cited both Romans 13:13 ('Not in rioting and drunkenness') and also Augustine.[66] However, his primary argument for the sinfulness of drunkenness was derived from the logical consequentialist argument that drunkenness impairs reason, and that reason is the basis both of virtuous deeds and of the avoidance of sin. Drunkenness thus impairs the ability to act virtuously and also enhances the risk of acting sinfully. In support of this argument, he quoted Ambrose and also made reference to the story of Noah's drunkenness in Genesis 9 as an example of drunkenness without sin.

Aquinas' differentiation between drunkenness as being without sin, as being venial sin or as being mortal sin was based upon cognisance of moderation and of the intoxicating nature of the drink.[67] In responding to Question 150, he argued that persons who realise neither that their drinking is immoderate, nor that the drink is intoxicating, should be considered to be without sin. Those who know that their drinking is immoderate, but who are unaware of the intoxicating nature of the drink, should be considered to have committed a venial sin. Those who are aware that they are being immoderate, and that the drink is intoxicating, should be considered to have committed a mortal sin. Interestingly, Aquinas did not consider here the possibility that persons might become drunk as a result of not

---

[62] There is also a reference in the Third Part (Q83.6) concerning the appropriate punishment for vomiting of the Eucharist as a result of drunkenness.

[63] *Summa Theologica*, Second Part of the Second Part, Q150.1.

[64] Ibid.    [65] Ibid., Q150.1, 2.    [66] *Confessions*, book 10, chapter 31.

[67] *Summa Theologica*, Second Part of the Second Part, Q150.1, 2.

realising that they are being immoderate in drinking, despite knowledge that the drink is intoxicating. Presumably this would also be a venial sin.[68]

Elsewhere, in responding to Question 88 of the First Part of the Second Part, a question on venial and mortal sin, Aquinas argued that drunkenness may be a venial sin if it is due to

some sort of ignorance or weakness, as when a man is ignorant of the strength of the wine, or of his own unfitness, so that he has no thought of getting drunk, for in that case the drunkenness is not imputed to him as a sin, but only the excessive drink.[69]

It is not completely clear how exactly the venial sin of drunkenness was distinguished by Aquinas from the venial sin of 'excessive drink'. It would appear that Aquinas understood drunkenness to be essentially a mortal sin,[70] but that it could be so only by virtue of the formation of the intention to get drunk. Where this is lacking, due to ignorance of the likely consequences of one's actions, it is effectively not drunkenness at all, but merely 'excessive drink'. Thus, frequent drunkenness can only be a mortal sin:

If, however, he gets drunk frequently, this ignorance no longer avails as an excuse, for his will seems to choose to give way to drunkenness rather than to refrain from excess of wine: wherefore the sin returns to its specific nature.[71]

It is interesting that in his response to Question 88 he included an additional factor by means of which drunkenness may be considered a venial sin. In addition to ignorance concerning the strength of the wine, Aquinas added ignorance of the person's own unfitness. Thus, Aquinas appears to have recognised that knowledge of the strength of the drink, awareness of what constitutes 'moderation' in drinking, and knowledge of one's own constitutional capacity to tolerate alcohol are all required in order to inform the intention for or against drunkenness.

Aquinas argued against viewing the sin of drunkenness as 'the gravest of sins' on the basis that it is opposed only to the 'good of human reason' and that it is not a sin directly against God himself:

---

[68] The oversight appears to betray a presumption that the drinker will know what constitutes moderation.

[69] *Summa Theologica*, First Part of the Second Part, Q88.5.

[70] E.g. 'It is a mortal sin by reason of its genus; for, that a man, without necessity, and through the mere lust of wine, make himself unable to use his reason, whereby he is directed to God and avoids committing many sins, is expressly contrary to virtue' (*Summa Theologica*, First Part of the Second Part, Q88.5).

[71] Ibid.

A thing is said to be evil because it removes a good. Wherefore the greater the good removed by an evil, the graver the evil. Now it is evident that a Divine good is greater than a human good. Wherefore the sins that are directly against God are graver than the sin of drunkenness, which is directly opposed to the good of human reason.[72]

That drunkenness is primarily to be construed as opposed to human reason, or as a cause of impairment of reason, is a recurring theme among the references to drunkenness in *Summa Theologica*.[73] As has already been mentioned, Aquinas had two understandings of drunkenness, and the first of these essentially defined it on the basis of the impairment of reason:

First it may signify the defect itself of a man resulting from his drinking much wine, the consequence being that he loses the use of reason.[74]

It is interesting that he did not refer to the consequences of drunkenness for health, impaired psychomotor function, memory, mood disturbance or even, and most notably, any direct effect that it might have upon the appetitive faculty or will. For Aquinas, a consequentialist argument against drunkenness was to be built entirely upon its adverse effect on human reason.[75]

Whether or not drunkenness excuses from sin was understood by Aquinas to depend upon the sinfulness of the act of drunkenness itself. If the act of drunkenness is 'without sin', or unintentional, then 'the subsequent sin is entirely excused from fault'.[76] Aquinas[77] cited Augustine's[78] consideration of Lot as a possible example of this kind, based upon Genesis 19:30–36, where Lot's daughters make him drunk in order to commit incest with their father.[79] Conversely, if the act of drunkenness is due to

---

[72] Ibid., Second Part of the Second Part, Q150.3.

[73] See, for example, First Part of the Second Part, Q46.4; 48.3; 55.3; 77.2; 88.5; and Second Part of the Second Part, Q150.1, 3; 153.5. Elsewhere, the theme is still implicit, if not specifically stated.

[74] *Summa Theologica*, Second Part of the Second Part, Q150.1.

[75] Following Aristotle, he recognises that varying degrees of impairment of reason may occur as a result of drunkenness, from mere 'hampering' through to complete incapacitation (*Summa Theologica*, First Part of the Second Part, Q46.4).

[76] *Summa Theologica*, Second Part of the Second Part, Q150.4.     [77] Ibid.

[78] *Reply to Faustus the Manichaean*, book 22, paras. 43–44.

[79] In fact, a reference to Augustine's text shows that it is far from clear that Augustine did consider that Lot was without guilt in this matter. Augustine states that '[Lot's] guilt therefore is not that of incest, but of drunkenness' (para. 44). Aquinas translates this as: 'Lot's guilt is to be measured, not by the incest, but by his drunkenness.' If Lot is considered not to be guilty of an intentional act of drunkenness, on the basis that his daughters somehow made him drunk without his consent, then Aquinas' principle holds good, i.e. Lot was not to be held guilty of incest. However, Augustine actually dismisses various hypotheses in support of this and seems to veer towards the likely conclusion that Lot was at least partly to blame for allowing himself to be made drunk. It is further interesting to note that both Augustine and Aquinas appear to overlook the fact that Lot was made drunk by his

sin, then responsibility for other sinful acts committed in the drunken state is retained, albeit to a lesser degree:

If, however, the preceding act was sinful, the person is not altogether excused from the subsequent sin, because the latter is rendered voluntary through the voluntariness of the preceding act, inasmuch as it was through doing something unlawful that he fell into the subsequent sin. Nevertheless, the resulting sin is diminished, even as the character of voluntariness is diminished.[80]

In considering the specific example of murder committed in a state of drunkenness resulting from a sinful act of drunkenness, Aquinas suggested that the offender is guilty of two sins (i.e. drunkenness and murder), and therefore deserving of a double punishment, but that the 'resulting sin' of murder is diminished by virtue of ignorance. Despite this, he acknowledged that expediency might require that a harsher punishment be imposed, 'since more harm is done by the drunk than by the sober'.[81]

Although it is never explicitly stated in the *Summa Theologica*, it would appear that Aquinas considered the drinking of wine to be a virtue. Certainly, he considered the use of wine to be 'lawful'.[82] It is also clear that he considered drunkenness to be a vice of excess or gluttony. According to his theory of the mean of virtues, it is therefore to be expected that this must be opposed to a contrary vice of an opposite kind, and he did indeed discuss this possibility in his response to Question 150:

the vice opposed to drunkenness is unnamed; and yet if a man were knowingly to abstain from wine to the extent of molesting nature grievously, he would not be free from sin.[83]

In summary, drunkenness was understood by Aquinas as being both a state of impaired reason, and an act of drinking which leads to such a state. It is implicit that drinking wine in itself is a virtue, and that prudence is required to discern the mean of this virtue, such that neither should reason be impaired as a result of drunkenness, nor should nature be 'molested' by abstinence. Aquinas quoted scripture and the Church Fathers in support of

daughters on two separate occasions, on each of which one of them committed incest with him. Did he not remember what had happened on the first occasion? If he did, then this suggests culpability for not avoiding a repetition of events. If he did not, then this implies that the impairment of memory by drunkenness is a further factor which must be taken into account in ascribing responsibility for acts committed in repeated states of drunkenness.

80 *Summa Theologica*, Second Part of the Second Part, Q150.4. See also First Part of the Second Part, Q77.7.
81 *Summa Theologica*, First Part of the Second Part, Q76.4.
82 *Summa Theologica*, Second Part of the Second Part, Q149.3.
83 *Summa Theologica*, Second Part of the Second Part, Q150.1.

his arguments, but he relied principally upon philosophical argument and natural law as the basis for his conclusions. Human beings are created for the ultimate end of the *ratio boni*, and drunkenness, by impairing reason, acts contrary to this good.

## MARTIN LUTHER

Born in Saxony in 1483, Luther studied at Erfurt University from 1501 to 1505, and in 1505 entered the Augustinian order. Two years later, he was ordained priest, and in the following year became Professor of Moral Philosophy at the University of Wittenberg. In 1511 he became Professor of Biblical Exegesis at the same university, and retained this chair until his death in 1546.[84]

Luther is perhaps best known for his role in the European Reformation, and for his doctrine of justification through faith alone. His theology was eventually to reject human works as a basis for salvation, emphasising the grace of God and the person and work of Christ alone. He understood scripture as foundational to revelation, and rejected philosophy, seeing it as contrary to Christian theology and ethics.[85] In 1517 he posted his ninety-five theses against indulgences on the church door in Wittenberg. He was excommunicated in 1520 by Pope Leo, and in 1521 his teachings were condemned in the Edict of Worms. During the course of his lifetime, he published a considerable number of works, including a defence of his understanding of the impotence of human free will (*De Libero Arbitrio*), a commentary on Galatians, and an informal record of conversations which took place over his dinner table between 1529 and 1545.[86]

Luther's ethics were based upon his theology. Assured of salvation through Christ, Christians are to direct their reason and works towards the good of their neighbour. The guidance for this life is to be found in the direction offered to the individual believer by the Holy Spirit, working through scripture, the Church and prayer. He developed a doctrine of two realms: of creation and redemption. In the former, God the Creator rules all sinful creatures, working through secular authorities. In the latter, God the Redeemer rules all Christian people through Christ and the gospel, by means of personal faith and love.[87]

---

[84] Cross and Livingstone, 1997, p. 1007.
[85] Ferguson, Wright and Packer, 1988, pp. 401–404; Macquarrie and Childress, 1986, pp. 360–363.
[86] Cross and Livingstone, 1997, pp. 1007–1010.
[87] Macquarrie and Childress, 1986, p. 361.

Luther clearly understood drunkenness to be a sin, both on the grounds of theological analogy with the sin of Adam, and also because it is expressly forbidden by scripture:

The apparent cause why God passed so sharp a sentence upon Adam, was, that he had eaten of the forbidden tree, and was disobedient unto God, wherefore, for his sake, the earth was cursed, and mankind made subject to all manner of miseries, fears, wants, sicknesses, plagues, and death. The reason of the worldly-wise, regarding only the biting of the apple, holds that for so slight and trivial a thing it was too cruel and hard a proceeding upon poor Adam, and takes snuff in the nose, and says, or at least thinks: O, is it then so heinous a matter and sin for one to eat an apple? As people say of many sins that God expressly in his Word has forbidden, such as drunkenness, etc.: What harm for one to be merry, and take a cup with good fellows? – concluding, according to their blindness, that God is too sharp and exacting.[88]

In his commentary on Galatians, Luther commented briefly on Paul's reference to drunkenness as a work of the flesh:

Paul does not say that eating and drinking are works of the flesh, but intemperance in eating and drinking, which is a common vice nowadays, is a work of the flesh. Those who are given to excess are to know that they are not spiritual but carnal. Sentence is pronounced upon them that they shall not inherit the kingdom of heaven. Paul desires that Christians avoid drunkenness and gluttony, that they live temperate and sober lives, in order that the body may not grow soft and sensual.[89]

He also referred to drunkenness as a work of the flesh in his *Large Catechism*:

For in the flesh we dwell and carry the old Adam about our neck, who exerts himself and incites us daily to inchastity, laziness, gluttony and drunkenness, avarice and deception, to defraud our neighbor and to overcharge him, and, in short, to all manner of evil lusts which cleave to us by nature, and to which we are incited by the society, example and what we hear and see of other people, which often wound and inflame even an innocent heart.[90]

For Luther, Paul's concept of the 'flesh' was to be understood as meaning 'the whole nature of man, inclusive of reason and instincts'.[91] This 'whole nature of man' is corrupted by sin, and is thus characterised by excesses and lusts such as those of drunkenness. Salvation from sin is to be found only through faith in Christ. But even then there is a tension between the Spirit of Christ and the flesh:

[88] *Table Talk*, Of God's Works (para. 96).
[89] *Commentary on St Paul's Epistle to the Galatians*, chapter 5, v. 20.
[90] *Large Catechism*, Part Third – Of Prayer (The Lord's Prayer): The sixth petition.
[91] *Commentary on St Paul's Epistle to the Galatians*, chapter 2, v. 16.

The trouble is, our flesh will not let us believe in Christ with all our heart. The fault lies not with Christ, but with us. Sin clings to us as long as we live and spoils our happiness in Christ. Hence, we are only partly free from the Law. 'With the mind I myself serve the law of God; but with the flesh the law of sin.' (Romans 7:25)[92]

And again:

Christ reigns in the heart with His Holy Spirit, who sees, hears, speaks, works, suffers, and does all things in and through us over the protest and the resistance of the flesh.[93]

Because of this tension, Christians will not be perfect in this world. They will still sin, and may not differ greatly from others in outward appearance:

If we sin, we sin not on purpose, but unwittingly, and we are sorry for it. Sin sticks in our flesh, and the flesh gets us into sin even after we have been imbued by the Holy Ghost. Outwardly there is no great difference between a Christian and any honest man. The activities of a Christian are not sensational. He performs his duty according to his vocation. He takes good care of his family, and is kind and helpful to others. Such homely, everyday performances are not much admired. But the setting-up exercises of the monks draw great applause. Holy works, you know. Only the acts of a Christian are truly good and acceptable to God, because they are done in faith, with a cheerful heart, out of gratitude to Christ.[94]

Luther thus saw drunkenness as a sin of excess, or intemperance, which is a work of fallen human nature, or a work of the 'flesh'. Luther also saw the bad example of others in society as 'inciting' drunkenness and other such works. The solution is to be found only through faith in Christ, through whom the Holy Spirit enters the heart and rules over the flesh. And yet, the acts of a Christian (including presumably the eschewing of drunkenness) are also freely offered 'out of gratitude to Christ'. A tension between the grace of God and human free will is evident here, and this is reflected in Luther's recognition that in practice Christians will continue to experience the 'protest' and 'resistance of the flesh' against the rule of the Spirit of Christ.

    Luther elsewhere recognised the potential seriousness of the consequences of drunkenness:

Yet Alexander could not leave off his foolishness, for often he swilled himself drunk, and in his drunkenness stabbed his best and worthiest friends, and afterwards drank himself to death at Babylon.[95]

---

[92] Ibid., chapter 3, v. 25.    [93] Ibid., chapter 2, v. 20.    [94] Ibid., chapter 4, v. 6.
[95] *Table Talk*, Of Jesus Christ (para. 237).

In regard to the culpability of those who commit offences when drunken, he appears to have taken a firm line:

It has been asked: Is an offence, committed in a moment of intoxication, therefore excusable? Most assuredly not; on the contrary, drunkenness aggravates the fault. Hidden sins unveil themselves when a man's self-possession goes from him; that which the sober man keeps in his breast, the drunken man lets out at the lips. Astute people, when they want to ascertain a man's true character, make him drunk. This same drunkenness is a grievous vice among us Germans, and should be heavily chastised by the temporal magistrate, since the fear of God will not suffice to keep the brawling guzzlers in check.[96]

Luther therefore appears to have seen drunkenness not so much as a state of impaired reason as one of impaired will (or 'self-possession'). This allows the 'unveiling' of 'hidden sins' and should be treated more seriously, not less seriously, than comparable faults committed in sobriety. Why exactly he believes that the fault is 'aggravated' in this way is not clear. However, he clearly saw this as being a common contemporary failing,[97] and recognised an important role for the secular authorities, in the created realm, in controlling the problem. Perhaps his motivation here was on the basis of social concern, and a desire to keep the problem 'in check'.

In summary, Luther saw drunkenness as sinful on the basis that it is expressly forbidden in scripture. It is thus analogous with the sin of Adam and Eve. Insofar as it was a problem in the 'created realm', it was a matter for the attention of the courts, and one which he believed should be treated severely in order to keep the problem in check. Insofar as it was a problem in the 'realm of redemption', it was a sign of the resistance of 'the flesh' to the work of the Spirit of Christ. The Christian is enjoined to eschew drunkenness, and other works of the flesh, out of gratitude to Christ. And yet, Luther still recognised that Christians may sin 'unwittingly' and that the reign of the Spirit of Christ in the believer's heart may not make him or her greatly different from 'any honest man'.

### GEORGE WHITEFIELD

George Whitefield was born in Gloucester in 1714. He travelled to Georgia with the Wesleys in 1738, and was ordained priest later that year. He became known for his spectacular open-air preaching, despite opposition from

---

[96] *Table Talk*, Of Offences (para. 695).
[97] A comment elsewhere in *Table Talk* suggests that it was in fact a longstanding problem in Germany (Of Vocation and Calling, para. 849).

ecclesiastical authorities. His Calvinistic theology led to a break with the Wesleys in 1741. He saw himself as an 'Awakener' of all the churches, and was a significant figure in the 'Great Awakening' in the United States, as well as in the Evangelical revival in the United Kingdom. His published works include notably his *Journal*, and many of his sermons.[98]

Whitefield's sermon on 'The heinous sin of drunkenness' was published in 1771–2.[99] It is an impassioned address, approximately 4,600 words in length, on the text of Ephesians 5:18: 'Be not drunk with Wine, wherein is Excess; but be filled with the Spirit.' The text is well structured, with an introduction followed by six reasons against the sin of drunkenness, and then three means to overcome the sin of drunkenness. It concludes with an exhortation to temperance and self-discipline. It is permeated throughout with allusions to scripture, although explicit references are few. It appears that Whitefield expected his audience to recognise his allusions to scripture, and the authority of scripture is taken for granted.

The introduction makes clear that drunkenness was a widespread problem, and that it continued despite the best efforts of the civil magistrates to combat it with deterrent sentences. It was therefore 'high time', he said,

for thy ministers, O God, to lift up their voices like a trumpet; and since human threats cannot prevail, to set before them the terrors of the Lord, and try if these will not persuade them to cease from the evil of their doings.[100]

Whitefield identified drunkenness as a sin, 'which must be highly displeasing to God; because it is an abuse of his good creatures'.[101] He referred to the creation of Adam, and to the giving of other creatures to Adam for food, a privilege which was forfeited because of Adam's sin, but restored through the death of Christ. However, he then identified a divine limitation upon the restoration of this privilege:

For God, by the death of Jesus, has given no man license to be intemperate; but, on the contrary, has laid us under the strongest obligations to live soberly, as well as godly, in this present world.[102]

No scriptural or other basis for identifying this divine limitation is offered, though an allusion to Titus 2:12 is possibly intended. However, it is then seen as being the basis for asserting that intemperance in respect of wine has turned 'that wine which was intended to make glad [the human] heart,

---

[98]  Cross and Livingstone, 1997, pp. 1737–1738.
[99]  Although this sermon, listed as Sermon 52, is in the public domain, and widely available, I have been able to find no record of the date on which it was originally delivered, or the place and circumstances in which it was preached. The text referred to here is taken from version 4 of the Christian Classics Ethereal Library CD-ROM produced by Calvin College, Grand Rapids, USA.
[100]  Sermon 52: Introduction.     [101] First reason against drunkenness.     [102] Ibid.

into a deadly poison'. For this reason, the drunkard will be subject to God's judgement.

Whitefield identified drunkenness as being the more sinful because it is a sin against a person's own body. In support of this contention he quoted, by analogy, 1 Corinthians 6:18:

'Flee fornication, brethren; for he that committeth fornication, sinneth against his own body.' And may not I as justly cry out, Flee drunkenness, my brethren, since he that committeth that crime, sinneth against his own body?[103]

He proceeded to list 'diseases and distempers', 'pains in the head', 'rottenness in the bones', 'redness of eyes', loss of beauty, and death of body and soul as being the consequences of drunkenness.

Whitefield then turned to the impact of drunkenness upon reason:

Drunkenness . . . robs a man of his reason. Reason is the glory of a man; the chief thing whereby God has made us to differ from the brute creation. And our modern unbelievers have exalted it to such a high degree, as even to set it in opposition to revelation, and so deny the Lord that bought them. But though, in doing this, they greatly err, and whilst they profess themselves wise, become real fools; yet we must acknowledge, that reason is the candle of the Lord, and whosoever puts it out, shall bear his punishment, whosoever he be.[104]

Another reason against drunkenness was to be found in the other sins to which it leads:

We may say of drunkenness, as Solomon does in strife, that it is like the letting out of water; for we know not what will be the end thereof. Its name is Legion; behold a troop of sins cometh after it.[105]

Like Augustine and Aquinas before him, Whitefield referred to the story of Lot. It is not clear whether he held 'righteous Lot' or his daughter primarily responsible for the sin of incest that was committed, but Lot is referred to as being the one who committed it. The text refers also to the story of Nabal (1 Samuel 25:1–42), who insulted David when drunk.

Most seriously, Whitefield understood drunkenness as leading to separation of the believer from the Holy Spirit:

But now, drunkards do in effect bid this blessed Spirit to depart from them: for what has he to do with such filthy swine? . . . They have chased him out of their hearts, by defiling his temple; I mean their bodies. And he can no more hold communion with them, than light can have communion with darkness, or Christ have concord with Belial.[106]

---

[103] Second reason against drunkenness.    [104] Third reason against drunkenness.
[105] Fourth reason against drunkenness.    [106] Fifth reason against drunkenness.

According to Whitefield, the text upon which he was preaching (Ephesians 5:18) itself implies 'that drunkenness and the Spirit of God could never dwell in the same heart'.[107]

Finally, Whitefield considered that drunkenness 'unfits a man for the enjoyment of God in heaven, and exposes him to his eternal wrath'.[108] He is vivid in his portrayal of the fate of the drunkard:

A burning Tophet, kindled by God's wrath, is prepared for your reception, where you must suffer the vengeance of eternal fire, and in vain cry out for a drop of water to cool your tongues. Indeed you shall drink, but it shall be a cup of God's fury: for in the hand of the Lord there will be a cup of fury, it will be full mixed, and as for the dregs thereof, all the drunkards of the land shall suck them out.[109]

In case any should not believe that this fate awaits the drunkard, he made implied reference to scriptural authority:[110]

But if you believe not me, believe eternal truth itself, which has positively declared, that no drunkard shall ever enter into his kingdom.[111]

In the final part of his sermon, Whitefield offered hope for salvation of the drunkard by means of prayer, the avoidance of 'evil company', and a life of 'strict self-denial and mortification'. He referred again to scripture, making especial reference to the example of self-discipline to be found in St Paul. However, he appears to have considered the work of the Holy Spirit to be the ultimately important factor:

But why urge I the apostle's example, to excite you to a strict temperance in eating and drinking? Rather let me exhort you only to put in practice the latter part of the text, to labor to 'be filled with the Spirit of God,' and then you will no longer search the scriptures to find arguments for self-indulgence; but you will deal sincerely with yourselves, and eat and drink no more at any time, than what is consistent with the strictest precepts of the gospel. O beg of God, that you may see, how you are fallen in Adam, and the necessity of being renewed, ere you can be happy, by the Spirit of Jesus Christ!

In summary, Whitefield understood drunkenness as sin, primarily on the authority of scripture. However, he was not averse to citing consequentialist arguments where he saw these as supporting scripture. He also found a theological basis against drunkenness, in the doctrines of creation and redemption. Drunkenness is the cause of numerous harms and vices, and most especially was understood as incompatible with the presence of the

---

[107] Ibid.    [108] Sixth reason against drunkenness.    [109] Ibid.
[110] This is presumably an allusion to 1 Corinthians 6:10 and Galatians 5:21.
[111] Sixth reason against drunkenness.

Holy Spirit, by which alone salvation is assured. There is no hint that responsibility might be reduced in respect of acts committed in a state of drunkenness. While drunkenness was seen as impairing reason, this was but one of many adverse consequences, and seems only to emphasise the heinousness of the sin still more.

Whitefield referred to potential remedies to drunkenness within what Luther would have understood as being the realm of creation. In particular, he referred to the work of civil magistrates and the importance of avoiding 'evil company'. However, it is clear that he was pessimistic that these alone would avail. It is the realm of redemption that is decisive. Prayer and self-discipline were seen as being more important, and ultimately it is being 'filled with the Holy Spirit' that brings about temperance in behaviour.

### CONCLUSIONS

Augustine, Aquinas, Luther and Whitefield represent different perspectives upon the Christian ethics of drunkenness prior to the nineteenth century. All of them understood drunkenness as being in some sense sinful, and all of them employed scripture in support of their arguments. All of them quoted or alluded to Galatians 5:21 in the course of their arguments, and Pauline theology appears to have been generally influential in their thinking. However, for Augustine and Aquinas, philosophy was also important. For Aquinas it featured more prominently in his writings on this subject than did scripture, although in principle he recognised scripture as the primary basis for revelation. For Augustine and Aquinas the tradition and teaching of the Church were also important considerations. To varying degrees, all four employed consequentialist arguments, but these usually seem to have been subsidiary – especially so in the case of Luther and Whitefield. Only Augustine wrote from obvious direct pastoral experience of addressing problems of drunkenness in the church. Whitefield's sermon was obviously addressed to a large, nominally Christian congregation, but the text betrays no evidence of the ongoing pastoral responsibility or sensitivity that Augustine showed towards specific groups of people known to him within his church.

For Augustine and Aquinas, drunkenness obviously fails to contribute to the ultimate good. For Augustine, it represented a failure to strive to please God alone. For Aquinas, it was understood as impairment of the ability of human beings to fulfil the rational function for which they were created. For Aquinas, the sinfulness of drunkenness and the degree of sinfulness of any particular act of drunkenness depend upon the extent to which the drinker is aware of the likely outcome of his or her actions.

For Luther, drunkenness was analogous to the sin of Adam and Eve in Eden, but he needed to offer no other verdict than that it is expressly forbidden in scripture. It is a state of impaired will rather than a state of impaired reason. For Whitefield, the first Genesis creation story, understood in the context of the fall and the subsequent work of Christ, was relevant by virtue of an interpretation that emphasises the proper stewardship of God's creatures (including wine), and an injunction against abuse or misuse of them. Again, however, the express injunction of scripture against drunkenness was primary.

For Augustine and Luther, drunkenness was a work of the flesh. For Augustine this meant that it arises, as do other works of the flesh, from human pride. It tends to lead to other vices in turn. For Luther, it meant that drunkenness arises from a corrupt human nature which is prone to excesses and self-indulgence.

The story of Lot and his daughters was taken up by Augustine, Aquinas and Whitefield. Augustine and Aquinas believed that responsibility for other sins committed in a state of drunkenness may be reduced or removed. According to Augustine, Lot was therefore guilty of drunkenness, but not incest. For Aquinas, Lot was not guilty of either drunkenness or incest, since he saw the responsibility for both sins as falling upon his daughters, who made him drunk without his consent. For Whitefield, this story was simply an illustration of the sins into which drunkenness can lead. Although he did not explore the matter in detail, he leaves the impression that he considers Lot to have been guilty of incest. Although Luther did not specifically comment on this story, his general principle was that responsibility for sins committed in a state of drunkenness is aggravated, not mitigated.

For Augustine, drunkenness could be overcome only through the grace of God. This creates a tension with his understanding of the role of human free will. However, this is partly solved by his recognition that God responds graciously to prayers freely offered. Drunkards therefore have a responsibility to pray to be set free from their drunkenness. For Luther, the civil authorities had a part to play in overcoming drunkenness in the 'realm of creation', but in the 'realm of redemption' faith in Christ was to be understood as the only solution. Despite this, he saw good works as being offered out of gratitude to Christ, and thus a tension between grace and free will is again evident. Whitefield was much more pessimistic than Luther about the benefits of action against drunkenness in the realm of creation. In the realm of redemption, it was the work of the indwelling Holy Spirit that he emphasised, in combination with prayer and self-discipline.

Augustine, Aquinas, Luther and Whitefield all appear to have accepted the moderate drinking of wine as a good, or at least morally neutral, thing. For Aquinas, this was understood according to his theory of the mean of virtues. Moderate drinking, but not excessive drinking, is a virtue. In theory, and perhaps rarely in practice, he understood that complete abstinence may also be a vice. For Augustine and Aquinas, it was a matter of the grace of God that some people avoid drunkenness, but for Aquinas (following Aristotle), the virtue of moderate drinking was also understood as a personally acquired habit. The tension between grace and free will thus emerges for Aquinas in the issue of the avoidance of drunkenness, as well as in the matter of redemption from it.

The question whether Christians should be obviously different from others in respect of drunkenness is also a recurrent theme. Augustine clearly believed that they should be different, but recognised that the sin of drunkenness had in practice been tolerated in various parts of the Church at different times. Luther did not generally expect to see any markedly obvious difference between the Christian and 'any honest man', and allowed for the sin that is committed 'unwittingly'. However, he did expect to see evidence of Christian faith in the ordinary and unglamorous affairs of home and family life, and he would therefore surely have expected an absence of drunkenness in this context. For Whitefield, the presence of the Holy Spirit was incompatible with drunkenness. The implication of his teaching thus appears to be that the Christian believer, almost by definition, will not engage in acts of drunkenness.

Does the ethical thinking of Augustine, Aquinas, Luther and Whitefield on the subject of drunkenness have relevance to contemporary Christian ethics? Three aspects would seem to be of particular importance.

First, Augustine's concept of the divided will has enormous relevance to an understanding of how people engage with desires or appetites that impel them towards goals that they recognise as being inherently undesirable. The phenomenon of psychological dependence, unknown to Augustine, arguably describes exactly the same phenomenological state, but has not been subject to the same philosophical and ethical analysis. Augustine offers us the possibility of constructing a more sophisticated moral framework for the use of 'anti-craving' drugs and of psychological treatments directed at eliminating strongly reinforced harmful behaviours such as heavy drinking or smoking.

Secondly, Aquinas' concept of the mean of virtues offers a potentially broad base for an understanding of the ethics of drinking. Such a concept has the potential to relate 'normal' drinking ethically to drunkenness and to other alcohol-related problems. Given that scientists now consider that alcohol use and misuse are closely related at the population level, this would appear to offer a closer correspondence between epidemiology, social psychology and ethics than would an ethical framework which treats drunkenness as a completely separate issue.

Aquinas also identified the need for the drinker to have awareness of the intoxicating effects of the drink, his or her own vulnerability to the effects of the drink, and the parameters of what might be considered 'moderate' consumption. To a greater or lesser extent, each of these considerations is recognised in contemporary health education. However, Aquinas treated drunkenness as if it either is present or is not present. In reality, it is a continuous variable which is correlated with the probability of social, physical or psychological harms. Furthermore, he did not fully account for the influence of the cultural and social milieu with its norms and expectations. These contribute to the nature and occurrence of drunkenness at least as much as do the properties of drink, drinker and drinking pattern. Aquinas' ethics of drunkenness need to be extended to take these variables into account. Similarly, contemporary ethics might benefit from giving greater attention to Aquinas' understanding of the importance of drinkers' awareness of the likely effects of their drinking behaviour.

Thirdly, there is need for a contemporary debate on the most appropriate Christian foundations for an ethics of drunkenness. Are simple and direct scriptural injunctions against drunkenness (e.g. Galatians 5:20) equally relevant today, given all that is now known about the way in which social and cultural processes, genetic vulnerability and psychology all contribute to the nature and consequences of drunkenness? What about the broad range of other alcohol-related problems which occur in the absence of 'drunkenness' (e.g. cirrhosis, brain damage, accidents)? How should the *summum bonum* of Augustine, or the *ratio boni* of Aquinas, now be understood? What about Whitefield's theology of the proper use of created things? What about Paul's concept of the flesh? It would seem that contemporary Christians might be just as divided on these priorities as were Augustine, Aquinas, Luther and Whitefield. However, such diversity requires a debate which goes beyond simple injunctions against drunkenness, which take into account neither the scientific realities nor the breadth of Christian opinion.

Augustine, Aquinas, Luther and Whitefield offer relevant and creative insights into ways in which contemporary Christian understandings of the ethics of drunkenness might be further explored, enhanced and developed.

# CHAPTER 5

# *Temperance redefined: the nineteenth-century temperance movement*

Temperance, along with prudence, justice and fortitude, was understood in classical thought as being one of the four cardinal virtues.[1] For Aquinas, temperance was the virtue of moderation or temperateness which resulted from the exercise of human reason,[2] and was chiefly concerned with the human passion for 'sensible and bodily goods' or 'desire and pleasure'.[3] In contemporary usage, it might best be described as 'self-control' or 'self-restraint' or 'a capacity for acting appropriately with respect to the fundamental organic processes of human life: appropriate consumption of food, appropriate use of stimulants and intoxicants, appropriate sexual behaviour'.[4] In the nineteenth century, however, in Europe and North America, the word 'temperance' became associated particularly with a concern about the use of alcohol, and in particular with a movement dedicated to complete abstinence from the use of alcohol. This was to have a profound and far-reaching influence upon the Christian ethics of alcohol use and misuse.

This chapter will trace briefly, and selectively, some of the different strands of the history, ethics and reasoning of the temperance movement, and in particular its relationship with Christian theology and the Church. It will be argued that changing social and medical conceptions of the vice of drunkenness were associated with a redefinition of temperance as abstinence in many Protestant churches. This led to hermeneutical and doctrinal controversy, as well as to Christian ethical debate concerning the most appropriate means of combating intemperance. It raises important questions for the contemporary Christian analysis of the ethics of alcohol misuse.

---

[1] Macquarrie and Childress, 1986, pp. 617–618; Cross and Livingstone, 1997, p. 1583.
[2] *Summa Theologica*, Second Part of the Second Part, Q141.1.
[3] *Summa Theologica*, Second Part of the Second Part, Q141.3.
[4] Porter, 2002, p. 170.

### DRUNKENNESS AS A DISEASE

In 1785, in Philadelphia, Dr Benjamin Rush published *An Inquiry into the Effects of Ardent Spirits upon the Human Body and Mind with an Account of the Remedies for Curing Them.*[5] Referring to drunkenness as a disease, he enumerated and described the acute and chronic adverse effects of distilled spirits upon body and mind. The paroxysms of this disease of drunkenness were observed by Rush to occur with increasing frequency, until finally sobriety would be the exception rather than the rule. The moral consequences of the disease process were all too clear: 'The demoralising effects of distilled spirits . . . produce not only falsehood, but fraud, theft, uncleanliness, and murder. Like the demoniac mentioned in the New Testament, their name is "legion," for they convey into the soul a host of vices and crimes.'[6] The solution to the problem was also clear to Rush. It could be prevented by the consumption of water, cider, beer, wine, sugar and water, or coffee rather than distilled spirits.[7] Before proceeding to outline more medical treatments, Rush also noted that 'many hundred drunkards have been cured of their desire for ardent spirits, by a practical belief in the doctrines of the Christian religion'.[8]

Other physicians also began to view drunkenness, or at least chronic drunkenness, as a disease. In 1804, the Scottish physician Dr Thomas Trotter published *An Essay, Medical, Philosophical, and Chemical on Drunkenness and Its Effects on the Human Body.*[9] Curiously silent about Rush's earlier work, and much less positive than Rush about the role of the Christian religion in addressing drunkenness,[10] Trotter was, however, quite clear: 'In medical language, I consider drunkenness, strictly speaking, to be a disease; produced by a remote cause, and giving birth to actions and movements in the living body, that disorder the functions of health.'[11]

The first half of the nineteenth century saw chronic drunkenness established in the eyes of the medical profession as a medical disorder.[12] By the end of the nineteenth century however, Dr Norman Kerr, another Scottish physician and first president of the Society for the Study and Cure of Inebriety,[13] while still apparently recognising all drunkenness as sin, also recognised that not all drunkenness resulted from disease. His concern, as a physician, was with 'those in whom either the habit of drinking, or some

---

[5] Rush, 1943.    [6] Ibid., p. 328.
[7] Ibid., pp. 330–332. Even 'wine and opium' was to be preferred to distilled spirits (p. 335)!
[8] Ibid., p. 338.    [9] Trotter, 1988.    [10] Ibid., pp. xiv, 3.
[11] Ibid., p. 8. Later he refers to drunkenness as '*a disease of the mind*' (p. 172, original emphasis preserved).
[12] Ibid., p. xiv.    [13] Later the Society for the Study of Addiction; Berridge, 1990, pp. 991ff.

inherited or other cause, has set up the diseased condition we designate inebriety, which may be defined as an overpowering impulse to indulge in intoxication at all risks'.[14] Drunkenness, or at least inebriety, thus came to be understood as a disease which could overpower the will.

### THE BIRTH OF THE TEMPERANCE MOVEMENT

Rush's work was read by Dr Lyman Beecher, an American Protestant minister who in 1826 wrote and delivered *Six Sermons on the Nature, Occasions, Signs, Evils, and Remedy of Intemperance*.[15] This work was published, and was in its turn widely read, proceeding to many subsequent editions,[16] so that Beecher is credited with a significant role in the establishment of a national temperance movement in the United States of America.[17] However, the first American temperance society was started at Moreau, Saratoga, in New York State in 1808 by Dr C. J. Clark. The members pledged not to drink spirits or wine, except for medicinal purposes, at public dinners or at Holy Communion.[18] In 1826, the American Temperance Society was formed, and by 1829 over 1,000 societies had been formed, with a total of 100,000 members. The chief proponents of the movement appear to have been physicians and clergymen.[19] In order to co-ordinate the work of these societies, the United States Temperance Union was created in 1833, and in 1836 was renamed the American Temperance Union, in order to incorporate the Canadian societies. There was debate as to whether the objective of the Union should be temperance or complete abstinence, but the latter was adopted.[20]

Before the confusion becomes too great, it is as well to pause here to note that some later nineteenth-century temperance writers were themselves clear that the term 'temperance' was by then being misused. For example, in his history of the temperance movement, *The Temperance Movement and Its Workers*, published in 1892, P. T. Winskill wrote:

> It may perhaps be well to remark here that in the early days of the movement the terms 'temperance' and 'total abstinence' – afterwards expressed in the word 'teetotalism' – had distinct and specific meanings, and were never, as they now are, deemed to be synonymous, which they certainly are *not*. Many societies, strictly teetotal, or on abstinence principles, and others based on the principles of the early

---

[14] Kerr, 1888, p. 10.  [15] Beecher, 1845.
[16] I am aware that it reached at least the tenth edition, which was published in 1845.
[17] Hyslop, 1931, pp. 15–16; Cross and Livingstone, 1997, p. 1584.
[18] Hyslop, 1931, p. 16; Cross and Livingstone, 1997, p. 1584.
[19] Hyslop, 1931, p. 16.  [20] Cross and Livingstone, 1997, p. 1584.

societies, bear the somewhat dubious title of temperance societies, and some of the former date their origin from the introduction of the first or anti-spirit pledge of the society, when teetotalism was not known or recognised by them. This is misleading, and tends to mystify dates, &c., causing students of the history of the movement much trouble and annoyance.[21]

However, according to other writers, the term was simply to be defined differently. For example, in an introduction to *The Temperance Movement and Its Workers*, Dr F. R. Lees employed what he referred to as the 'Socratic' definition of temperance: 'Temperance is to know (φρονησις) how to *use* what is good, and *avoid* what is bad.'[22] On this basis, if alcohol is good, then, temperance will be concerned with its use. But if alcohol is 'bad', temperance will be concerned with its avoidance. The main strand of the temperance movement became increasingly convinced that alcohol was 'bad', at least insofar as its consumption as a beverage is concerned.

By the 1830s, the essential tenets of temperance thinking were established. According to Levine,[23] these were as follows:

1. Alcohol was an inherently addictive substance. Regular use of alcohol was the cause of habitual drunkenness.
2. Alcohol weakened drinkers' control of their own moral behaviour, released animal passions, and led to poverty and crime.
3. Alcohol was a poison which caused or predisposed to a wide range of physical diseases.

Alcohol was the problem. Abstinence was promoted as the solution. From about 1840 onwards,[24] the habitual drunkard was treated with sympathy as suffering from a disease, and was seen as being in need of help. A number of temperance organisations (such as the Washingtonians, the Sons of Temperance, and the Good Templars) especially concerned themselves with the reclamation and reformation of inebriates.

The temperance movement was divided between those who believed that the primary means of combating the evil of drink should be 'moral suasion' and those who supported prohibition. In 1846 the state of Maine was the first among the United States to introduce legal prohibition.[25] This represented

---

[21] Winskill, 1892a, p. 59.
[22] Ibid., p. xxii. Lees does not give his source for this quotation, and it might be debated whether it is a truly 'Socratic' definition. It might also be observed that removal of the comma from the English text could change the meaning to a definition rather different from the one that Lees apparently has in view.
[23] Levine, 1984.
[24] Maxwell, 1950, pp. 411–412; Levine, 1984. In fact, earlier attitudes towards the drunkard had not been uniformly unsympathetic, and the redemption of the drunkard from sin was seen as the desirable goal (Lender, 1973, pp. 357–358).
[25] Macquarrie and Childress, 1986, p. 619.

the beginning of the first of three waves of state prohibition laws, which culminated in 1919 with national prohibition under the Eighteenth Amendment to the Constitution.[26]

## THE TEMPERANCE MOVEMENT IN BRITAIN AND IRELAND

In 1829, inspired by news of the temperance movement in America, John Edgar, Professor of Theology in Belfast, initiated an anti-spirit campaign in Ulster, and John Dunlop began a similar campaign in Glasgow and Greenock.[27] Professor Edgar, a Presbyterian minister, was joined by six other Christian ministers of various Protestant denominations, and one layman from his own church, in establishing the Belfast Temperance Society.[28] John Dunlop was similarly influential in establishing the Scottish temperance societies.[29] Both men began their involvement in the temperance movement with a concern for moderation in the use of alcohol, primarily by means of abstinence from distilled spirits.[30] Professor Edgar, at the outset of his temperance career, rather dramatically poured out a gallon of 'fine malt whisky' into the gutter in front of his house.[31] He remained committed to moderation throughout his life, and strongly opposed the movement to total abstinence.[32] Dunlop, a great believer in the importance of prayer for the temperance movement, later underwent a 'conversion' to total abstinence.[33]

The Bradford Temperance Society, the first of its kind in England, held its first meeting in February 1830. The Society was established by a businessman, Henry Forbes, who had come into contact with the temperance movement in Glasgow, while on a business trip. He obtained a supply of temperance literature, including Beecher's *Sermons*, to distribute to his acquaintances. At the first public meeting, in June 1830, Professor Edgar was among the speakers.[34]

In 1832 a number of temperance societies adopted total abstinence pledges. For example, the Greenlaw Temperance Society adopted the following pledge, which was initially available in addition to the original moderation pledge: 'We do resolve that, so long as we are members of this association, we shall abstain from the use of distilled spirits, wines,

---

[26] The three waves of state legislation were in the 1850s, 1880s and 1910s. The Eighteenth Amendment was repealed in 1933 (Stark and Bainbridge, 1996, p. 86).

[27] Hyslop, 1931, p. 16.    [28] Winskill, 1892a, pp. 50–51.    [29] Ibid., p. 57.

[30] 'Moderation' at this time seems to have had as much to do with using alcohol only in moderate concentration as with using it only in moderate amount.

[31] Winskill, 1892a, p. 50; Hyslop, 1931, p. 16.

[32] Ibid., p. 51.    [33] Ibid., p. 7.    [34] Ibid., p. 63.

and all other intoxicating liquors, except for medicinal and sacramental purposes. Adherence to this principle will be notified by prefixing * to the name.'[35] Pledges of this kind were apparently adopted, fairly independently, in temperance societies in various parts of North America and the United Kingdom.[36]

Particular national and international significance has been attributed to the 'Seven Men of Preston', members of the Preston Temperance Society, who signed a total abstinence pledge in September 1832. It is to this movement that the origins of the word 'teetotal' are credited. One of their later members, an illiterate man with a history of 'hard drinking', wishing to emphasise the benefits of total abstinence when speaking at one of their meetings, but unable to find the right word, apparently said: 'I'll be reet down and out and t-t-total for ever.'[37] The neologism caught on, and was adopted as a name for the new movement.

Another member of the Preston Society, Thomas Swindlehurst, known as the 'King of Reformed Drunkards', is quoted as saying that the original moderation pledge of that society was

nothing but sheer humbug, botheration, and nonsense, for I find that, after I have had one glass of ale, I have a greater desire for the second than I had for the first, for the third than I had for the second, for the fourth than the third, &c . . . and the pledge does not prevent me from going to public-houses and giving drink to others . . . I am quite sure, from my own experience, that nothing short of *total abstinence from all intoxicating drinks can either reform drunkards, or prevent moderate drinkers from becoming drunkards.*[38]

Although not one of the 'Seven Men', it would seem that Swindlehurst had a valid claim to being the true founder of total abstinence principles in the Preston area. It would further seem that the living testimony of 'reformed drunkards', including Swindlehurst and his two sons, was particularly influential in the ascendancy of the total abstinence movement in that locality.[39]

At an early stage, it was realised that the reformation of drunkards alone was not enough, and that steps must be taken to prevent drunkenness by enlisting the young to total abstinence. In 1832 the Paisley Youths' Total Abstinence Society was a pioneer in such work, which was rapidly followed by others. The first national juvenile movement, known as the Band of Hope, held its first regular meeting in 1847.

---

[35] Ibid., p. 83.    [36] Ibid., p. 84.    [37] Hyslop, 1931, p. 21.
[38] Winskill, 1892a, p. 90, original emphasis preserved.    [39] Ibid., pp. 88–92.

In 1853, following visits to Britain by representatives of the American prohibitionist movement, the United Kingdom Alliance was founded.[40] The stated object of the Alliance was 'to call forth and direct an enlightened public opinion to procure the total and immediate legislative suppression of the traffic in all intoxicating liquors as beverages'.[41]

Until 1838, the temperance movement in Ireland generally paralleled that in England and the United States. It was largely directed against the use of spirits, and was led by clergy and professional men. The very poor, and especially drunkards, were beyond redemption.[42] For example, one Roman Catholic bishop wrote: 'I would be . . . glad to heal the drunkard; but if he were obstinate, and obstinately persevered in his vice, I would feel upon his death, as I would upon the death of the murderer dying on the scaffold – that he had paid the forfeit of his life to the offended justice of earth and heaven.'[43]

After 1838, the temperance movement in Ireland took a different course, largely as a result of the work of one Roman Catholic priest. A charismatic and controversial figure, Father Theobald Matthew, a Fransiscan friar, was engaged in parish ministry in Cork, in Ireland, from 1814 to 1838.[44] Father Matthew's concern with the problems of intemperance appears to have arisen partly from his work with the poor in Cork, and partly from the heavy drinking of his own family. He joined the new Cork Total Abstinence Society in 1838, accompanying his signature of the register with the words 'Here goes, in the name of God'.

Father Matthew's popularity grew rapidly. In September 1839, in three days in Limerick, he administered the pledge to an estimated 150,000 people, and in Waterford 90,000 people signed the pledge in two days. According to some estimates, half the population of Ireland eventually signed the pledge during the course of his ministry, and the national consumption of spirits was halved. Popular superstition was fuelled by reports of miracles, including the healing of the deaf, blind, dumb and crippled. However, in the 1840s his crusade waned as rapidly as it had risen.

In the 1860s there was a resurgence of Catholic temperance societies in Ireland.[45] Eventually this movement led to the formation of the Pioneer Total Abstinence Association, established by Father James Cullen in 1901. Father Cullen was a very different man from Father Matthew. He was a gloomy and modest man, who worked for thirty years with the temperance

[40] Macquarrie and Childress, 1986, p. 619.
[41] Winskill, 1892d, p. 280.   [42] Malcolm, 1986, pp. 99–100.   [43] Ibid., p. 84.
[44] Hyslop, 1931, pp. 32–33; Malcolm, 1986, pp. 101–150.   [45] Malcolm, 1986, pp. 293–321.

movement before forming the Pioneer Association. His work was char-acterised by a careful organisation that Father Matthew's lacked. In 1862 he was apparently shocked by contact with a drunken priest, but it has been suggested that it was his work among the boatmen of Enniscorthy that brought home to him the full seriousness of the problem of intemper-ance.[46] Initially unimpressed with the value of the pledge, he saw religious devotion and alternative forms of recreation as being important antidotes to intemperance. From 1881 to 1883 he retreated from temperance work and, following an appropriate programme of study, was received into the Society of Jesus. In 1887 he was appointed Director of the Apostleship of Prayer in Ireland, a movement which emphasised prayer and devotion to the Sacred Heart of Jesus.

Cullen came to see total abstinence as an essential part of the devotional life of devout Catholics. In 1889 he established the Total Abstinence League of the Sacred Heart as a branch of the Apostleship of Prayer. Despite the name of the League, it allowed for three classes of membership: lifetime abstinence, temporary abstinence, and those who did not abstain but who supported the suppression of intemperance with their prayers and money. Gradually, Cullen increased the emphasis on the pledge as an act of sacrifice for God, and as a part of a life of total commitment. The Pioneers, when they were formed, were an elite group, a Catholic devotional society which was a 'special regiment in the great temperance army'.[47]

Protestants in Ireland were divided between those who continued to advocate moderation (meaning largely avoidance of spirits) and those who believed that total abstinence was required. The extremes were observable in those who replaced communion wine with grape juice on the one hand, and the Church of Ireland, which was apparently content for drink manufac-turers to fund its church buildings, on the other.[48] Moderationist societies in Ireland tended to be almost entirely Protestant.[49] The debate focussed partly on differences in interpretation of scripture,[50] and partly upon more pragmatic considerations. For example, Professor Edgar considered total abstinence unscriptural, equating it with the Manichaean heresy.[51] In con-trast, Jonathan Simpson, a Presbyterian minister, argued for legislative

---

[46] Ibid., p. 308.    [47] Ibid., p. 317.    [48] Ibid., pp. 158–159, 279, 293.
[49] Ibid., p. 89.    [50] Ibid., pp. 277–279.
[51] Ibid., p. 73. Manichaeism originated in the third century in Mesopotamia. It was a religion of radical materialistic dualism (E. Ferguson, McHugh and Norris, 1999, pp. 707–709; Mann, 2002, pp. 40–41). The Manichees were total abstainers who considered wine to be evil. According to Augustine, they considered wine to be 'the poison of the princes of darkness' (*On the Morals of the Manichaeans*, ch. 16, para. 24) or 'the poisonous filth of the race of darkness' (*Reply to Faustus the Manichaean*, book 16, para. 31).

prohibition on largely utilitarian grounds.[52] For Protestants, temperance was also linked to revivalism. Temperance was seen as a necessary prerequisite for evangelism,[53] but revival was also associated with a reduction in drinking and drunkenness.[54]

In 1862, the Church of England and Ireland Temperance Reformation Society was founded. Under the influence of this society, a *Report on Intemperance* was presented to both Houses of Convocation of the Provinces of Canterbury and York.[55] The report included an extensive appendix detailing the results of inquiry concerning the problems of intemperance as encountered by clergy, police, magistrates, judges, coroners, governors of workhouses, superintendents of asylums, and others. It made a series of recommendations for non-legislative and legislative remedies for the evil of intemperance.

In 1873, the society was renamed the Church of England Temperance Society. The new society had three objects:
1. 'the promotion of the habits of temperance'
2. 'the reformation of the intemperate'
3. 'the removal of the causes which lead to intemperance'
The third object was largely to be conducted in accordance with the report previously presented to the Houses of Convocation of the two provinces. Membership was allowed according to two classes, one of which was open to abstainers and non-abstainers, but the second of which was restricted to total abstainers. The Archbishops of Canterbury and York became presidents, and Her Majesty the Queen became patroness.[56]

The close of the nineteenth century found some nonconformists considering total abstinence a *de facto* requirement for ministerial office, and even for church membership.[57] In contrast, the Church of England remained open to those who espoused moderation as well as those who championed total abstinence.

Frederick Temple (1821–1902), as Archbishop of Canterbury at the turn of the century, was an enthusiastic temperance reformer, who identified intemperance as the biggest social evil of his time, and who campaigned vigorously for legislative reform.[58] His own conviction of the need for total abstinence, which he did not seek to impose upon others, appears to have been born out of his experience of drunkenness among the clergy, and out of a belief that his own example would have a positive effect upon others:

---

[52] Malcolm, 1986, pp. 154–156.   [53] Ibid., p. 160.   [54] Ibid., p. 165.
[55] Winskill, 1892c, p. 152; Committee on Intemperance, 1869.
[56] Ibid., pp. 152–153.   [57] Briggs, 1994, pp. 338–339.
[58] Carpenter, 1997, pp. 397–398; Winskill, 1892c, p. 155.

I have been for many years a total abstainer from all intoxicating liquors – not because I found it at all necessary for my own life, but because I found that the influence I could bring upon other people in this particular might be so far greater when I was abstaining entirely than if I simply checked myself to very careful moderation, and laboured in other ways to keep people from yielding to such temptation.[59]

## NINETEENTH-CENTURY TEMPERANCE LITERATURE

The temperance movement spawned a voluminous literature. As it would be a Herculean task to attempt to read and review this entire literature, three examples only will be studied here in detail.

Lyman Beecher's *Six Sermons on Intemperance*[60] has been chosen for consideration both because it was so influential, and also because it provides an example of American Protestant literature from a very early phase of the movement. Dawson Burns's *Christendom and the Drink Curse*[61] provides an example of a much later, and thus more highly developed, work, written by an English Baptist minister, when the movement was (almost) at its height. Both of these writers saw the root of the problem as being inherent in alcoholic beverages. In the case of Lyman Beecher, the concern was specifically with distilled spirits. For Dawson Burns, the 'drink curse' was associated with all alcoholic drinks.

Thomas Bridgett's *The Discipline of Drink*[62] is a very different work from either of these. Written by an English Roman Catholic priest, a contemporary of Burns, it adopts a different theological perspective, and views drunkenness, not drink, as the core problem. It is also a historical work, looking both for the lessons that can be learned from the mistakes of history, and also for the authority and grace associated with the traditions of the Catholic Church.

## LYMAN BEECHER'S *SIX SERMONS ON INTEMPERANCE*

Lyman Beecher (1775–1863) was born in New Haven, Connecticut, and studied at Yale University. He was a pastor of various Presbyterian and Congregational churches and President of Lane Theological Seminary (1832–1850). He was a leading figure in the Second Great Awakening. His concern

---

[59] Dant, 1903, p. 177.
[60] Delivered and written in 1926. All quotations here, however, are from the tenth edition (Beecher, 1845).
[61] Burns, 1875.    [62] Bridgett, 1876.

for social reform included women's suffrage and the anti-slavery movement as well as temperance. He was an opponent of both Unitarianism and Roman Catholicism. In 1835 he was accused of heresy, but was vindicated by both Presbytery and Synod.[63]

Beecher wrote extensively, and with great care, writing, amending, destroying and rewriting his manuscripts, which were not easy to read. Towards the end of his life this process seems to have been so emphasised as to prevent him from publishing his work at all.[64] In addition to *Six Sermons on Intemperance* (written and delivered at Litchfield, Connecticut, in 1826),[65] Beecher's published works included *Plea for the West* (1835). Recognising the importance of the Midwest for the future of the United States, this tract was outspoken against the supposed interests of the Roman Catholic Church and European powers in these territories.[66]

Beecher apparently dressed simply, and was diffident in ordinary conversation. In the pulpit, however, 'his voice rang clear and loud, his sentences became compact and earnest, and his manner caught the glowing fervour of his thought'.[67] His greatest passion was revival. When on his deathbed, he was asked, 'What is the greatest of all things?' His reply: 'It is not theology; it is not controversy; it is to save souls.'[68]

Beecher was quite clear that he considered intemperance to be a sin.[69] The first two sermons of the *Six Sermons on Intemperance* are prefaced by a quotation of Proverbs 23:29–35.[70] 'This is a glowing description of the sin of intemperance,' wrote Beecher as the opening line of the first sermon.[71] 'No sin has fewer apologies than intemperance,' he continued. And yet, he then immediately proceeded to provide apologies in the form of references to the 'undefined nature of the crime', and the problems of ignorance and unawareness of the signs of intemperance.[72] Later he stated that 'the habit is fixed, and the hope of reformation is gone, before the subject has the

---

[63] Cross and Livingstone, 1997, p. 178.

[64] One of his daughters apparently said that there were three rules which enabled her to read her father's work: 'If there is a letter crossed it is not a *t* . . . If there is a letter dotted it is not an *i* . . . If there be a capital letter it is not at the *beginning* of a word' (Winskill, 1892a, p. 38).

[65] Beecher had been pastor of the Congregational church in Litchfield since 1810. In the same year that his *Six Sermons* were written and delivered, Beecher requested an increase in his salary, which was refused by his church. Consequently, he left Litchfield that year and became pastor of another Congregational church, in Boston (Winskill, 1892a, p. 36).

[66] Cross and Livingstone, 1997, p. 178.    [67] Winskill, 1892a, p. 25.    [68] Ibid., p. 38.

[69] He later indicates that it is also both a disease and a crime (see p. 37).

[70] His quotations from scripture all appear to have been from the Authorized (King James) Version.

[71] Beecher, 1845, p. 6.    [72] Ibid., pp. 6–7.

least suspicion of danger'.[73] It appears that he hoped his sermons would remove the need for the use of these apologies: 'Nothing, therefore, seems to be more important, than a description of this broad way, thronged by so many travellers, that the temperate, when they come in sight of it, may know their danger and pass by it and turn away.'[74]

Beecher proceeded immediately to the task of defining intemperance. He wished to dispel the 'common apprehension' that intemperance is that which 'supersede[s] the regular operations of the mental faculties and the bodily organs' such that a man loses command of 'his mind, his utterance, and his bodily members'.[75] By this he appears to have had in mind a view of intemperance as drinking 'to insensibility'.[76] He wished rather to broaden the concept of intemperance to include such factors as 'inordinate desire', the expense incurred, present effects on health, temper and 'moral sensibilities', and the future consequences for mental and physical health. Most especially, he was concerned about 'the moral ruin which it works in the soul, that gives it the denomination of giant wickedness'.[77]

Beecher considered it 'a matter of undoubted certainty, that habitual tippling was worse than periodical drunkenness'.[78] His reasoning for this was that the quantity consumed by the daily drinker will inevitably increase, with deleterious effects for mental and physical health. Furthermore, he estimated that in more than half of cases, drunkenness (or 'inebriation') would also inevitably follow. In other words, daily drinking, more often than not, leads inevitably to drunkenness. Thus he concluded

THAT THE DAILY USE OF ARDENT SPIRITS, IN ANY FORM, OR IN ANY DEGREE, IS INTEMPERANCE.[79]

Beecher spent a little time in his first sermon outlining some of the physical effects of 'ardent spirits' upon the human body. However, it was clearly his concern for the salvation of souls which was his priority and passion. It is perhaps worth quoting an extract from his first sermon at greater length, in order to convey something of his feeling for this. It is easy to imagine his impassioned delivery from the pulpit!

These sufferings, however, of animal nature, are not to be compared with the moral agonies which convulse the soul. It is an immortal being who sins, and suffers; and as his earthly house dissolves, he is approaching the judgement seat, in anticipation of a miserable eternity. He feels his captivity, and in anguish of spirit clanks his chains and cries for help. Conscience thunders, remorse goads, and as the gulf

---

[73] Ibid., p. 16.    [74] Ibid., p. 7.    [75] Ibid.    [76] Ibid., p. 8.    [77] Ibid.    [78] Ibid., p. 9.
[79] Ibid., p. 11, capitalisation preserved from the published text.

opens before him, he recoils, and trembles, and weeps, and prays, and resolves, and promises, and reforms, and 'seeks it yet again' – again resolves, and weeps, and prays, and 'seeks it yet again!' Wretched man, he has placed himself in the hands of a giant, who never pities, and never relaxes his iron grip. He may struggle, but he is in chains. He may cry for release, but it comes not; and lost! lost! may be inscribed upon the doorposts of his dwelling.[80]

Having defined the nature of intemperance, he proceeded to outline its occasions. These were:

'The free and frequent ardent use of spirits in the family'[81]
'Ardent spirits given as a matter of hospitality'[82]
'Days of public convocation'[83]
'Evening resorts for conversation, enlivened by the cheering bowl'[84]
'All convivial associations for the purpose of drinking'[85]
'Feeble health and mental depression'[86]
'Medical prescriptions'[87]
'The vending of ardent spirits, in places licensed or unlicensed'[88]
'A resort to ardent spirits as an alleviation of trouble'[89]
'Ardent spirits employed to invigorate the intellect, or restore exhausted
    nature under severe study'[90]
'The use of ardent spirits, employed as an auxiliary to labor'[91]

In each case, Beecher refuted any argument that ardent spirits might be of value, and showed how the occasion may lead to regular drinking and a habit of intemperance.

In his second sermon, Beecher considered the signs or symptoms of intemperance as they affect both body and mind. These were:

1. Associations of drinking with particular times and places, such as holidays, festivals, taverns and meetings with friends[92]
2. 'A disposition to multiply the circumstances which furnish the occasions and opportunities for drinking'[93]
3. The 'desire of drinking ardent spirits returning daily at stated times'[94]
4. The 'desire of concealment' which leads to drinking 'slily and in secret places'[95]
5. Drinking in company 'so much as [a man] may think he can bear without awakening in others the suspicion of inebriation'[96]
6. Opposition of the 'reformation of intemperance'[97]

---

[80] Ibid., p. 15.    [81] Ibid., p. 17.    [82] Ibid.    [83] Ibid., p. 18.    [84] Ibid.    [85] Ibid., p. 19.
[86] Ibid.    [87] Ibid.    [88] Ibid.    [89] Ibid.    [90] Ibid., p. 21.    [91] Ibid.
[92] Ibid., pp. 26–28.    [93] Ibid., pp. 28–29.    [94] Ibid., pp. 29–31.    [95] Ibid., p. 31.
[96] Ibid., pp. 31–32.    [97] Ibid., p. 32.

7. Redness of eyes and/or 'countenance', 'impaired muscular strength and tremour of the hand', dysfunction of the liver, loss of appetite, indigestion, inflammation of the lungs, blistering of the tongue and lips, 'irritability, petulance, and violent anger', 'extinction of all the finer feelings and amiable dispositions of the soul' (including any religious affections)[98]

Eventually, Beecher concluded, intemperance leads to death of both body and soul.

But what was the remedy? First, there was a communal need for an 'all-pervading sense of the danger . . . of falling into this sin'.[99] The prudent use of ardent spirits is simply not possible and it is folly to attempt it. Secondly, the distinction between intemperance and drunkenness must be observed:

So long as men suppose that there is neither crime nor danger in drinking, short of what they denominate drunkenness, they will cast off fear and move onward to ruin by a silent, certain course, until destruction comes upon them, and they cannot escape.[100]

Bottles of ardent spirits should be labelled in the same way as bottles of laudanum, Beecher exhorted: 'TOUCH NOT, TASTE NOT, HANDLE NOT.'[101] If this applies to all people, it applies especially to the reformation of those for whom intemperance has become habitual. Immediate and complete abstinence is the only solution.

It is interesting that, at this point alone in the *Sermons*, Beecher distinguished between 'ardent spirits', 'strong beer' and wine. He was quite clear that all of these drinks are to be avoided by the intemperate if they wish to reform. However, he indicated that strong beer 'may not create intemperate habits as soon'[102] and left open the possibility that people may not '*become* intemperate on wine'.[103] Given his opening of this and his previous sermon with a quotation from Proverbs concerning the dangers of wine, a passage which he had already described as 'a glowing description of the sin of intemperance', it is curious that he was willing to allow such a distinction.

Beecher's third sermon was devoted to the evils of intemperance. This, along with the remaining three sermons, was prefaced with a quotation

---

[98] Ibid., pp. 32–37.     [99] Ibid., p. 37.     [100] Ibid., p. 39.
[101] Ibid., p. 40, capitalisation preserved from the published text. This is presumably an unacknowledged quotation from Colossians 2:21, but the context of that quotation makes it curiously inappropriate for Beecher's purpose. Indeed, taken in context, the quotation would appear to offer strong biblical support *against* total abstinence!
[102] Ibid., p. 41.     [103] Ibid., p. 42, my emphasis.

from Habakkuk 2 (vv. 9–11, 15–16). The text was taken as the basis for a consideration of the effects of intemperance upon the nation.

Beecher enumerated the following points:

1. 'The effects of intemperance upon the health and physical energies of a nation, are not to be overlooked, or lightly esteemed.'[104]
2. 'The injurious influence of general intemperance upon national intellect, is equally certain, and not less to be deprecated.'[105]
3. 'The effect of intemperance upon the military prowess of a nation, cannot but be great and evil.'[106]
4. 'The effect of intemperance upon the patriotism of a nation is neither obscure nor doubtful.'[107]
5. 'Upon the national conscience or moral principle the effects of intemperance are deadly.'[108]
6. 'Upon national industry the effects of intemperance are manifest and mischievous.'[109]

Beecher pursued the sixth of these points at great length. Going beyond the impairment by intemperance of the workforce and thus of industrial productivity, he considered the burden that the intemperate posed to the national economy. Becoming poor, as inevitably they must, the intemperate and their families must be cared for at the expense of other citizens. Intemperance transferred 'larger and larger bodies of men, from the class of contributors to the national income, to the class of worthless consumers'.[110] The intemperate were portrayed as idle, irreligious, ignorant, criminal, a threat to the economy of the nation and to civil liberty.

The fourth, fifth and sixth sermons took up in greater depth the need for a remedy against intemperance. Voluntary abstinence, the efforts of clergy or the press, civil legislation, voluntary associations, and local measures in town or state were all alike portrayed as worthy but futile. The manufacturers, distributors and vendors of ardent spirits were not to be held to blame; or at least they were not solely to blame. It was the 'temperate' drinkers whom Beecher held responsible, for they had created the demand, and it was national repentance that he sought.

However, Beecher did also require a legislative solution. He enjoined that ardent spirits should cease to be a lawful article of commerce, other than for medicinal purposes. Commerce in ardent spirits employs large numbers of men, and large sums of money, for no good purpose, and at the same time results in great evil. Beecher further saw such commerce

---

[104] Ibid., pp. 48–49.   [105] Ibid., pp. 49–51.   [106] Ibid., pp. 51–52.   [107] Ibid., p. 52.
[108] Ibid., p. 52.   [109] Ibid., pp. 53–58.   [110] Ibid., p. 55.

as a manifest violation of the command 'Thou shalt love thy neighbour as thyself',[III] since it causes harm to the neighbour of anyone who
engages in it. He noted that those who engage in this trade are themselves at greater risk of intemperance, and are also moral accessories to the
crimes committed by the intemperate. It should, therefore, be considered
unlawful.

Beecher advocated education on the topic of the nature, causes, evils and
remedy of intemperance. He advocated the formation of societies such as
the American Society for the Promotion of Temperance. He urged employers to discourage the use of ardent spirits in the workplace, young men to set
an example of voluntary abstinence, and professionals to use their influence
in support of abstinence. He advocated consumer pressure, encouraging
people to boycott those shops which sold ardent spirits. In particular, he
saw an important role for the Christian Church. Those who were 'past
reformation' should be 'cut off', and the use of ardent spirits should be
proscribed within the churches. The churches should lobby the States and
Congress, and pray for reform.

Beecher closed his sixth sermon with an impassioned plea to his reader
(and presumably originally his listener) to 'resolve upon reformation by
entire abstinence'[112] and to encourage the same in family and community.
The plea was supported by scriptural quotations of Matthew 5:30, and
Habakkuk 2:9–13.

Although Beecher commenced each sermon with a quotation from scripture, he employed only two different passages to introduce a total of six
sermons. Other quotations from, or allusions to, scripture were infrequent,
albeit strategic. The direct links between scripture and his arguments for
temperance were few, and were rarely spelled out in detail (apart perhaps
from the command to love one's neighbour). For example, he states that
'drunkards, no more than murderers, shall inherit the kingdom of God',[113]
but nowhere explicitly quotes 1 Corinthians 6:10. This seems at first sight
a little surprising for a Protestant clergyman to whom scripture was, presumably, of huge importance in matters of faith and conduct.

However, Proverbs 23:29–35 seems to have symbolised for Beecher the
whole range of harms that were caused by 'ardent spirits', even though
the passage actually refers to 'wine'. Similarly, Habakkuk 2:9–16 seems
to have represented for him the condemnation of scripture, and of God,
on all who destroyed their lives, families and communities as a result of
intemperance.

---

[III] Ibid., p. 75.     [112] Ibid., p. 105.     [113] Ibid., p. 36.

It might also be argued that Beecher made little reference to scriptural passages which directly condemn drinking, because his concern was especially with ardent spirits, which are not specifically mentioned in scripture at all. This does not exactly explain his apparent failure to address the contradiction inherent in his second sermon, where he began with a text which drew attention to the dangers of drinking wine, and then proceeded to minimise concern about wine in favour of his concern with ardent spirits. However, it does draw attention to the fact that he was arguing from principle rather than from 'proof texts'.

Three underlying principles may be identified in Beecher's *Sermons*. First, he was concerned with the salvation of souls. His social concern was ultimately rooted in his belief that the intemperate, unless they reform, are destined for hell. However, there was also a patriotic aspect to his concern for salvation. The closing words of his sixth sermon are given over to this soteriological theme. He hoped that his book might:

save millions from temporal and eternal ruin. I pant not for fame or posthumous immortality, but my heart's desire and prayer to God for my countrymen is, that they may be saved from intemperance, and that our beloved nation may continue free, and become great and good.[114]

Secondly, his concern to bring an end to commerce in ardent spirits derived from his belief that to be involved in this trade, even indirectly, constitutes a breach of the command to 'love thy neighbour as thyself'. He saw ardent spirits as being at the root of many social and personal evils, and therefore it is a breach of the command to love one's neighbour to do anything other than work and pray for an end to intemperance. Curiously, this principle did not appear to extend to an expression of compassion for those who are unreformed. He referred to them as 'worthless consumers', seeing some at least as 'irreclaimable' in their habits and needing to be 'cut off' from the Church.

Thirdly, his sermons include considerable argument of a consequentialist nature. His definition of intemperance included those whom many of his contemporaries would not have thought intemperate. His justification for this was based primarily upon an argument concerning the adverse consequences of regular consumption of ardent spirits. The point was clearly debatable, and he therefore took trouble to refute what he perceived might be the responses of his critics. In order to do so, he adduced evidence based upon his own experience or opinion.

[114] Ibid., p. 107.

DAWSON BURNS'S *APPEAL TO THE CHRISTIAN WORLD*

Dawson Burns (1828–1909) was born in Southwark. His father, a noncon-
formist minister, and prolific religious writer, was said to have been the first
clergyman of any denomination to preach teetotalism in church.[115] Dawson
himself signed the pledge at the age of eleven years, gave his first speech at a
temperance society meeting at the age of twelve years, and within another
year had written his first temperance tract. He entered training for the Baptist ministry at the General Baptist College in Leicester in 1847. Although
a pastor of at least two Baptist churches, over a period of some thirty years,
he gave up his local church ministry in 1881 so as to devote himself wholly
to temperance work. He held offices in the National Temperance Society,
the Leicester Temperance Society, the Manchester and Salford Temperance
Society and the United Kingdom Alliance. His publications included the
*Temperance Bible Commentary* (1862), which he wrote jointly with Dr F. R.
Lees; *The Bases of the Temperance Reform*, a prize-winning essay which was
published in 1873; *Christendom and the Drink Curse* (1875); and his two-
volume history of the temperance movement, *Temperance History* (1890).[116]

In the preface to *Christendom and the Drink Curse: An Appeal to the
Christian World for Efficient Action against the Causes of Intemperance*, Burns
indicated that he intended to attempt

to trace the relations subsisting between the Drinking System and those great
interests which ought to be dear to all Christians, and the relations which, on that
account, Christians should sustain to the Drinking System.[117]

In fact, the book is concerned not merely with the Church and the 'Drinking
System', but with three forces explicitly identified by Burns, 'The Christian
Church, Drinking Customs, and the Temperance Movement',[118] and a
fourth, 'Modern Society', which is a major concern of at least two of his
chapters. Burns systematically examined the relationships which existed
between these forces and drew conclusions as to the appropriate responses
which should be offered by society and the church. He closed the book
with impassioned exhortations to various classes of individual Christians,
and finally made an appeal to 'each and every Christian'.[119]

---

[115] Stephen and Lee, 1908, p. 423. Lyman Beecher's sermons were delivered ten years before Jabez Burns
signed the pledge, and in any case the cause of total abstinence was further advanced in the USA
than in Britain. It would therefore appear that any claim of this sort that Jabez may have had could
have applied only to England, or perhaps the United Kingdom. According to Briggs's history of
the English Baptists, the claim pertained only to London (Briggs, 1994, p. 334). However, he also
lectured widely on temperance during a tour of the USA.

[116] Winskill, 1892b, p. 288; Lee, 1920, pp. 272–273.    [117] Burns, 1875, p. iii.

[118] Ibid., p. xi.    [119] Ibid., pp. 311–312.

Burns distinguished early on between gluttony on the one hand, and drunkenness and intemperance on the other.[120] While gluttony is clearly also a vice, he saw drunkenness and intemperance as vices which are specific to beverages containing alcohol.

> The beverages containing Alcohol act in a way peculiar to themselves. They alone can produce what is called 'drunkenness' or 'intemperance' . . . so that this pestiferous vice would be wholly unknown but for the manufacture and consumption of Strong Drink.[121]

He was quite clear that it was alcohol which was the substance of concern, and that no distinction is to be made between distilled spirits, wine or beer, except in potency.[122] Throughout the book, his use of the term 'Strong Drink' appears to apply to any or all intoxicating (i.e. alcoholic) drinks.

He was careful to rebut accusations of Manichaeism:

> Temperance teaching does not ascribe moral evil to the substance itself, but shows how it is connected with evil in the moral agent who imbibes it. To attribute the evil to drunkenness is to admit the Temperance position; for what causes drunkenness is not all drink, but Alcoholic Drink.[123]

However, it is clear that he considered alcohol to be at the root of the problem of intemperance. The reference of the title of the book to the 'Drink Curse' made this clear enough. He also understood fermentation as symbolic of moral and doctrinal corruption. Alcohol 'pollutes', generates 'unholy passion' and leads to death.[124]

'Drunkenness', at least in popular usage, he considered to be equivalent to 'intoxication'. Intoxication in turn, again according to popular usage, was understood as referring to 'the aggravated symptoms of alcoholic poisoning'.[125]

While recognising that intemperance was, in fact, 'indicative of sensual indulgence in general', he stated that 'in popular usage' it had gradually become narrowed in meaning to 'indulgence of the appetite for Strong Drink' or 'indulgence in some alcoholic drink'.[126] He considered intemperance to be a broader term than either drunkenness or intoxication.

---

[120] Ibid., p. 5 (and see also p. 221). He later states that 'drunkenness, according to its etymology, was a term of quantity indicating excessive drinking, as gluttony indicated excessive eating, without any particular reference to the intoxicating effect of the potations' (p. 56). This appears a little contradictory, but seems to be explicable on the basis of his belief that the meaning of the word has changed.

[121] Ibid., p. 5.    [122] Ibid., p. 221.

[123] Ibid., p. 13. In contrast, in his *Temperance Bible Commentary*, he and Dr Lees stated that 'the Bible teaches, clearly and fully, by a series of continuous and consistent testimonies, *that intoxicating drink is an evil article*; poisonous to the body, seductive to the soul, and corrupting to the circumstances of man' (Lees and Burns, 1880, p. xxviii, original emphasis preserved).

[124] Ibid., p. 192.    [125] Ibid., p. 57.    [126] Ibid., pp. 56–57.

Intemperance begins 'when Alcoholic liquor originates a desire for itself, which is gratified for the sake of the indulgence'.[127] Once the appetite is formed, alcohol produces 'a craving for itself, in larger quantities, and at shorter intervals'.[128] Eventually, 'complete restoration' becomes very difficult.

> The love of Intoxicating liquor is a disease, a vice, and a sin, all in one: how is this compound evil to be overcome? The answer is unanimous – by Abstinence and by Abstinence only.[129]

As abstinence is the only effective treatment, and as restoration becomes increasingly difficult, it is therefore vital that treatment is not delayed. Indeed, it is better that complete abstinence is adopted in the first place, in order to ensure that intemperance does not develop at all:

> But wherefore wait till the evil exists in any degree, and why incur any risk of its formation? If it is referable, as it is, to one particular substance (variously mixed in different intoxicating beverages), and if its action is of the most insidious character, resulting in a vice of national proportions, and inconceivable destructiveness, *how can the Christian Church be doing its appointed work by encouraging, in any measure, the manufacture, sale and common use of such a substance?*[130]

It is quite clear that Burns did not consider habitual alcohol consumption to be either desirable or defensible. It is implicit that he considered any regular alcohol consumption whatsoever to constitute intemperance. For example:

> Looking abroad upon British Society, we may ask ourselves how many who habitually use these drinks are quite free from the appetite for them in at least an incipient degree?[131]

Burns systematically enumerated and described the harms attributable to intemperance. Considering first the prosperity of the Christian Church,[132] he saw intemperance as a cause of apostasy, and also as a barrier to conversion to the faith. Conversely, he saw a direct relationship between 'the spread of Temperance and the increase of Church communicants and members'.[133] Intemperance hinders the Church in her mission both by weakening her from within, and by rendering those without impervious to her good actions. He also argued that Christian priorities in the use of wealth demand that expenditure upon alcohol should be reviewed. He estimated the annual national expenditure upon alcohol to be £130 million, and then estimated that perhaps a half of this was spent by persons 'in recognised

---

[127] Ibid., p. 60.  [128] Ibid.  [129] Ibid., p. 220.  [130] Ibid., p. 62, original emphasis preserved.
[131] Ibid., p. 63.  [132] Ibid., pp. 3–52.  [133] Ibid., p. 24.

connection with some Christian communion'.[134] He asserted that this far exceeded all that was contributed annually to the Church or her various societies and missions. Furthermore, he argued, it profited neither Church nor society, it was diverted from deserving causes, it was the cause of great evil and misery, and further encouraged the sale of alcohol – itself the commodity at the root of the problem.

Burns then turned to 'modern society' and considered first the 'radical social evils' which arise as a result of the consumption of 'Strong Drink'.[135] Among the moral evils that he identified, in addition to intemperance itself, were improvidence, ignorance, profligacy, neglect of duty, and criminal offences. The physical evils were considered under the headings of destitution, and disease and death. The economical evils were considered at the levels of national interest and the family. Secondly, consideration was given to the 'ameliorative institutions' of modern society.[136] These institutions were taken to include a wide range of legal measures and philanthropic institutions, such as asylums, sanatoria and reformatories for drunkards, provident societies, schools, refuges, efforts to support families, the criminal justice system, efforts to improve the conditions of the poor, hospitals, infirmaries and dispensaries, and economic counsels. Together, it was argued, they had had only an ameliorative effect upon the problem of intemperance, since they had only indirectly addressed its root cause. Thirdly, attention was turned to the educational forces of modern society.[137] These were taken to include culture, social intercourse, law and liberty. Each in turn was seen to have been impeded and counteracted by the drinking habits of the nation.

Having considered the harms and evils of intemperance in relation to Church and society, Burns proceeded to consider responses to intemperance under similar headings.

Burns was clear that he saw temperance reform as a 'child of the Church', and he therefore also saw an intimate relationship between temperance organisations and the Christian Church.[138] The work was begun by 'men whose hearts God had touched', all the churches had been affected by temperance reform, and leaders of the temperance movement were often leaders of the churches.

He understood temperance associations as having two main objects: curative and preventive.[139] Both objects were to be achieved by the same means: total abstinence. He believed that moderation was ineffective as a

---

[134] Ibid., p. 39.    [135] Ibid., pp. 56–88.    [136] Ibid., pp. 89–105.    [137] Ibid., pp. 106–115.
[138] Ibid., p. 215.    [139] Ibid., pp. 220–232.

treatment, and that it was because of this that 'few drunkards were per-
manently reclaimed under the first Temperance (anti-spiritous) *regime*'.[140]
Moderation[141] was seen as equally ineffective as a means of prevention.
Burns argued:

It has been shown that . . . [moderation] is itself attended with many disadvantages,
and with great waste of wealth, health and moral power, so that were drunkenness blotted out, the injurious effects of drinking would be both numerous and
alarming.[142]

Furthermore, he argued:

Small quantities distinctly lead to the use of larger quantities, at first occasion-
ally, and afterwards habitually, till the intemperate condition is induced and confirmed.[143]

It was absurd, therefore, to imagine that moderation could prevent intemperance – and neither could education, self-discipline or religious principle
be relied upon to provide immunity from intemperance. Total abstinence
was essential.

After considering the objects of the temperance societies, Burns turned
to considering their methods.[144] In fact, these methods appear to comprise
principally the 'Temperance Pledge', with the remainder of the section
devoted largely to replies to objections to the existence and practice of
temperance societies.[145] Even about the pledge itself, little was said, with
most space being devoted to the rebuttal of objections.[146] The wording of
pledges was not uniform, and some were made as verbal declarations, while
others required signature of a document.

Burns saw society as having a vital role to play in addressing the problems
of intemperance, by means of legislation.[147] He considered three possible
approaches: passive, regulative and prohibitive. According to the passive
approach, the manufacture and sale of alcoholic beverages should be left
unregulated, in the same way as other commodities. The licensing system
should be abolished, and taxation used only for generation of revenue,

---

[140] Ibid., p. 221.    [141] Defined here as drinking not associated with drunkenness.
[142] Ibid., p. 226.    [143] Ibid., p. 227.    [144] Ibid., pp. 232–239.
[145] Christian objections to the temperance societies apparently included the involvement of Christians
with unbelievers, the diversion of time and money which might be used for better purpose, objections to the secrecy and rituals of certain societies, and the causing of divisions with the churches
(ibid., pp. 233–239).
[146] For example, objections included the views that violation of the oath would amount to perjury, that
it was binding upon the conscience, and that it was unnecessary or inappropriate in the context of
baptismal vows, 'in which all moral obligations are included' (ibid., pp. 232–233).
[147] Ibid., pp. 249–290.

if at all. For Burns, it was clear that experience had proved that this would not remedy the situation. According to the regulative approach, the drink traffic should be controlled by legislative measures. Having considered the practical problems encountered in such an approach, he concluded that it was intrinsically defective and incapable of achieving its objectives.

Burns clearly favoured the prohibitive approach to legislation against intemperance. He saw it as being premised upon two principles. First, the Liquor Traffic was the source of many evils. Secondly, no other measure for preventing these evils would be effective while the traffic continued. The first of these Burns saw as being based upon an overwhelming amount of historical evidence. The second was deducible from the first. Objections being refuted, Burns proceeded to outline a practical means of approaching such legislation, in the form of a 'Permissive Bill'. This Bill would allow local prohibition to be introduced in districts where public opinion was supportive. He clearly saw this as a practical approach to introducing prohibition gradually, which would be likely to gain support in at least some parts of the country.

It is interesting that, whether or not one accepts them, all of Burns's arguments described thus far follow a coherent and logical train which is internally consistent and self-supporting. They make perfect ethical sense, whether or not they are considered to be valid, on largely consequentialist grounds. However, in the middle of the book is a chapter entitled 'The Church, strong drink, and the Word of God'.[148] The scriptures, Burns argues, are 'God's Word of Truth and Grace – the record of God's way on Earth, and the revelation to every humble seeker of the way of Life Eternal'.[149] Their precepts, principles, and examples demand our attention if we would 'be guided to a conclusion which their Divine Author will approve'.[150] This high view of scripture, and the centrality of the chapter to the book, should probably be taken as indicating the importance that Burns attributed to scripture in his defence of the temperance movement. However, it is interesting to note that this chapter is not first in his book, and that the arguments of the rest of the book do not depend upon it. It was not the foundation of his argument. It appears rather to offer recognition that, if the temperance cause was to gain widespread acceptance in Christendom, it had to show itself to be consistent with Holy Scripture.

The position adopted in this chapter was based upon Burns's argument, outlined in much greater detail in the *Temperance Bible Commentary*, that

---

[148] Chapter 3, pp. 131–212.   [149] Ibid., p. 133.   [150] Ibid.

the various Hebrew and Greek words translated as 'wine' in the English Authorized Version of the Bible do not necessarily refer to fermented or intoxicating drink. In particular, he asserted that the Hebrew יין, and the Greek οινος, can both be used in reference to either the fermented or unfermented juice of the grape. It is possible to distinguish between these meanings only by reference to context.[151] In a supplement to the fifth edition of the *Temperance Bible Commentary*, written by Dr Norman Kerr, another hermeneutical principle was also set forth. Although not written by Burns and Lees themselves, this supplement was referred to by them as an 'admirable tract', and their own approach would appear to be entirely consistent with it: 'Believers in the Bible who are acquainted with the fact that alcohol is a poison, and that all alcoholic liquors are poisonous, are therefore certain that the Inspired Volume cannot sanction the use of intoxicating beverages.'[152] In other words, their knowledge of the nature of alcohol, combined with a doctrine of inerrancy, led them to ensure that their interpretation of scripture would not conflict with their temperance principles. The possibility of translating words such as יין and οινος, as referring variously to fermented or unfermented grape juice, as well as a complete lack of inhibition at speculation on matters about which scripture is silent, conveniently removed most of the difficulties that this undertaking might otherwise have encountered.

Three examples of this approach to scriptural interpretation are offered here.

### Genesis 19:30–35

The story of Lot's incest with his daughters after they had made him drink wine was not discussed in detail in *Christendom and the Drink Curse*, but is to be found in the *Temperance Bible Commentary*.[153] It provides an interesting contrast here with the approach of Augustine, Aquinas and Whitefield, discussed in Chapter 4. Though the story is usually interpreted as a case of drunkenness, Burns and Lees introduced the highly speculative possibility that the wine that Lot drank was drugged. However, they clearly saw no difference in principle between wine that was 'corrupted' by being drugged and wine that was corrupted by fermentation. They drew three observations. First, on the basis of a dubious inference that Lot was habitually abstinent, they concluded that it was deviation from his practice of

---

[151] Ibid., pp. 133–134, 183–185ff. See also the *Temperance Bible Commentary*, pp. 431–433.
[152] Lees and Burns, 1880, p. 483.  [153] Ibid., pp. 12–13.

abstinence that led him into sin. Secondly, they noted the 'lustful influence' of wine upon Lot and, speculating that his daughters also drank the wine, commented that 'female chastity is never more imperilled than when plied with strong drink'. Thirdly, they quoted Matthew Henry as noting both that drunkenness leads to many other sins, and also that following this episode Lot is not heard of again in scripture. Drunkenness leads, therefore, to 'contempt and oblivion'.

### *John 2:1–11*

The miracle at Cana is discussed in both *Christendom and the Drink Curse*[154] and the *Temperance Bible Commentary*.[155] At Jesus' command, six waterpots of stone were filled with water (holding perhaps 120 gallons), and water drawn off from one of them was then found to have been turned into wine. Burns recognised that the traditional interpretation was that all the water was converted into wine. However, he saw no reason to assume that more than the small amount drawn off was actually miraculously changed into wine. He further saw no reason to assume that the water was changed into fermented or intoxicating wine. In fact, he argued that alcoholic wine was not considered to be 'the best', as the wine miraculously created by Jesus at Cana was described as being, and therefore inclined to the view that the latter was non-alcoholic wine. He further argued that, on the basis of 'moral considerations', it was preferable to see the miracle as an analogy to the turning of water into grape juice on the vine, rather than seeing it as 'for the gratification of a village company'. The Greek μεθυσθωσιν, in verse 10, was understood as referring to the large quantity of wine drunk by the guests (thus, in the Authorized Version, 'well drunk'), rather than to intoxication or drunkenness.

### *Galatians 5:21*

In *Christendom and the Drink Curse*, Burns did not quote from the New Testament vice lists as providing an injunction against drunkenness. One of his precepts (see below) was that scripture warns against and forbids drunkenness, but not only did he give little space to further discussion of this, he also offered no specific scriptural references. This strange contrast with the use of such passages by Augustine, Aquinas and the early Reformers

---

[154] Burns, 1875, pp. 188–189.    [155] Lees and Burns, 1880, pp. 301–308.

is further illuminated, but not completely explained, by his understanding of the concept of 'drunkenness' as unrelated to intoxication:

We are to understand by drunkenness in these passages drinking to excess – just as gluttony is eating to excess – without any exclusive or special regard to an intoxicating result of indulgence.[156]

In the *Temperance Bible Commentary*, when commenting on Galatians 5:21, he interpreted μεθαι thus:

'Intemperances' – copious indulgences in drinks, some of which would have the power of inebriating, though intoxication is not the *essence*, but only the *extreme* of the vice condemned by the apostle. The essential of the vice is, that men *drink for pleasure*, regardless of the law of God or the claims of man.[157]

Elsewhere, Burns identified the following 'scripture precepts':[158]

1. Warnings against, and forbidding of, drunkenness
2. Warnings against 'familiarity with wine' (e.g. Ephesians 5:18; 1 Timothy 3:3, 8; Titus 1:7; 2:3)
3. Inculcation of temperance and sobriety (e.g. 1 Corinthians 9:25; Galatians 5:23)
4. Regard to soberness (Philippians 4:5; 1 Thessalonians 5:6, 8; 1 Timothy 3:2; 2 Timothy 4:5; Titus 2:2, 6; 3:2; 1 Peter 1:13; 2:2; 4:7; 5:8)
5. Prohibition of wine or strong drink to certain classes of people (e.g. the Nazirites)
6. Condemnation of intoxicating drink 'because of its peculiar quality and effects' (e.g. Proverbs 20:1; 23:29–35)

The 'scripture principles' which he identified were in relation to 'God, to our Fellow-creatures, and to Ourselves'.[159] In relation to God, wine was seen as a 'defrauder or deceiver' (Habakkuk 2:5), a 'poison' (Habakkuk 2:15; Hosea 7:5), and a 'mocker' (Hosea 7:5), which had never enabled consecration to God, but only desecration and corruption. In relation to neighbours, love was understood as being our duty. The Christian who would use strong drink in moderation was challenged on whether this would reclaim the intemperate or prevent the spread of intemperance. The reader was reminded of St Paul's injunctions that we should not cause a weaker brother to 'stumble' (Romans 14:15ff.; 1 Corinthians 8:9ff.), and that the whole law is fulfilled in loving one's neighbour as oneself (Galatians 5:13, 14). The 'cardinal principle' was that '*Christians should resign what is*

---

[156] Burns, 1875, p. 135.   [157] Lees and Burns, 1880, p. 349.   [158] Burns, 1875, pp. 135–141.
[159] Ibid., pp. 142–166.

*pleasant, and even useful to themselves, if by this resignation they can prove their love and do good to others'.*[160]

In relation to self, Burns advised of duties 'of self-preservation and protection' and of 'individual improvement'.[161] The former duty was justified on the basis of the rules of 'do thyself no harm' and 'abstain from all appearance of evil', which he considered to be expressions of the 'law or principle' of prudence. The latter duty was considered to be a part of 'making sure the calling and election'[162] which were appropriate to each person's circumstances. The moral and religious character, and intellectual powers, were in fact said to be 'perverted and paralysed' by intoxicating liquors. He then pursued a long discourse, citing scientific rather than biblical authority, to the effect that alcohol is not necessary to good bodily health.

Burns offered examples of abstinence which are to be found in scripture.[163] In addition to the Nazirites (e.g. Samson, Samuel and John the Baptist) and Rechabites (Jeremiah 35:1–19), he quoted examples of less than complete abstinence (Daniel and the Levitical priests) and argued rather speculatively for the complete abstinence of Adam and Eve, and of the Israelites in the wilderness. He also argued that scripture nowhere unequivocally shows that Christ drank intoxicating wine, and further that

it is . . . clear that the use of wines of an inflaming character cannot be ascribed to Him without placing Him in opposition to the spirit and letter of the dispensation He came to fulfil and honour.[164]

Burns further argued at length that total abstinence was consonant with, if not demanded by, the 'spirit of scripture',[165] in contrast to what he apparently considered to be the 'dry, hard, Literalism' of his opponents.[166] He drew parallels between arguments from scripture that were used in support of slavery and the arguments of objectors to total abstinence,[167] and he argued that strong drink stands in the way of righteousness and love,[168] and that no express command is required for specific works of benevolence.[169]

Dawson Burns devoted his life to the temperance movement. It was clearly his perception that 'strong drink' brought many evils contrary to the good of both Church and society, and he saw it as his Christian duty

---

[160] Ibid., p. 148, original emphasis preserved.
[161] Although unreferenced by Burns, these are in fact quotations of Acts 16:28 and 1 Thessalonians 5:22 from the Authorized Version.
[162] Again unreferenced, and this time also not exactly quoted from the Authorized Version, this is an allusion to 2 Peter 1:10.
[163] Ibid., pp. 167–171.    [164] Ibid., p. 185.    [165] Ibid., pp. 172–182.    [166] Ibid., p. 173.
[167] Ibid., pp. 173–177.    [168] Ibid., pp. 178–179.    [169] Ibid., p. 180.

to do all that he could to combat the 'drink curse'. The solution was clear to him. Both in reclaiming the drunkard and in preventing intemperance, the requirement was the same. Total abstinence was imperative for all. Both moral suasion and legislative reform would be required to achieve this. He argued his case systematically and comprehensively, rebutting the objections of critics as he went.

For Burns, intemperance included almost any consumption of alcohol – especially on a regular basis. Alcohol, or the 'drinking system', constituted the focus of evil, rather than only drunkenness. Because the consumption of alcohol was itself the source of no good, but only increased the likelihood of further consumption, and thus eventually its attendant evils, any alcohol consumption at all was to be eschewed.

The predominant line of argument in Burns's work was based upon consequentialist reasoning. Clearly he was concerned, like Beecher, with the salvation of souls. However, this does not come across as being the foundational concern that it appears to have been in Beecher's *Sermons*. Clearly, Burns's understanding of the 'spirit of scripture' was important to him, and in many ways resembled and overlapped with Beecher's recognition of the importance of the love command. However, his primary arguments would be likely to appeal beyond the boundaries of Christendom, and did not require acceptance of the scriptural precepts and principles which he developed.

### THOMAS BRIDGETT AND THE DISCIPLINE OF DRINK

Thomas Edward Bridgett (1829–99) was born in Derby, England. Brought up in a Protestant family, and educated at a Congregationalist college and Church of England school, he proceeded to Cambridge University in 1847. Unable to take the oath of Royal Supremacy, he left in 1850 without a degree. Soon afterwards, having been strongly influenced by John Henry Newman's lectures at the London Oratory, he was received into the Roman Catholic Church. He received his theological education at Wittem in Holland, and was ordained priest in 1856. He then spent five years in ministry in Clapham, England, followed by nine years in Limerick, Ireland. In 1871 he returned to Clapham, where he spent most of his remaining years.[170]

Bridgett's published works were mainly historical and controversial. His first book, *In Spirit and in Truth*, based originally upon a sermon on ritual, was published in 1867. His later works included a book on medieval devotion to the Blessed Virgin Mary, *Our Lady's Dowry* (1875); a historical work

---

[170] Herbermann et al., 1907, pp. 782–783.

on the Eucharist, *The History of the Holy Eucharist in Great Britain* (1881); and a book written in collaboration with Father Knox, *The True Story of the Catholic Hierarchy Deposed by Queen Elizabeth* (1889). His most popular work was perhaps the *Life of Blessed Thomas More* (1891). He also published some volumes of devotional verse.[171]

*The Discipline of Drink*, published in 1876, included an 'Introductory letter to the author' by Cardinal Manning. Some 'Words' of Cardinal Manning, delivered originally at a meeting of the Holy Family Confraternity in 1875, were also quoted in the appendix. Manning, who became Archbishop of Westminster in 1865 and was made a cardinal in 1875, had himself been a Tractarian who had left the Church of England in 1851.[172] As a Roman Catholic cardinal, he was active in various social concerns, including the temperance movement. He became a total abstainer in 1871 and soon afterwards formally instituted the Catholic League of the Cross, a Roman Catholic total abstinence society.[173] It would seem that *The Discipline of Drink* was probably written by Bridgett at the request of Manning.[174] Bridgett himself does not appear to have been very active in the temperance movement, and *The Discipline of Drink* does not appear to have been seen by Bridgett, or his biographers, as being among his most important works.[175]

Manning's introductory letter is revealing of some of the tensions that existed between Protestants and Roman Catholics engaged in the temperance movement. Writing of the problems that emerge when Roman Catholics engage in 'societies not in the unity of the Catholic Church', he stated:

Abstinence could not be put before them with the Catholic motives of penance, self-humiliation, reparation, and expiation for themselves and for others; and I am sorry to know that at times they were beset by great temptations to a spirit of self-consciousness and self-manifestation fatal to the spirit of penance. More than this, they could not help hearing a great deal of wild talk, worthy of the Manichees, and they were therefore in danger of learning the same language, if not of adopting also the same wild ideas.[176]

Manning, in his endorsement of the position taken by Bridgett, was clear that 'drunkenness was not the sin of the drink but of the drunkard'.[177] In Bridgett's appendix, his quoted words are even stronger:

---

[171] Ibid., pp. 782–783; McDonald et al., 1967, pp. 799–800.
[172] Cross and Livingstone, 1997, p. 1028.   [173] Winskill, 1892c, pp. 224–225.
[174] Ryder, 1906, p. 139.
[175] Ibid., pp. 127–178; Herbermann et al., 1907, pp. 782–783; McDonald et al., 1967, pp. 799–800.
[176] Bridgett, 1876, p. xiv.   [177] Ibid., p. xv.

Any man who should say that the use of wine or any other like thing is sinful when it does not lead to drunkenness, that man is a heretic condemned by the Catholic Church. With that man I will never work.[178]

Seeing temperance as incumbent upon all baptised Christians, Manning believed that total abstainers and moderationists[179] should work together 'to extinguish drunkenness'.[180] Yet he also, like Dawson Burns, saw St Paul's injunctions concerning the weaker brother (Romans 14:21) as applying to the need to have care for those who would easily be drawn (back) into drunkenness:

The law of liberty is the law of charity; and if any self-denial on our part, in things that are lawful and to us altogether safe, shall help, or encourage, or support, or give even a shadow of strength to those to whom such lawful things are not only dangerous but often deadly, then assuredly the love of souls will prompt us to place ourselves at their side, and, in sharing their acts of self-denial, to give them a hand and a heart of sympathy.[181]

With an echo of Lyman Beecher's passion for saving souls, Manning ended his introductory letter with an expression of trust that Bridgett's book 'may powerfully help the work of saving souls from the pestilence of drink'.[182]

In his Preface, Bridgett indicated that his book was published in the hope that it may

be serviceable to the lay advocates of temperance, who, from want of accurate instruction in Christian morals, sometimes condemn drink which is the work of God, while attacking drunkenness which is the work of man. They will find in the first part of this inquiry what has been in all ages the teaching of the Catholic Church – taught herself by the Holy Ghost – on the subject of alcoholic drinks . . . The present little work is an attempt to treat [drunkenness] historically, at least in its moral aspects, and with a distinctly practical purpose. The writer was led to investigate, for his own guidance in the pulpit and Confessional, the methods by which the vice of drunkenness has been met, in different ages and countries, by the Catholic Church.[183]

The book was therefore intended to provide practical instruction, and to dispel false teaching. It adopts a historical approach, and places a high value on the authority and teaching of the (Roman) Catholic Church.

Bridgett's book is divided into two parts. The first was devoted to 'doctrine and discipline of the church in general' and the second to 'the preceding doctrine and discipline studied in their results in the British Isles'. The

---

[178] Ibid., p. 231.
[179] The 'mortified who never taste drink' and the 'temperate who never abuse it' (ibid., p. 232).
[180] Ibid., p. xvi.     [181] Ibid., pp. xviii–xix.     [182] Ibid., p. xix.     [183] Ibid., pp. vii–viii.

second part is the longer, occupying some two-thirds of the whole book. It focusses in more detail on an account of the subject which is specific to the British Isles.

Bridgett began with a survey of 'the doctrine and discipline of the church as to the voluntary use and disuse of alcoholic liquors'.[184] He surveyed the teaching of the Church, quoting extensively from scripture and from such authorities as Clement of Alexandria, Origen, Augustine, Isidore of Pelusium, Julianus Pomerius, St Gildas, Antiochus, Nicetas of Constantinople, Bernard of Clairvaux and Cardinal Pullen. That this survey of the teaching of the Catholic Church was meant to provide a rebuttal of the position adopted by his opponents was apparent from the outset:

It is important at the present day, that the action of the Church in the cause of temperance should be clearly marked off from that of certain sects and associations, which seem to pursue the same end.[185]

Clement of Alexandria was first among the sources from which Bridgett quoted, and was described by Bridgett as being the 'earliest Christian writer who treats expressly of this subject'.[186] It is interesting to note that, at the head of the first chapter of *Christendom and the Drink Curse*, Dawson Burns also quoted from Clement:

I admire those who desire no other beverage than water, avoiding wine as they do fire.[187]

In contrast, and conveying a rather different meaning, Bridgett quoted more fully and accurately:

I praise and admire those who have chosen an austere life, who take water as the preserver of moderation, and flee wine like a threatening fire.[188]

He went on, with the support of further quotations from Clement, to argue that the moderate use of wine is good, and that Jesus drank wine.

Quoting from Origen, he addressed the argument of Paul concerning the circumstances where eating meat or drinking wine might offend a brother (Romans 14:21). Like Manning and Burns, he saw this as clearly applicable to the question of drinking wine. Unlike Burns, he saw it as indicating that

---

[184] Ibid., pp. 1–22.    [185] Ibid., pp. 1–2.    [186] Ibid., p. 2.    [187] Ibid., p. 3.

[188] Ibid., p. 2. The quotation is from book 2, ch. 2, of Clement's *Paedagogous*. It is interesting to compare both of these quotes with the text of the Nicene and Ante-Nicene Fathers edition, taken here from version 4 of the Christian Classics Ethereal Library CD-ROM, produced by Calvin College, Grand Rapids, USA : 'I therefore admire those who have adopted an austere life, and who are fond of water, the medicine of temperance, and flee as far as possible from wine, shunning it as they would the danger of fire.'

abstinence is not to be commended for any or every reason, and should not be dictated on the basis of any heretical notion that wine is bad in itself, but only as a means of encouraging a brother in faith.[189]

Bridgett alluded to, or drew attention to, the variety of early heresies which he saw as being similar or identical to those of his contemporary opponents within the temperance movement, including the teachings of the Manichees, Gnostics, and Encratites:

To assert that alcohol is a kind of evil principle, and its use prohibited, *is* a heresy. It is to contradict the whole of the teaching of the Old and New Testaments, and the universal traditions of the Catholic Church.[190]

In contrast, the proper motivation for abstinence is

the subjugation of the flesh, obedience to lawful authority, or charity and conde-scension to others.[191]

Furthermore, Bridgett recognised that any form of asceticism carries the danger of lack of humility, and must be accompanied by other virtues, such as charity and purity of heart.[192]

On the other hand, he equally saw the need to defend the teaching of the Catholic Church against those who would reject the place of asceticism. He saw the teaching of the Church as recognising a place both for the moderate use of alcohol and also for complete abstinence. In support of this he discussed the contrasting examples of Jesus and John the Baptist as portrayed in chapter 11 of Matthew's gospel.[193] Again, using the teaching of St Paul, he considered the place in Christian life both for 'gladness arising from plenty' and also for 'fasting and tears'.[194] There is more than a hint that he considered abstinence to be 'the most perfect' thing,[195] but equally he was clear that it is not required of all and that it may be inappropriate at particular times or circumstances.

In his second chapter,[196] Bridgett turned his attention to drunkenness, and this time quoted extensively from Augustine of Hippo, writing in fourth-century Africa, Caesarius of Arles in sixth-century France, and Rabanus Maurus in ninth-century Germany. In each case, the message was clear. Drunkenness was a widespread problem, an evil, a vice, and a sin which affected even the clergy, and disturbed the discipline and well-being of the Church. Further, effective response was possible. One of Augustine's letters was, according to Bridgett, followed by a canon restraining feasting

---

[189] Ibid., pp. 3–5.    [190] Ibid., p. 6, original emphasis preserved.    [191] Ibid., p. 8.
[192] Ibid., p. 19.    [193] Ibid., pp. 12–15.    [194] Ibid., pp. 16–17.    [195] Ibid., p. 15.
[196] Ibid., pp. 23–51.

in the African church, and, a century and a half after Caesarius wrote, the vice was apparently not widespread in Provence, Gaul or Lombardy.

In the final chapter of the first part of his book, Bridgett focussed on 'Church discipline', or the various ways in which the Church had historically responded to the problems of drunkenness which it had encountered.[197] He considered in turn the discipline of the clergy, of ascetics (primarily those in religious orders) and of the laity, the fast of Lent, the treatment of drunkards, and the sacrament of penance.

Bridgett emphasised that total abstinence had never been imposed upon the clergy by the Church, although drunkenness was forbidden. The option of total abstinence was open to them, however, and Bridgett argued (on the basis of scant evidence) that this option was taken up by some from the earliest times, following apostolic example. Among the more recent examples that he cited were St Boniface, St Anselm and St Jerome, and he asserted that it 'would be easy to gather a long list of similar examples'.[198]

Bridgett recognised that some ascetics, through individual choice, pursued total abstinence, but was unaware of any monastic rule that ever imposed this. His quotation from Humbert, a thirteenth-century general of the Dominican order, is interesting in that it specifies the faults that may be encountered in regard to drinking wine in monastic life. In particular, these concern excessive quantity or strength, 'indecent' variety (one kind is enough), excessive cost ('a religious should not in one draught consume what would relieve many poor'),[199] excessive time spent drinking, excessive conversation about drinking, and finally, excessive interest in judging wines. Humbert apparently emphasised that the option of complete abstinence is permissible and commendable for those who choose it as a means of subduing 'the flesh'.

For the laity also, Bridgett was clear, the Church had never imposed total abstinence. The testimonies of Clement, Origen, St Bernard, Gregory the Great and even Christ himself[200] were here brought to bear in support of the argument. Abstinence is 'beyond the necessary rules of morality',[201] but this does not mean that it is not of value for some individuals or in certain circumstances. Furthermore, while feasting was to be tolerated at certain times, fasting at certain times was prescribed by the Church. However, even

---

[197] Ibid., pp. 52–74.　　[198] Ibid., p. 58.　　[199] Ibid., p. 60.

[200] The words of Christ which Bridgett quotes are those of Matthew 19:12: 'He that can take, let him take it.' Although these words were attributed to Christ, by the evangelist, in relation to the issue of celibacy, Bridgett considers celibacy and total abstinence from alcohol to be similar issues; both may be virtuous, but neither is to be imposed.

[201] Ibid., p. 63.

here, it seems, the fasting did not necessarily include complete abstinence. Thus, for example, the Lenten fast might include abstinence from wine, but not beer, and in any case the avoidance of 'strong drink' as a part of the fast may have been 'a counsel of perfection rather than a strict precept'.[202]

Bridgett was able to find little historical or theological information about the treatment by the Church of 'habitual and confirmed drunkards'.[203] He noted, without alluding to any source, that they were told to avoid places and company associated with drinking, and that they were told to make 'clear and well-defined resolutions'.[204] He noted also the advice of St Caesarius that such persons should gradually reduce their consumption until they have 'returned to a reasonable and moderate manner of drinking'.[205]

Bridgett asserted that, before the sixth century, drunkenness was considered too lightly, and treated too leniently. From the sixth century onwards, however, it began to make specific appearances in various penitential codes. Not only was abstinence considered to be an appropriate penance for intemperance, but it would also be imposed as a part of the penance of other sins. Indeed, he considered that the neglect of the sacrament of penance in the three centuries prior to his writing should be considered a significant factor underlying an increased prevalence of drunkenness.

In the second part of the book, Bridgett began by reviewing the history of drunkenness as an 'English vice', the kinds of alcoholic drinks consumed, the drinking customs associated with them, and the civil legislation related to the same. His historical survey noted in passing the association with drunkenness of such sins as gluttony and sexual immorality. However, little was said by him about the specific nature of the adverse consequences of drunkenness. In general, Bridgett saw drunkenness itself as being both the problem and the sin.

In this context, he proceeded to a more detailed historical review of the actions of the British Church in response to the problems of drunkenness. In 569, at synods held by St David, penances were specified for priests who were drinking prior to conducting the daily office, for persons who became drunk through ignorance or negligence, and for those who forced others to become drunk. Penance (although not specified in these canons) would have included fasting and abstinence from wine and beer. The penance would be more or less severe according to intention, with 'contempt' treated more severely than negligence, and 'hatred or wickedness' in causing the

---

202 Ibid., p. 66.　　203 Ibid., p. 68.　　204 Ibid., p. 67.　　205 Ibid., p. 68.

drunkenness of others being considered the equivalent of the murder of souls.[206]

Canons drawn up by St Cummian Fota (d. 662) for the Irish Church were later in use in various parts of Europe in the eighth to eleventh centuries. These included reference to bishops, priests and deacons with 'a habit of drunkenness'; drunkenness among monks, priests, deacons and lay people; and the act of compelling another to become drunk. Again, intention was significant in determining penance. 'Inadvertence' was considered less seriously than 'carelessness', which in turn was less serious than 'contempt'. 'Hate' was considered to be more serious than 'evil hospitality'. Drunkenness of lesser degree and frequency (not associated with vomiting, and/or occasional) attracted a lesser penance than that which was more gross (associated with vomiting, and/or habitual). Penance was more severe for priests than deacons, and for clergy and religious than for laity.

In the Anglo-Saxon Church, St Egbert,[207] St Theodore[208] and the Venerable Bede all adopted the penitentials of St Cummian.[209] In 960, St Dunstan[210] drew up a code with the following canons:[211]

Canon 26:  'Let no drinking be allowed in the church.'
Canon 28:  'In the festivals of the church all should be very sober and pray diligently, with neither drinking nor useless pastimes.'
Canon 57:  'Let priests beware of drunkenness, and be diligent in warning and correcting others in this matter.'
Canon 58:  'Let no priest be given to beer or buffoonery.'

Another collection of canons was assembled by Aelfric[212] in 970:[213]

Canon 30:  'A priest should not drink in taverns like laymen.'
Canon 35:  'Do not exult over dead men, nor seek a corpse, unless any one accuses you. Then prohibit heathen songs and noisy laughter, and do not eat and drink where there is a corpse, lest you join in their heathendom.'[214]

---

[206] Ibid., pp. 134–136.
[207] Archbishop of York, d. 766 (Cross and Livingstone, 1997, p. 533).
[208] *Circa* 602–690, Archbishop of Canterbury (Cross and Livingstone, 1997, p. 1600).
[209] In the cases of Theodore and Egbert, with minor modifications or explanations, which Bridgett details (ibid., pp. 145–149).
[210] *Circa* 909–988, Archbishop of Canterbury (Cross and Livingstone, 1997, pp. 514–515).
[211] Ibid., pp. 149–150.
[212] *Circa* 955–c. 1020, Abbot of Eynsham (Cross and Livingstone, 1997, p. 22).
[213] Ibid., p. 150. Bridgett also provided a translation of an alternative and longer version of the thirty-fifth canon (pp. 150–151).
[214] Drunkenness at funeral wakes had been a particular problem in the English Church (ibid., pp. 105–106).

Although there had always been a decree of discretion and flexibility in the administration of penitential discipline,[215] the system was gradually subject to further relaxation in the Middle Ages.[216]

In 1102 St Anselm proclaimed a canon:

That priests should not go to drinking assemblies nor drink down to the pegs.[217]

The Fourth Lateran Council (1215) provided a decree against drunkenness of clergy, on pain of suspension from benefice or office.[218]

A series of attempts was made during the thirteenth century, mainly by decrees of bishops at diocesan level, to prevent or suppress the problems associated with 'scot-ales'.[219] These variously forbade the announcement of scot-ales in church, forbade the participation of clergy in scot-ales, and required clergy to discourage members of their congregations from attending them. Bridgett concluded that these measures were effective, but noted that in the fourteenth and fifteenth centuries various similar measures were still being introduced in regard to such concerns as wakes, taverns, drinking assemblies, excess drinking among clergy, and the like.[220]

In the seventeenth century, in Ireland, a number of provincial synods prohibited excessive eating and drinking at various festivities, regulated against clergy drinking in taverns, and (in one case) regulated against the drinking of distilled spirits by clergy.[221]

It was Bridgett's belief that, in England, the Reformation brought about an increase in drunkenness, and thus an increasing need for civil legislation to address the problem.[222] He believed that the pre-Reformation Church had been at least partially successful in limiting and moderating drunkenness in the British Isles, and that the Reformation had the effect of removing her beneficial influence.

It is not exactly clear how Bridgett wished to explain this change. On the one hand, he recognised that Protestants continued to condemn the vice of drunkenness. On the other hand, he believed that their doctrines indirectly and unintentionally 'loosened the bonds of morality'. He clearly

---

[215] Ibid., pp. 151–166.   [216] Ibid., pp. 167–168.

[217] Ibid., pp. 168–169. In order to try and restrict drunkenness, Dunstan had arranged that pegs would be inserted in drinking bowls, with the proviso that no-one should drink in one draught so much that the level of drink would fall below the peg. Unfortunately, the practice had developed of not drinking any less than this (pp. 104–105)!

[218] Ibid., pp. 169–170.

[219] Ibid., pp. 170–176. An 'ale' was 'a gathering of persons by appointment to drink ale', often with some other object in view (such as a wake, or wedding) and a 'scot' was a payment. A scot-ale was thus a drinking gathering, where each participant paid for his share of the drink (pp. 106–117).

[220] Ibid., pp. 176–178.   [221] Ibid., pp. 179–183.   [222] Ibid., pp. 184–197.

believed that the removal of the 'sacrament of penance' had had a particularly unhelpful influence.[223] There was enough evidence, in his view, to support the contention that 'Catholics . . . need not look outside the Church for methods of combating vice'.[224]

Bridgett allowed himself relatively little space for dwelling upon the lessons of history and their contemporary application. However, those lessons and applications were nonetheless clear to him:

1. The civil powers should legislate so as to address the causes of drunkenness so far as is possible, or at least so as not to make the problem worse.[225]

2. Catholics should not co-operate with, or align themselves with, 'morality divorced from religion'.[226] The Holy See had condemned such organisations as the 'Sons of Temperance' in America, and the Catholic bishops in England and Ireland warned against the 'Good Templars'.

3. In all efforts to promote temperance, or combat intemperance, the need for divine grace should not be overlooked:[227]

   Even could we assure ourselves of perseverance in sobriety without the use of the appointed channels of grace, we should require God's help to make our abstinence fruitful to salvation.[228]

   Temptation cannot be conquered without grace or, if it appears that it has been, it is only because another vice has taken its place. Bridgett bemoaned the 'pride and fanaticism' of the reformed drunkard, and the neglect of the penitential system which tended to keep such problems at bay.

4. The 'pledge' was considered by Bridgett to be 'a legitimate and most beneficial discipline'.[229] However, it must be 'guarded from abuse'. It is to be taken only 'with a correct knowledge of its purpose and its obligation, and made a help and not a substitute for religion'.[230] On the one hand, 'mortification', the edification of others and protection against danger were all considered to be worthy motives. On the other hand, he cautioned against drunkenness following completion of a temporary period of abstinence, and he warned against taking the pledge

   as if, by the supposed holiness of him who gives it, it would work a sudden physical or moral change, and relieve him who takes it from his unnatural craving or make him victorious without a combat . . . It . . . has no sacramental grace unless taken in the Sacrament of Penance.[231]

---

[223] Ibid., pp. 196–197.   [224] Ibid., p. 197.   [225] Ibid., pp. 199–201.   [226] Ibid., pp. 201–203.
[227] Ibid., pp. 203–205.   [228] Ibid., p. 204.   [229] Ibid., pp. 206–214.   [230] Ibid., p. 209.
[231] Ibid., pp. 209–210.

The different penitential disciplines for clergy and religious as compared with the laity, and for indeliberate as opposed to deliberate sins, for Bridgett, had parallels with drunkenness among those who had taken the pledge and those who had not.[232] Paradoxically, he saw drunkenness among those who had taken the pledge as incurring less guilt:

> A fall into drunkenness by a man who has taken the pledge – if the pledge has not been intended for a vow, but only for an earnest resolution – will involve a less degree of guilt than an act of drunkenness committed by one who has refused to put himself under such restriction.[233]

5. Bridgett affirmed the formation of temperance associations, but also affirmed their variety of rules and objectives at a time when agreement could not be reached as to 'all the measures which prudence will prescribe'.[234] Quoting from St Bernard's writing about the rivalry between Cistercians and Cluniacs in the twelfth century, he warned also against the dangers of jealousy or mutual deprecation which such confraternities, like religious orders, might generate.

6. While recognising that abstinence might legitimately be a remedy, precaution, virtue, or act of charity or of self-denial, Bridgett was concerned that abstinence should also be seen as an act of expiation or propitiation within the context of the Catholic sacrament of penance.[235]

7. Bridgett expressed concern that recreation had become associated with alcoholic liquor, and wished to dispel any idea that his advocacy of penitential discipline should be seen to cast him as an enemy of amusement.[236]

8. Aware of the great problems of drunkenness on a Saturday evening, Bridgett proposed that, in honour of the Blessed Virgin Mary, Catholics might abstain from the use of fermented and distilled drinks on that day.[237] A vow might be taken, or resolution made, to observe 'Our Lady's Abstinence' either for a limited period of time or for life. Mindful of a fourteenth-century tradition, and the contemporary problems of drunkenness among women, he felt that Our Lady's Abstinence might be especially appropriate for women.

9. Bridgett encouraged the practice of inducing children to resolve not to consume alcoholic drinks until the age of twenty-one years.[238]

10. While he appreciated history and tradition, Bridgett noted the flexibility of the Church's approach to the problem of intemperance, and

---

[232] Ibid., p. 144.    [233] Ibid.    [234] Ibid., p. 215.    [235] Ibid., pp. 218–221.
[236] Ibid., pp. 221–222.    [237] Ibid., pp. 222–225.    [238] Ibid., pp. 225–226.

its variations in discipline according to circumstances.[239] In order to respond to 'new conditions of life, and new temptations to intemperance, new methods have to be devised'.[240]

Bridgett concluded his book with an extended quotation from the pastoral address of the Archbishops and Bishops of Ireland, delivered at the National Synod of Maynooth in 1875. The closing lines of this quotation summarised much of his own perspective upon intemperance:

We bless from our hearts those zealous ecclesiastics, and others who, in accordance with the spirit of the Church, devote their time and energies to forwarding the cause of temperance; and we would remind all, that however valuable other help may be, there exists but one unfailing source whence human weakness can draw strength to resist temptation, and break the bonds of evil habits. That source is the Sacred Heart of Jesus, the overflowing fountain of mercy, from which, through prayer and the sacraments, we receive grace in seasonable aid. The habit of daily prayer faithfully persevered in; frequent and worthy approach to the Holy Sacraments; the devout hearing of the Word of God; and the avoiding of dangerous occasions, are the only sure means by which intemperance can be overcome.[241]

Bridgett's approach to intemperance reflected his interests as a historian, but also his theology as a Roman Catholic. The tradition of the Church was a vital source of authority to him, but he was also keen to support many of his arguments from scripture. Consequentialist reasoning was less clearly in evidence, but he did not eschew measures such as civil legislation, where these could be helpful in support of his cause. On the other hand, he did distance himself from potential allies whose reasoning seemed to him to be based upon heretical doctrine, or who failed to recognise the importance of divine grace.

For Bridgett, the response to the problems of intemperance could not be divorced from the discipline of the Church. Total abstinence could be helpful, but should be accepted voluntarily as a rule of life, or in penitential spirit as a part of reliance upon divine grace. If accepted carelessly, or based upon wrong motives, it could easily lead to vice rather than virtue, and could reflect a denial of the inherent goodness of God's creation.

Bridgett was clearly at pains, at various points in his book, to appeal to the open-minded Protestant reader. However, it is difficult to see that his appeal could have been very wide outside the Roman Catholic Church. Bridgett shared many of the underlying concerns of the secular and Protestant wings of the temperance movement, and also shared some of their methods. In broad principle, he also shared with Protestants recognition

[239] Ibid., pp. 226–230.     [240] Ibid., p. 228.     [241] Ibid., p. 230.

of the importance of divine grace and salvation. However, he diverged from them in his reasoning and in points of doctrine. His methods were unlikely to appeal (e.g. Our Lady's Abstinence, and abstinence as a penitential discipline), and his doctrine led him into opposition with other temperance groups (e.g. the Sons of Temperance and the Good Templars).

Bridgett was much more open than most Protestants (with notable exceptions in, for example, the Church of England) to working alongside those who espoused moderation rather than total abstinence. Indeed, he was antipathetic towards those who were not willing to accept any place for moderation. For Bridgett, intemperance was equated with gluttony and drunkenness. Alcohol was still a part of God's good creation.

### THE NINETEENTH-CENTURY TEMPERANCE MOVEMENT: A SOCIOLOGICAL AND HISTORICAL PERSPECTIVE

Arguing in sociological terms, Gusfield proposed that the temperance debate in America was symbolic of larger issues.[242] In his view, which has been very influential, the imposition of temperance became a means by which a declining middle class could maintain status. However, this understanding has been criticised. Whatever the symbolic importance of alcohol policy, intemperance in nineteenth-century America was in itself a very serious social problem. Some kind of social response was required, and the temperance movement offered a logical solution.[243]

Similarly, Brian Harrison, in his review of the temperance movement in Victorian England, has noted the role that the movement played both in upward social mobility for its members and in stabilising society.[244] Harrison also recognises the great achievements of the movement in drawing social attention to the scale of the problem of drunkenness and in inducing in society a concern to do something about it.[245] But he further notes that the movement failed, both in its assessment of the underlying causes of the problem, and in its prescription for their treatment. Because it saw social ills as the result rather than the cause of drunkenness, and because drunkenness and addiction were viewed in turn as moral failings, it failed to examine in any systematic and unbiased way the nature and causes of the problem which it sought to address. Because of its strongly negative focus on drink it alienated itself from large and influential sections of society and failed to

---

[242] Summarised by Stark and Bainbridge, 1996, p. 84. See also Gusfield, 1962.
[243] Stark and Bainbridge, 1996, pp. 84–85.
[244] Harrison, 1971. See for example pp. 150, 366–368.     [245] Ibid., p. 365.

consider positive measures such as the provision of counter-attractions to alcohol.[246]

Levine[247] has argued that the changing conceptual framework for understanding addiction in nineteenth-century America is intelligible in terms of the sociology of knowledge. Rush was known for his broader reconstruction of madness as mental illness, and not only for his work on drunkenness as disease. With Philippe Pinel and William Tuke,[248] he is credited with the introduction of the 'moral treatment', in which physical restraint of lunatics was replaced by expectations of self-control. This new view of madness, according to Levine, can be understood in Foucaultian terms as an expression of the economic and political power of the nineteenth-century American middle class.

According to this understanding, Enlightenment optimism enabled the middle classes to deny the existence of evil and to construe social problems as soluble or curable. Evil was redefined as deviance, or as a 'disease of the will'. Social order thus depended upon the self-control of the individual. Levine argued that this tendency was carried further in America than elsewhere because the United States is an uniquely middle-class nation. In this context, liquor was demonised, because it impaired self-control and prevented people from living ordered and temperate lives. Addiction emerged as a concept concerned with the difficulty that people experienced in handling their own desires.

### CHANGING MEDICAL AND THEOLOGICAL PERSPECTIVES

The disease concept of habitual intemperance, which characterised much of the nineteenth-century temperance thinking about alcohol consumption, was clearly a significant change from the earlier views of drunkenness as the result of personal choice.[249] In 1673, Increase Mather, a New England Puritan, wrote: 'Drink is in it self a good creature of God, and to be received with thankfulness, but the abuse of drink is from Satan; the wine is from God, but the Drunkard is from the Devil.'[250] This would appear to summarise the main stream of teaching within the Christian Church for centuries before.[251] Drunkenness was sinful; drinking was not. Drunkards were sinners, because they followed their sinful desire to drink and did not truly desire the virtue of temperance. In 1754 Jonathan Edwards, in *The Freedom of the Will*, also exemplified this earlier position:

---

[246] Ibid., pp. 353–368.  [247] Levine, 1978, pp. 163–167.  [248] Gelder et al., 1996, p. 644.
[249] Levine, 1978, p. 144.  [250] From *Wo to Drunkards*, quoted in Lender, 1973, p. 353.
[251] See Chapter 4.

A drunkard, who continues in his drunkenness, being under the power of a love, and violent appetite to strong drink, and without any love to virtue; but being also extremely covetous and close, and very much exercised and grieved at the diminution of his estate, and prospect of poverty, may in a sort *desire* the virtue of temperance . . . but still he goes on with his drunkenness; his wishes and endeavours are insufficient and ineffectual: such a man has no proper, direct, sincere willingness to forsake this vice, and the vicious deeds which belong to it; for he acts voluntarily in continuing to drink to excess: his desire is very improperly called a willingness to be temperate; it is no true desire of that virtue.[252]

For Edwards, desire and will were one and the same. However, Benjamin Rush, and subsequently Lyman Beecher and Dawson Burns, along with many others of their era, saw things differently. Habitual intemperance was the result of moderate alcohol consumption (whether specifically distilled spirits, in the case of Rush and Beecher, or any alcoholic beverage, as in the case of Burns). They understood distilled spirits, or intoxicating beverages, as creating a strong (perhaps uncontrollable) desire, such that the will was not in harmony with desire. Desire and will were to be distinguished. The habitual drunkard was seen as victim more than sinner, a sufferer from a cruel disease, and generally worthy of sympathy. Moderate alcohol consumption was seen as sinful, and alcohol was understood as being the evil cause of intemperance.[253]

Changing medical perspectives thus seem to have been associated with changing theological perspectives. It is tempting to argue that the former brought about the latter. However, this would be difficult to prove, and in any case would seem to be somewhat simplistic. Physicians such as Rush and Kerr wrote from a clearly Christian perspective, albeit as doctors. Theology may have influenced medicine as much as the reverse, and both were clearly influenced by recognition of a major social problem with serious adverse medical and spiritual consequences. In the nineteenth century, both medicine and the Christian Church sought to find new ways of addressing the problem of drunkenness, and both adopted a new perspective upon the problem in the process.

---

[252] J. Edwards, [1754] 1969, p. 152.
[253] Levine, 1978, pp. 151–161. However, this did not prevent some of the early temperance reformers, such as Beecher, from being rather unsympathetic toward the habitual drunkard at times. As quoted above, Beecher, saw the habitual drunkard as being a drain upon civilised society. Others saw such persons as being beyond help. Some of the societies and reformers were apparently more sympathetic than others.

## TEMPERANCE REDEFINED AS ABSTINENCE

The early pioneers of the temperance movement espoused moderation rather than complete abstinence as the means to prevent intemperance. However, 'moderation' in this context usually meant complete abstinence from distilled spirits. Wine and beer were seen as much less cause for concern. For some, such as Edgar, this remained their belief. However, many, perhaps most, who conceived of moderation in these terms appear to have been drawn later to adopt the position of requiring complete and life-long abstinence from all alcoholic drinks for all people. Because drunkenness was essentially conceived as being a disease of the will, caused by alcohol itself, temperance in the traditional sense of moderation resulting from the use of reason was viewed as an oxymoron insofar as alcohol was concerned. There were only two alternatives for members of the temperance movement. Drinking led sooner or later to intemperance. Abstinence was the logical choice of reason, and alone preserved the use of reason, and thus alone could be conceived as temperance.

For others, such as Bridgett, complete abstinence was seen to have its virtues but was not to be required of all people. Moderation was the virtue that was to be expected of all who drank, and drunkenness was to be eschewed by all, but abstinence was not required of everyone, and was not necessarily to be life-long for those of whom it was required. Bridgett nowhere addressed directly (at least not within the pages of *The Discipline of Drink*) the scientific argument that regular alcohol consumption inevitably led to intemperance. This is not surprising, and is hardly an oversight on his part. His thesis rested upon the historical observation that, for centuries, temperance as moderation had been preserved by the traditions of the Church. Historical evidence and the teachings of the Church gave him no reason to change his understanding of the virtue of temperance. Even where Roman Catholics such as Manning did adopt total abstinence, it would seem that their view of temperance was essentially different from that of Protestants such as Dawson Burns.

## THE CONSEQUENCES OF REDEFINING TEMPERANCE AS ABSTINENCE

The reconstruction of the virtue of temperance as requiring complete abstinence from alcohol consumption had implications for interpretation of scripture, understanding of the doctrine of salvation, the bases for ethical debate, the means of addressing intemperance and the spirituality of the Christians involved.

## Problems in interpretation of scripture

A redefinition of temperance as abstinence created hermeneutical difficulties. Did not scripture have positive things to say about wine, as well as negative things to say about drunkenness? Was wine not the 'good creature of God', just as Increase Mather had said? What about sacramental wine? And, perhaps most significantly of all, did not Jesus himself drink wine? Surely, if Jesus Christ drank wine, temperance could not be equated with total abstinence, and total abstinence could not be required of all Christians, let alone all people in society.

The major hermeneutical debates within the temperance movement were thus concerned with the scriptural justification (or lack of it) for total abstinence and the nature of the wine referred to in the Bible.[254] In response to these questions, Beecher, Burns and Bridgett each gave different emphasis to scripture, and they interpreted it in markedly different ways.

Beecher made relatively few quotations, and did not seem to grapple with the inherent contradiction in the application of a passage about wine to his concern with distilled spirits, while apparently simultaneously condoning continued drinking of wine. For Beecher, drunkenness was still the main concern, and it was distilled spirits which he saw as the main cause of drunkenness. When he employed scripture, he was concerned with what it said about drunkenness.

Burns, in contrast, analysed scripture in great depth in regard to all that it said about fermented drinks. His main concern was a justification for total abstinence, especially in places where the Bible might appear not to support this. However, his hermeneutical key presupposed the principles of the temperance movement; and his flexible approach to the translation of key words, combined with his willingness to speculate, enabled him to explain with ease any difficult passages that might appear to refute his argument.

Bridgett also used scripture in support of his arguments, perhaps even more than Beecher, but certainly much less than Burns. Where he did so, it was generally to support a position contrary to that of the total abstainers. For Bridgett temperance did not equate with total abstinence,

---

[254] See, for example, Malcolm, 1986, pp. 277–280.

and traditional interpretations of scripture were both unproblematic and authoritative.

### *Changes in understanding of the relationship between temperance and Christian salvation*

It is clear that in a broad sense the whole temperance movement was concerned with the salvation of human beings from intemperance. For the larger part of the movement, this was also understood in some specifically Christian sense of 'the provision of God for . . . human plight'.[255] However, variation in understandings of the specific nature and form of this salvation are apparent.

The history of the temperance movement in Ireland shows that Protestants identified an inverse relationship between revivalism and intemperance. Similarly, in America and England eternal salvation and temperance as abstinence were closely linked in the Protestant mind. For Beecher, salvation from intemperance was a part of the broader need of all human beings for salvation from sin of every kind. His concern was the eternal salvation of souls. Drunkenness led to death and to hell. Salvation required abstinence from distilled spirits. Burns also saw intemperance as a hindrance to the mission of the Church. It renders people inaccessible to the Christian message, it leads Christians to apostasy, and it drains the resources of the Church to no good purpose. However, for Burns the primary problem was alcohol, not drunkenness, and accordingly salvation required abstinence from all forms of alcohol.

The emphasis upon abstinence as a virtual requirement for eternal salvation led to a paradoxical move away from traditional Protestant concerns. Even during the nineteenth century, some Protestant clergy were concerned that this was leading to neglect of the central mission of the Church.[256] A century later, the emphasis on total abstinence found commonly among nineteenth-century Baptists can appear to a modern Baptist as an almost heretical threat to the Reformation doctrine of justification by faith alone.[257]

Ironically, among the three works reviewed here, it was the Catholic author, Bridgett, who drew attention to the fact that abstinence alone is ineffective for salvation without God's grace. Salvation from intemperance alone, however that was to be defined, still left ample room for other vices to flourish, and for eternal salvation thus to be lost.

---

[255] S. B. Ferguson, Wright and Packer, 1988, p. 610.　　[256] Stark and Bainbridge, 1996, p. 86.
[257] Briggs, 1994, pp. 338–339.

Perhaps Burns and others were simply influenced by the force of their own arguments in the face of such pressing need. But it would still appear that social reconstruction of the understanding of drunkenness, and the disconnection of the relationship between will and desire, led to a reorientation of theological priorities among Protestant clergy. If drunkenness was the result of a disease which rendered the will impotent in the face of overpowering desire, then the prevention and cure of that disease would have to be addressed before traditional evangelism could play its part. Paradoxically, this led to an emphasis on human action, in the form of abstinence, as a prior requirement to make souls accessible to the soteriological efficacy of an omnipotent God.

### *Variation in emphasis upon the different bases of Christian Ethics*

Beecher clearly saw the problem of intemperance as being one of fallen, sinful humanity in need of salvation. For him, a response to intemperance was required as a part of a Protestant evangelical desire for revival. The primary bases for his ethics of drunkenness were to be found in his doctrines of sin and salvation, and it was a concern with the salvation of souls which provided the motivation for his preaching on temperance. However, for Beecher, temperance had not been completely redefined as abstinence.

Burns developed his scriptural arguments more fully than Beecher and Bridgett, and probably more fully than most other temperance advocates, but his underlying argument was a rational one, and it led him, along with many of his peers, to redefine temperance as abstinence from all alcoholic drinks. It became his hermeneutical key, it influenced his doctrine, and it provided the primary basis of his ethics of intemperance.

Bridgett, in contrast to both Beecher and Burns, relied heavily upon the evidence of history and the traditions of the Church. His concerns were with Catholic doctrine and spirituality, but doctrine was employed to counter any suggestion that temperance should be redefined as abstinence, and abstinence was an optional aid to the spiritual life. Manning, the probable commissioner of *The Discipline of Drink*, who was clearly familiar with the temperance debate and its social realities, presumably identified doctrine and tradition as Catholic priorities, and saw Bridgett as being uniquely able to marshal these arguments for his cause. With Bridgett's support, he was able to remain both a personal abstainer and an ally of the temperance movement without accepting any redefinition of temperance as abstinence.

To some extent, then, each author was true to denominational form. However, there were anomalies. In particular, the redefinition of temperance as abstinence, based as it was upon a social and medical reconstruction of the nature of drunkenness, led Burns to rely heavily upon reasoned argument as foundation of his cause, with scripture apparently playing only a supportive role. His largely consequentialist argument is cogent and sustainable for any non-Christian reading his book who may wish to dispense with scripture altogether. While his work may have been motivated by his understanding of scripture, the foundation of his argument was situated solidly in the ground of human reason.

### *Prohibition as the means of achieving temperance in society*

There were differences of emphasis within the temperance movement in terms of the methods perceived to be necessary in pursuit of their cause. However, during the course of the nineteenth century, the emphasis shifted from moral suasion to prohibition.[258] Medicalisation of the concept of drunkenness thus led, via a redefinition of temperance as abstinence, to a moral imperative which the movement sought to impose on all members of society.

Lyman Beecher believed that strong drink should no longer be a legal commodity for commerce, but his sermons were primarily a powerful form of moral suasion. Father Matthew's approach relied almost entirely upon moral suasion, and was at least temporarily spectacularly successful. However, as the century drew on and intemperance remained an enormous social problem, it became clear that moral suasion alone would not suffice.

Dawson Burns attempted to persuade the hearts and minds of readers to his cause, and he was willing to approach his goal gradually by means of 'permissive' legislation, but there is no doubt that he perceived total prohibition as being the only realistic and ethically justifiable goal for society. Temperance, originally a personal virtue, once it was construed as congruent only with total abstinence, thus became seen eventually as a social necessity which must be imposed upon others.

Other Christians were not convinced. Thomas Bridgett saw a minor and (at least in *The Discipline of Drink*) somewhat vague role for legislation. However, he strongly opposed the imposition of a view of temperance which for him ran quite contrary to Christian tradition and the teaching of the Catholic Church. Yet others, including Frederick Temple, were prepared to take a more pragmatic and relaxed approach. Espousing abstinence themselves, they did not necessarily require it of others. Recognising that

---

[258] Or, in more sociological terminology, from 'assimilative reform' to 'coercion' (Levine, 1978, p. 161).

it was either unnecessary, or else unrealistic, to expect everyone to adopt total abstinence, they were happy to accept heterogeneity of practice.[259]

### *Changes in understanding of the relationship between temperance and Christian spirituality*

For Beecher and Burns, temperance, redefined as complete abstinence from distilled spirits or all alcohol respectively, was seen as a requirement of all good citizens, and especially of all Christians. For Dunlop, prayer was an important means of achieving the abstinence goals of the temperance movement. For Cullen and Bridgett, however, abstinence was not required of all, and assumed a rather different role in the Christian life.

For Cullen, total abstinence was required of all devout Catholics. His permissiveness of moderation among members of the Total Abstinence League of the Sacred Heart was not so much an affirmation of moderation as a realistic recognition that not all Catholics would pursue it. Abstinence came to be regarded by Cullen as an essential element in the devotional life of all pious Catholics. Whereas the Protestant Burns required temperance (and thus abstinence) of all, the Catholic Cullen saw it as a voluntary sign of devotion which would be found only among the most committed.

For Bridgett, total abstinence was not an essential element of the devotional life, even for the most committed Catholic. It was, however, likely to be helpful to any or all Christians for short periods of time, as a part of a life of Christian discipline, and as a penitential act. For some, life-long abstinence was a worthy vocation to which they had a special calling. However, he was adamant that it was not to be *required of,* or imposed upon, anyone.[260]

### CONCLUSIONS

Popular attitudes to alcohol use and misuse, medical understanding of concepts such as inebriety, and theological analysis of the nature and virtue of temperance are all part of a complex interplay of ideas which are dependent upon each other and upon their social context in important and various ways. In the nineteenth century, a medicalisation of the concept of drunkenness as a disease of the will caused by regular moderate consumption of

---

[259] Malcolm, 1986, p. 301.
[260] Presumably, he would have excepted the habitual drunkard who had found himself or herself incapable of maintaining moderation. However, he does not give any detailed consideration to this circumstance.

alcohol led many Protestants to a redefinition of temperance as complete abstinence from alcohol. The paradoxical consequence of this was that moderate consumption of alcohol was viewed as intemperance, and thus as sin. The habitual drunkard was viewed more generously as a victim, albeit in some cases also as virtually beyond salvation.

The ramifications of this process of the medicalisation of drunkenness and the demonisation of alcohol were various and often paradoxical insofar as Christian ethics and theology were concerned. Advocates of the new temperance found themselves in heated disagreement with Christians who adhered to a more traditional understanding of that virtue. Temperance (i.e. abstinence) was required of all, even if that necessitated its imposition by force of law. The real bases of the Christian ethics of drunkenness were shifted towards consequentialism and rational argument. Hermeneutical debate became defensive rather than foundational, and the hermeneutical key of the advocates of the redefined virtue of temperance was to be found in the rational principles of the temperance movement rather than in Christian tradition or theology. Indeed, the nature of this key was such as to allow virtually any interpretation sympathetic to temperance principles in the face of virtually any passage, no matter how inconvenient it might at first appear. Perhaps the most surprising theological outcomes of this process of redefinition of temperance, however, were that Catholic theologians could find themselves emphasising the need for grace, and Protestants sailed amazingly close to the social wind of salvation by abstinence.

Contemporary debate on the Christian ethics of alcohol use and misuse may learn much from the experiences, both successes and mistakes, of the nineteenth-century Church. Social contexts have changed, although a disease model of addiction is still prevalent in North America and elsewhere. Complete abstinence for all would now seem to be an almost completely untenable political solution in either North America or Europe. However, recognition of the importance of drinking at the population level as a determinant of drunkenness and other alcohol-related problems, and the understanding of the policy initiatives that can influence these variables, are far more scientific and far more sophisticated than ever they were in the nineteenth century.[261]

A theological and ethical understanding of alcohol use and misuse is now required which will take into account scientific developments in understanding of alcohol misuse and dependence at both the individual and the population level. A more sophisticated understanding of the nature of the

[261] G. Edwards et al., 1994.

relationship between will and desire is also required, one which will recognise that disease and sin are not necessarily mutually exclusive categories. While disease may perhaps alter both the experience of desire and/or the perceived freedom of the will, a simple model of habitual drunkenness as disease of the will does not do justice either to the longitudinal process of development of alcohol dependence or to the complex interaction between the biological, social and psychological aspects of its aetiology.[262]

Christian theology also needs to give attention to the nature of the relationship between methods of prevention and treatment of alcohol dependence and other alcohol-related problems on the one hand, and Christian salvation on the other. If the aetiology of alcohol dependence does involve both disease process and human choice, and if recovery is possible (which research evidence suggests it is),[263] what does this tell us about the relationship between medical or psychological treatment and Christian salvation? Perhaps it is possible to find a Christian theology of alcohol dependence (and thus of addiction generally) which affirms human autonomy and responsibility, while also recognising the realities of human vulnerability and disease. Indeed, for a faith tradition which places great weight upon the doctrine of the creation of material things by God and the redemption of humanity by God incarnate in Christ, surely such a theology should not be too hard to find? In this way, perhaps Christian theology may bring a genuinely original, creative and redemptive contribution to the ethical debate on alcohol use and misuse.

[262] Cook, 1994.     [263] G. Edwards, Marshall and Cook, 2003.

# CHAPTER 6

# Addiction as sin and syndrome: the divided self

The aim of this chapter is to reflect theologically upon the concept of addiction with a view to exploring some possibilities for the construction of a theological model of addiction. This is not exactly a proposal for a dialogue between Christian theology and science,[1] but it does presuppose that a kind of conversation can be established between Christian theology and the scientific study of addiction.

Alistair McFadyen[2] has drawn attention to the twin dangers that contemporary theology faces. On the one hand, it is at risk of reducing conversation about God to purely secular terms, such that it has no real contribution to make to the discussion. On the other hand, it is at risk of withdrawing completely from secular discourse about material reality and confining itself to the non-material fields of the spiritual and the moral. Both are perceived by McFadyen as essentially 'non-Christian' positions; forms of collusion with the 'pragmatic atheism' of secular discourse. For McFadyen, the 'one possibility by which modern theology may live'[3] is that it might engage in a critical dialogue with the secular. Thus 'the business of Christian theology . . . is to understand both God and reality from the perspective of God's concrete presence and activity in the world, and in relation to our concretely lived experiences of being in the world'.[4] McFadyen proceeds to illustrate this in relation to the doctrine of sin. His study, published under the title *Bound to Sin*, sets out to test the proposition that the doctrine of sin holds 'explanatory and descriptive power in relation to concrete pathologies'.[5] He endeavours to achieve this aim by means of the study of two particular pathologies: childhood sexual abuse and the Holocaust. His specific claim is both exacting and challenging: 'the concrete pathologies operating in child sexual abuse and the holocaust cannot *adequately* be understood except with reference to the denial and opposition to God

---

[1] At least not in terms of the dialogue between science and religion proposed by Ian Barbour and others (Barbour, 1998, pp. 90–98).
[2] McFadyen, 2000.     [3] Ibid., p. 43.     [4] Ibid., p. 44.     [5] Ibid., p. 5.

which characterises sin.'[6] Focussing primarily upon the Augustinian doctrine of original sin, McFadyen skilfully marshals extensive evidence in support of his claim. This includes evidence that, for victims of both childhood sexual abuse and the Holocaust, any notion of willing as based purely upon free decision and arbitrary choice is clearly simplistic.[7] Just as the doctrine of original sin would suggest, people in practice find themselves 'embedded' in sin for which they are not morally accountable on the basis of moral culpability understood solely in terms of the exercise of free will.[8] More importantly, however, McFadyen believes that both pathologies can be construed in terms of worship and idolatry.

For McFadyen, worship 'is actively to orientate and order one's life, whether more or less explicitly, around a reality as primary to and constitutive of meaning, worth, truth and value'.[9] Whereas 'loving joy' is the mark of worship of God, idolatry is characterised by the blocking and disorientation of this joy.[10] Sin, even when its agent is also a victim and not morally accountable in the usual sense, leads to constriction of joy. Thus, McFadyen finds that his dialogue between the doctrine of sin and the concrete pathologies that he chose to study leads to both an enriched understanding of the pathologies in question and also an enriched understanding of the doctrine of sin.[11] His exploration of these two concrete pathologies of sin thus leads him to understand sin in relation to joy in worship of God as Trinity:

> Sin now appears as energised resistance to the dynamics of God and, thereby, as constriction in the fullness of being-in-communion and of joy. Sin is thus construed primarily in dynamic terms, as highly energised, comprehensive disorientation in, through and of all relationships. Such energised disorientation is also communicable and, whilst the claim of biological transmission has not been amenable to testing in relation to these pathologies, it is clear that this disorientation is transmittable through the dynamics of social relationships.[12]

McFadyen makes an extremely convincing case in respect of the explanatory and descriptive power of the doctrine of sin in relation to both his chosen pathologies. It is, perhaps, more debatable whether or not he shows that these pathologies can be *adequately* understood *only* in the context of a theistic (specifically Christian) doctrine of sin. What would it mean *adequately* to understand either childhood sexual abuse or the Holocaust in any context?[13] However, his methodology at least allows an interesting

---

[6] Ibid., p. 54, original emphasis preserved.     [7] Ibid., p. 126.     [8] Ibid., p. 129.
[9] Ibid., p. 227.     [10] Ibid., p. 232.     [11] Ibid., p. 246.     [12] Ibid., pp. 246–247.
[13] McFadyen seems to be asking whether or not the language of moral responsibility offers a *sufficient* description of the pathologies in question (ibid., p. 112). However, even if it is accepted that he has

dialogue to emerge and arguably does result in an enriched understanding of both the two pathologies and the Christian theology with which he brings them into dialogue. The important question in the present context is whether or not a similar methodology might assist in developing a creative or illuminative dialogue between Christian theology and the pathology of addiction.

It is argued here that McFadyen's methodology is well suited to a theological reflection upon the phenomenon of addiction. Addiction certainly shares the characteristics according to which McFadyen selected his two pathologies, namely an almost universal recognition of the reality of, and the pathological nature of, the phenomenon,[14] an extensive descriptive and research literature, and obvious complexity. It is true that addiction is morally more ambiguous. The moral model of addiction is now unpopular, and those who subscribe to the disease model would argue that it is not primarily a matter of moral culpability that one suffers from the disease of addiction. On the other hand, there is a long Christian tradition of recognising addiction (e.g. as 'habitual drunkenness') as sin. However, this moral ambiguity may make the dialogue more interesting, and may allow more opportunity for Christian theology to demonstrate explanatory power (or not). Scientific theories of addiction also incorporate a biological dimension of aetiology, which is not a prominent factor in either of the pathologies selected by McFadyen. This may be of relevance to Augustine's belief in the biological transmission of original sin, an aspect of the doctrine which McFadyen found could not be tested by his chosen pathologies. Furthermore, the present task is fundamentally a similar one to that intended by McFadyen – namely to show that Christian theology holds explanatory power in relationship to a specified concrete pathology (i.e. addiction).

However, McFadyen set out to test the explanatory power of Christian theology, exemplified by the doctrine of sin, in the context of the

succeeded in showing that such language alone is insufficient, and that Christian theology does offer a sufficient description, his methodology does not allow him to prove conclusively that a Christian doctrine of sin offers the *only* sufficient description of these pathologies.

[14] This statement should not be taken to imply assent to the disease model, and neither should this footnote be taken to imply dissent from that model. It is rather argued that there is common assent, in a general and pragmatic way, to the 'pathological' nature of addictive behaviour as maladaptive, deviant or dysfunctional. Even when alcoholism or addiction as a disease is described as 'myth', it is still recognised that alcohol misuse and addictive behaviours are real social problems to which appropriate social and individual responses are required (see, for example, Fingarette, 1989; Davies, 2000). In passing, it is important also to note that, in *Bound to Sin*, McFadyen uses the term 'pathology' extensively, and even describes sin as 'a way of speaking of the pathological aspects of the world encountered by human beings as they live in it' (McFayden, 2000, p. 44) but yet does not define what he means by that term. He appears to have in mind a broad understanding, including both sin and sickness.

contemporary secular understanding of two concrete pathologies. The present exercise is concerned less with demonstrating the explanatory power of Christian theology in principle, and more with understanding the problem of addiction in theological terms, or with showing that Christian theology has a useful contribution to make to discourse about addiction. It is therefore by definition concerned with only one concrete pathology: namely, addiction. Furthermore, this pathology is already capable of description according to diverse, and sometimes contradictory, explanatory models. It is therefore proposed that some minor modifications of McFadyen's methodology are required.

First, following McFadyen, the concrete pathology (i.e. addiction) has already been described, in Chapters 1 and 2, according to understanding developed in secular scientific discourse, using non-theological language. The description has largely focussed on one particular conceptual framework of understanding – that of the dependence syndrome – which has been chosen for reasons already outlined. The scope has been limited largely to one specific drug, alcohol, both in order to simplify the discussion and also to allow a longer historical context of theological reflection to be examined. It has been seen that addiction to alcohol can properly be understood only in the broader context of the use and misuse of alcohol by populations and by individuals. However, because the concept of the alcohol dependence syndrome has been extrapolated to other forms of drug misuse, and to other behaviours, the conclusions drawn here are of relevance to broader theological reflection on addiction.

Secondly, the theological focus of the discussion will be broadened slightly. Two theological perspectives on sin (albeit not unrelated) have been chosen rather than one, because the aim is to explore theological possibilities in relation to the concrete pathology of addiction, rather than to explore a particular doctrine in relation to different concrete pathologies. Limitations of space will prevent a comprehensive engagement with either of these theological frameworks. However, it is hoped that an initial exploration of the possibilities that they offer will provide at least a preliminary indication of the way in which theological language might assist in developing a more adequate understanding of the phenomenon of addiction.

The two theological perspectives that have been selected for consideration here are those of St Paul the apostle and St Augustine of Hippo. These two theological systems have been chosen partly with a view to the enduring influence that they have had upon Christian theology, and thus western culture, and partly because of the particular promise that they would appear to offer in relation to this field. Augustine (and probably Paul) also had relevant pastoral experience of dealing with drunkenness among members of his Christian community.[15]

In addition to their broader theological analysis of sin, both Paul and Augustine wrote about the subjective experience of inner conflict, or struggle, in relation to willed action. This theological attention to the way in which human beings find themselves behaving in ways that they personally dislike, or would wish not to do, would appear to be especially relevant to the understanding of a pathology which essentially involves habitual behaviour that people find difficult to control despite the pain and harm that it causes.

In each case, a particular text has been selected from the work of the author in question, in order to provide a focus for the discussion. These texts have been selected by virtue of the promise that they show as descriptions of subjective experiences which would appear to be similar to that of addiction. In the case of Paul, the selected text is the description of the divided self to be found in Romans 7:14–25. In the case of Augustine, the selected text is book VIII of his *Confessions*, in which he relates his own autobiographical experience of a divided will.

Thirdly, the engagement here with the theologies of Paul and Augustine will be set firmly in the historical context of Christian engagement with problems of drunkenness. It is important that any exploration of a possible theological model of alcohol addiction/dependence should be understood in the context of the differing Christian responses to problems of drunkenness over the centuries. This context has already been set in Chapters 3 to 5, but it will be recapitulated here and some further brief comments will be added.

The primary purpose of this exercise is to explore some possibilities for the construction of a Christian theological model of addiction. Secondarily, however, the methodology may allow some further reflection on McFadyen's question about whether or not a specifically Christian theological discourse can offer additional explanatory and descriptive power in relation to an area of secular discourse.

## THE HISTORICAL CHRISTIAN CONTEXT FOR A THEOLOGY OF ADDICTION

I have argued in Chapter 3 that drunkenness was recognised by Old and New Testament authors as a problem of excessive indulgence of an appetite,

---

[15] In relation to Paul, see Chapter 3. In relation to Augustine, see Chapter 4.

rather similar to gluttony as excessive indulgence in food. However, it was also recognised as a problem which led to a range of other vices, including 'sins of speech', sexual immorality, violence, strife and jealousy. In the New Testament, drunkenness is represented as a 'desire of the flesh'; a manifestation of a life under a power which is 'not God', and inappropriate to life in the eschatological kingdom of God. While early Christian understanding of the problem of drunkenness shared much with Jewish and Greco-Roman culture, it was also distinctive in this way. Drunkenness was seen to be the result of a desire which exerts a power over an individual, which competes with the call of God, and which results in a life which is inappropriate to, or unready for, the coming kingdom of God.

As the centuries passed,[16] drunkenness remained a problem for the Church, and successive Christian theologians resorted to scripture, philosophy and the traditions of the Church in a quest to understand it and respond to it. For Augustine, and later Aquinas, drunkenness was understood primarily as failing to contribute to the ultimate good. For Augustine, it represented a failure to strive to please God alone. For Aquinas, it was an impairment of the ability of human beings to fulfil the rational function for which they were created. With the Reformation came an increasing emphasis upon scripture as the basis for Protestant attitudes to the problem. For Luther, drunkenness was analogous to the sin of Adam and Eve in Eden, but it needed no other verdict than that it was expressly forbidden in scripture. It was a state of misdirected will rather than a state of impaired reason. For Whitefield, drunkenness was improper stewardship of wine, which was one of God's creatures, but again the express injunction of scripture against drunkenness was his primary basis for argument.

Augustine, Aquinas, Luther and Whitefield were all strongly influenced by Pauline theology, but, for Augustine and Aquinas, philosophy was also important. For Augustine and Luther, drunkenness was a work of the flesh. For Augustine this meant that it arises, as do other works of the flesh, from human pride. For Luther, it meant that drunkenness arises from a corrupt human nature which is prone to excesses and self-indulgence.

Augustine and Aquinas also left in their writings broader theological concepts with incompletely explored potential for a more sophisticated Christian theological exploration of contemporary problems of drunkenness and alcohol misuse. For example, Augustine's concept of the divided will has enormous relevance to an understanding of how people engage with desires or appetites that impel them towards goals that they recognise as

---

[16] See Chapter 3.

being inherently undesirable. Similarly, Aquinas' concept of the mean of virtues has the potential to relate 'normal' drinking ethically to drunkenness and to other alcohol-related problems in a manner which is harmonious with current scientific thinking.

Prior to the nineteenth-century, drunkenness was generally understood by all Christians as being sinful, but drinking alcohol was not. Drunkards were sinners, because they allowed their will to follow their sinful desire to drink excessively and did not sufficiently desire, or act upon their desire for, the virtue of temperance. However, during the nineteenth century, in the light of new medical conceptions of the problem, this all changed. Habitual intemperance came to be understood by large numbers of Christians (albeit mainly Protestants, and certainly not all of them) as the virtually inevitable result of almost any regular alcohol consumption, which would create a strong, and perhaps uncontrollable, desire for alcohol. The habitual drunkard came to be seen as victim more than sinner, a sufferer from a cruel disease, the evil cause of which was alcohol itself. Intemperance was reconceived as being moderate alcohol consumption, and temperance as complete abstinence from alcohol.[17]

During the twentieth century, these attitudes changed once more. As the temperance movement declined in influence, moderate alcohol consumption was again accepted by most western Christians as being good, and drunkenness was still understood as bad. However, this 'badness' was not a simple return to the attitudes of pre-nineteenth-century Christendom, and neither was it a simple continuation of nineteenth-century temperance thinking. For many, a specific problem of 'alcoholism' or 'alcohol addiction' was understood as being a disease.[18] Drunkenness was certainly to be distinguished from this disease, but was nonetheless also an important symptom of it. In contrast, the so-called 'moral model' of alcoholism was widely dismissed by secular discourse as being unhelpful. In fact, a variety of models of alcoholism was propounded and, to a greater or lesser degree, the models existed alongside one another.[19]

Contemporary scientific understanding, as described briefly above, now views alcohol dependence as a bio-psycho-social disorder. It is clear that this context provides an understanding of the nature of alcohol-related

---

[17] See Chapter 5.    [18] S. Y. Hill, 1985; Meyer, 1996.

[19] Siegler, 1968. Even by the end of the twentieth century, there is evidence that a significant minority of educated young people conceptualised alcohol abuse as both sin and disease, or as both sin and addiction. Furthermore, conceptualisation of illicit drug (cocaine) abuse as sinful was endorsed by 51 per cent of respondents – a similar proportion to that endorsing the disease concept (Cunningham et al., 1994).

problems radically different from that encountered by the apostle Paul, Augustine, Aquinas or the Church Reformers. It is a clear improvement on the medical and social understanding of nineteenth-century physicians and theologians. There is thus a need for a contemporary theological and ethical analysis of the most appropriate Christian foundations for understanding drunkenness, alcohol dependence, and other alcohol-related problems.

## A PAULINE THEOLOGY OF SIN AND ADDICTION

Paul has been referred to as 'the first and greatest Christian theologian'.[20] He was a zealous Jew, a native of Tarsus in Cilicia,[21] who had trained as a Pharisee.[22] He persecuted the young Christian Church,[23] until an experience on the Damascus road, probably in the early 30s CE,[24] left him with a conviction of being commissioned by God to take the gospel – the good news about Jesus Christ – to the Gentiles.[25] The missionary work that he undertook in response to this call was controversial, especially among Jewish Christians,[26] because of his insistence that circumcision should not be a requirement for Gentile converts[27] and his support for non-observance of food laws by Jewish Christians.[28] He was probably martyred in Rome, under Nero, around 62–65 CE.[29]

Paul was a Roman citizen, with a substantial Greek education.[30] He left seven epistles which are generally agreed to be of authentic authorship, all of which were probably written in the mid-50s CE.[31] From these writings it is possible to adduce that Paul saw his faith in Jesus Christ as the fulfilment of the faith of the Hebrew people, and not as a departure from it.[32] However, Christ was central to Paul's theology. Christ replaced the Torah as the defining characteristic of the people of God and of the purposes of God. The image of the body of Christ replaced the Temple cult as the defining context of the faith community. God was to be known definitively through Christ. Christ was the hermeneutical key to scripture. Salvation was to be found in increasing conformity to Christ. For Paul, Christianity *was* Christ.

---

[20] Dunn, 1998, p. 2.    [21] Acts 22:3; Dunn (1988a), p. xl.
[22] Philippians 3:5; Galatians 1:13–14.    [23] Galatians 1:13.
[24] Dunn, 1988a, p. xli.    [25] Galatians 1:15–16; Romans 1:5.
[26] See Dunn, 1988a, pp. xxxix–xliii.    [27] Galatians 2:1–10.    [28] Galatians 2:11–14.
[29] Cross and Livingstone, 1997, pp. 1234–1235.    [30] Dunn, 1988a, p. xl.
[31] Romans, 1 and 2 Corinthians, Galatians, Philippians, 1 Thessalonians and Philemon. In addition, various claims are made for Pauline authorship of Colossians, 2 Thessalonians, Ephesians and the pastoral epistles. Except perhaps for Colossians and 2 Thessalonians, these claims would appear dubious (see Cross and Livingstone, 1997, p. 1235).
[32] See Dunn, 1998, pp. 713–737, on which the following account of Paul's theology is largely based.

James Dunn has suggested that among the most innovative and enduring features of Christian theology which may be traced to Paul were his distinctive Christian understandings of gospel, grace and love.[33] The 'good news' of the death and resurrection of Jesus Christ, grace as the epitome of God's dealings with human beings, and love as the motive for divine giving and human living, together encapsulate the breadth and nature of Christianity. Of these, it is relevant here to say just a little more about grace.

For Paul, grace was to be understood as the activity of God in bringing about the redemption of human beings through Christ.[34] Grace is the opposite of sin, in that sin is self-centred whereas the grace of God is manifested in outgoing love.[35] Grace is offered by God as a gift to human beings. Grace is concerned with divine initiative, divine activity and divine power, all offered to the benefit of undeserving human beings.[36] It is expressed particularly in the event of Christ himself, but also in the divine enabling of human beings in the course of their daily lives.[37]

An innovation of Paul which has perhaps had less lasting impact is that of the distinction between 'body' and 'flesh'. Flesh (σαρξ), in Pauline thought, had a range of meaning, but was almost always concerned with the weakness and corruptibility of the creature as contrasted with the creator.[38] Body (σωμα) also had a range of meaning, but referred to somewhat more than just the physical body. It had a sense of the embodied 'I', standing in relation to the physical environment.[39] Thus, Dunn suggests that for Paul 'body' denotes a *being in the world*, whereas 'flesh' denotes a *belonging to the world*.[40] The anthropology defined by this distinction incorporated a positive evaluation of the createdness of human beings, derived from Hebrew thought, and also a more negative element to life in this world, the 'desiring, decaying flesh which . . . subverts existence before and for God',[41] derived from Greek thought.

This distinction also relates to the tension inherent in Paul's eschatology. For Paul, the Christian is situated simultaneously in two overlapping ages or epochs. The believer, who is still in this world in the flesh, is also in Christ, desiring to serve God and do his will. Therein lays a tension, a

---

[33] Ibid., p. 733.    [34] Ridderbos, 1977, pp. 173–174.    [35] Barrett, 1994, p. 90.
[36] Dunn, 1998, pp. 322–323.    [37] Ibid., p. 320.
[38] Dunn, 1988a, p. 363. Ridderbos emphasises more the inclusion of human sinfulness within the meaning of this term (Ridderbos, 1977, pp. 93–95).
[39] Dunn, 1998, p. 56. Ridderbos again has a slightly different emphasis, noting that the body has a spiritual and heavenly sense, as well as a material one, and that the body does not have the negative connotations of weakness and sin associated with the Pauline concept of flesh.
[40] Dunn, 1998, p. 72, original emphasis preserved.    [41] Dunn, 1998, p. 72.

warfare even, which will continue until the resurrection of the body after death.[42]

Paul understood sin as a power over human beings which has a tendency to enslave, and to cause them to forget their creaturely dependence upon God. Its influence is both upon individuals, their attitudes and actions, and also upon the values and practices of society as a whole.[43] For Paul, sin was concerned primarily with relationship with God. It involved the whole person, and the whole human race.[44] It was concerned with enmity, or rebellion, against God himself.[45] Paul offered very little analysis of where this power originated from. He was concerned much more with its reality in human experience.[46]

Dunn has suggested[47] that Paul saw three effects of the power of sin in the lives of human beings: misdirected religion, self-indulgence and sins. Misdirected religion is manifested as a perversion of the instinct to invest ultimate significance in God, such that religion is directed to other ends, which remain more easily under human control. Self-indulgence is concerned with the way in which neutral or good desires (e.g. sexual appetite) become transformed into harmful preoccupations (e.g. lust). Sins are those consequences of wrong judgement, made under the power of sin, exemplified by the lists of vices that Paul provided in various places.[48]

For Paul, sin was intimately linked with death.[49] Death was the inevitable consequence of sin, the end of life lived 'in the flesh', and the due punishment for sins.

### *Romans 7:14–25: the divided self*

At the time of writing his epistle to the Romans, Paul clearly hoped to visit Rome for the first time, *en route* to Spain.[50] Prior to undertaking this missionary journey, it was apparently his intention to visit Jerusalem to deliver money collected by Gentile Christians in his churches for the (primarily Jewish) Christian poor there.[51] He was concerned, in the wake of previous controversies, that this offering might not prove to be acceptable.[52] The epistle represents Paul's mature reflection upon, and understanding of, the Christian gospel, addressed to a church of some size and importance.[53]

---

[42] Ibid., p. 475.    [43] Ibid., pp. 111–114.    [44] Barrett, 1994, p. 64.    [45] Ridderbos, 1977, p. 105.

[46] Dunn, 1998, p. 113.    [47] Ibid., pp. 114–124.    [48] See Chapter 3.

[49] Dunn, 1998, pp. 124–127; Barrett, 1994, p. 64.

[50] Romans 1:11–15; 15:23–24; Cranfield, 1995, p. xiii; Ziesler, 1989, p. 3.

[51] Romans 15:25–29; Cranfield, 1995, p. xiii.    [52] Romans 15:31.

[53] Cranfield, 1995, p. xiii.

It incorporates an attempt to address missionary, apologetic and pastoral purposes.[54]

Paul's epistle to the Romans deals with the need of Jew and Gentile for the grace of God, the means by which they may both be engaged in an experience of that grace, and the way in which they should relate together as Christians. There is a strong Christological element to the letter, and Paul eventually describes a new ethical framework based upon an understanding of the community of faith as the body of Christ.[55] An important (and complex) subsidiary theme in the letter is that of the place of the law for those who are in Christ.[56]

That portion of the letter with which we are most concerned here is chapter 7, verses 14–25:

[14]For we know that the law is spiritual; but I am of the flesh, sold into slavery under sin. [15]I do not understand my own actions. For I do not do what I want, but I do the very thing I hate. [16]Now if I do what I do not want, I agree that the law is good. [17]But in fact it is no longer I that do it, but sin that dwells within me. [18]For I know that nothing good dwells within me, that is, in my flesh. I can will what is right, but I cannot do it. [19]For I do not do the good I want, but the evil I do not want is what I do. [20]Now if I do what I do not want, it is no longer I that do it, but sin that dwells within me.

[21]So I find it to be a law that when I want to do what is good, evil lies close at hand. [22]For I delight in the law of God in my inmost self, [23]but I see in my members another law at war with the law of my mind, making me captive to the law of sin that dwells in my members. [24]Wretched man that I am! Who will rescue me from this body of death? [25]Thanks be to God through Jesus Christ our Lord!

So then, with my mind I am a slave to the law of God, but with my flesh I am a slave to the law of sin.[57]

This passage must be understood within the context of the whole letter. However, the nature, position and detailed exposition of this section of the text are differently construed by different commentators. The end of chapter 7 clearly represents an important transition by all accounts, as chapter 8 changes focus to the more positive theme of 'life in the Spirit'. However, for some commentators, 7:14–25 is concerned primarily with the experience of the Christian who continues to struggle with sin, and for others it is concerned with non-Christian experience. Within the former group, some see this as being mature Christian experience and others as a way of Christian life which should be left behind. For some it is understood

---

[54] Dunn, 1988a, pp. lv–lviii.  [55] Ibid., pp. lxi–lxii; Ziesler, 1989, pp. 6–8.
[56] Dunn, 1988a, pp. lxiii–lxxii.  [57] Romans 7:14–25, NRSV.

as more or less autobiographical of Paul's own experience, and for others it is not.[58]

By way of example, the interpretations of Cranfield, Dunn and Ziesler will be reviewed here, as well as the more psychologically orientated analysis offered by Theissen. Cranfield and Dunn understand 7:14–25 as representing Christian experience, and Ziesler and Theissen as non-Christian experience.

Cranfield[59] is clear that verses 13–23 are concerned with 'the inner conflict characteristic of the true Christian, a conflict such as is possible only in the man in whom the Holy Spirit is active and whose mind is being renewed under the discipline of the gospel'.[60] For Cranfield, the inner conflict portrayed in verses 16, 18 and 19 is the result of a battle 'that is not possible until a man is sanctified by the Holy Spirit'.[61] His interpretation of the passage in question is that the Holy Spirit provides a growing knowledge and awareness of God's will as expressed in the law, and also a growing 'will to obey it'.[62] As this Christian growth continues, individuals become increasingly perceptive of, and sensitive to, the extent to which sin still has power over them.[63] This process should not be misunderstood, however, as a conflict between the Holy Spirit and sin. It is rather a reflection of the work and power of the Holy Spirit within the human mind and personality alongside the continuing power of sin over the self. Thus, Paul writes in the first person singular.[64] For Cranfield, Paul's understanding of 'the flesh' is interpreted in a Calvinistic sense of 'fallen human nature' and even his best actions will always be marred by egotism.[65]

According to this understanding, verses 24–25 provide a conclusion to the previous verses and a link to chapter 8.[66] Verse 25b is reflective of the eschatological tension experienced by the Christian living in this present age, and verse 25a is expressive of confidence in the expectation of future deliverance from this tension.

---

[58] See reviews of the possibilities in Cranfield, 1995, pp. 156–159; Ziesler, 1989, pp. 191–195. For Dodd, Romans 7 represents Paul's 'vivid personal recollection' of his pride in the law, the consequent repression of natural instincts that this brought about, and the inner conflict that it thus generated (Dodd, 1967, pp. 74–75).

[59] For Cranfield, 1:16b–17 represents a statement of the main theological theme of the body of the letter. The quotation from Habakkuk in v. 17, 'But he who is righteous by faith shall live', is then expounded in 1:18—8:39. In particular, 5:1—8:39 is understood as an exposition on the words 'shall live'. Within this section 7:1–25 is concerned with 'a life characterized by freedom from the law's condemnation', and 7:7–25 is considered to be a 'necessary clarification of what has been said concerning the law' (Cranfield, 1995, p. xv.)

[60] Cranfield, 1995, p. 155.   [61] Ibid., p. 166.   [62] Ibid., pp. 166, 169.

[63] Ibid., pp. 155, 166.   [64] See e.g. v. 16, and ibid., pp. 166, 168.

[65] Ibid., p. 167.   [66] Ibid., pp. 155, 169–172.

Dunn[67] portrays the inner conflict in verses 15–25 as a split in the 'I' between willing and doing.[68] He understands Paul as having become aware of the power of sin 'as never before' following his conversion.[69] He also sees a parallel between a split in the 'I' and a split in the law. The 'willing' 'I' agrees with the law, and wishes to obey it. This is the same 'I' that is identified with Christ in his death, that is no longer under the law of works, and that is obedient to the spiritual law, the law of faith. The 'impotent' 'I', however, is the 'man of flesh', the 'I' not yet identified with Christ in his resurrection, the 'I' which is still under the law used by sin to bring death. A liberation of the 'I' has been commenced, but is not yet complete. This is not a form of dualism. The flesh is still 'I', but life in this world is still life in the flesh. The split is therefore one between the two epochs: the old epoch of life in this world, in the flesh, over which sin still has power, and a new epoch of life in Christ, lived in the power of God.[70]

Dunn portrays verse 24 as a cry of frustration at the existential plight in which Paul finds himself. He too sees verse 25a as reflective of confidence in the deliverance that will come in Christ, and verse 25b as reflecting the eschatological tension inherent in the situation of the believer in this world, in whom the work of redemption has been begun but not yet completed.[71] The tension is initiated, not resolved, at the point of conversion, for it is only then that the 'eschatological "now" in Christ'[72] is introduced.

For Ziesler,[73] 7:14–25 is a description of the 'divided self' – a description of a pre-Christian state, experienced by people who are without Christ. Although he admits that this position is debatable, he feels that Paul would

---

[67] For Dunn, 1:16–17 also represents a summary of the letter's theme. However, for him, it is the whole of vv. 16–17 that provides this summary for the whole letter. A focus on the quotation from Habakkuk is considered misguided (Dunn, 1988a, pp. 46–49). The passage of interest to us here (i.e. 7:15–25) is located within a section concerned with the 'outworking of the gospel in relation to the individual' (6:1—8:39), and is a part of an answer to the question of whether or not grace might be understood as encouraging sin (ibid., pp. viii–ix). First, Dunn sees vv. 14–25 as redressing any possible misunderstanding created in v. 13 regarding the benefits of remaining under the law. Secondly, he sees vv. 14–25 as an exploration of the role of the law in the Christian's experience of the eschatological tension created by the continuing power of sin prior to full participation in the resurrection of Christ (ibid., p. 404).

[68] Ibid., p. 406.     [69] Ibid., p. 407.     [70] Ibid., pp. 407–409.

[71] Ibid., pp. 410–412.     [72] Ibid., p. 411.

[73] For Ziesler, 1:16–17 is again understood as a summary of the whole letter. It is also a bridge between the opening thanksgiving in 1:8–15 and the main body of the letter in 1:18—11:36 (Ziesler, 1989, pp. 35, 67). However, Ziesler sees 7:1–25 as being the third of four aspects of God's solution to human sinfulness as discussed by Paul (ibid., p. 36). The four aspects of Paul's understanding of this divine solution, according to Ziesler, are an end to divine condemnation [4:1—5:21], an end to bondage to sin [6:1–23], an end to the divided self [7:1–25], and an end to life in the flesh [8:1–25]). Romans 7:1–6 is concerned with the death of the Christian to the law, and 7:7–13 is concerned with the way in which the law is exploited by sin.

not have given such an extremely negative description of Christians as to suggest that they are 'sold under sin'.[74] However, he makes the point that this passage is concerned primarily with the failure of the law to solve the problem of sin, and not with the identity of the 'I'.[75]

Ziesler also considers that the nature of the conflict described in this passage is debatable. He recognises that the passage is reminiscent of a tradition exemplified by a quotation from Ovid, although he considers it not precisely the same: 'I see and approve the better things, but I pursue the inferior things.'[76] He points out that, although the notion of the divided self is pervasive, it varies throughout the passage. On the one hand are sin, the 'I' sold under sin, the flesh, and a law in 'my members'. On the other hand are the 'I' that wants to do good, the 'inmost self', 'the law of my mind', and the law of God. Up to verse 20, or perhaps verse 21, the division appears to be within the self, but after this it appears to be between different laws.[77] In verses 14–16, the opposition is between will and action, in verses 17–20 it is between self and sin.[78]

Rather more speculatively, Ziesler points out that the passage is preceded (vv. 7–13) by, and possibly even followed by (8:4), a concern with covetousness or 'wrong desire', and that the line of argument works best in respect of desires over which people do not have control.[79] Is Paul talking here primarily about conflicting desires?

For Ziesler, verse 24 is concerned with the person living under sin, without Christ. Verse 25a ostensibly presents Christ as the solution to the human dilemma. However, verse 25b appears to be an awkward return to that dilemma, and is unconvincingly explained by Ziesler as a possible gloss.[80]

For Theissen, 7:14–25 is a depiction of suffering 'under the flesh'.[81] It achieves this description by means of two strands of thought,[82] which are to be found respectively in verses 15–18 and 19–23. In each, the argument begins with the contradiction of willing and doing,[83] and then moves on to a consideration of the power of sin.[84] In the second strand of thought, the power of sin is dealt with rather more briefly, but the concluding assent to the law is emphasised more strongly, and the theme of a clash between the flesh and the law becomes a more greatly emphasised clash between two laws (the 'law of God' and 'another law').

---

[74] Romans 7:14; ibid., pp. 191–194.    [75] Ibid., pp. 194–195.
[76] *Metamorphoses*, 7.19f., quoted by Ziesler (Ziesler, 1989, p. 190).
[77] Zeisler, 1989, p. 190.    [78] Ibid., p. 196.    [79] Ibid., pp. 190–191.
[80] Ibid., pp. 192, 199.    [81] Theissen, 1987, p. 183.    [82] Theissen, 1987, pp. 186–188.
[83] Verses 15 and 19 respectively.    [84] Verses 17–18 and 20 respectively.

For Theissen, Paul has described a 'three tribunal' anthropological model, in which the tribunal of the 'I' stands between the antagonistic tribunals of the law which points to God, and the law of sin. The law of God is represented in the mind, the law of sin in the 'members' or the 'flesh' of the person. The 'I' stands between these two, being drawn in either one direction or the other.[85]

Theissen believes that, in 7:14ff., Paul was drawing implicitly upon the classical Greek tradition of understanding the conflict between willing and doing.[86] On the one hand, this tradition represented affect, in the form of passion, sloth or pleasure, as the cause of evil, by means of its power to override reason. This is exemplified by Medea, who was portrayed by Euripides as having killed her children because of her desire for revenge, and who was understood by Ovid as caught in conflict between love for Jason and the voice of reason: 'Some strange power holds me down against my will. Desire persuades me one way, reason another. I see the better and approve it, but I follow the worse.'[87] Seneca took this understanding a step further. Rather than portraying Medea's murder of her children as a conflict between passion and reason, he saw her as caught in a conflict between two emotions: love and anger.

On the other hand, the tradition included an argument that evil is due, not to passion, but to ignorance. This was exemplified by Socrates and Epictetus, for whom human beings were understood to make rational choices, based upon knowledge and interpretation. According to Epictetus, Medea deceived herself in her decision to murder her children. She acted according to her understanding, but lacked proper understanding and thus acted wrongly.

Theissen sees Paul as following in this tradition of reflection on the conflict between willing and doing. He argues that Paul inclines more towards the 'affective' model of Euripides than to the 'cognitive' model of Epictetus. For Paul, sin is the power which generates the conflict, but the flesh is the source of the passions which draw the subject away from right action. However, he sees Paul as going beyond tradition by virtue of his portrayal of two 'normative systems' in conflict: the law of the flesh and the law of the mind.

---

[85] Theissen later proposes a correspondence between these three tribunals and the id, ego and superego of Freudian psychoanalytic thought (Theissen, 1987, p. 244).

[86] Theissen, 1987, pp. 211–221.

[87] Quoted by Theissen (Theissen, 1987, p. 217), from Ovid, *Metamorphoses* (with removal here of the interpolations of the original Latin text).

For Theissen, in 7:7–23 Paul is engaged in relating 'an inner dialogue that leads more and more deeply into a destructive self-condemnation'.[88] Redemption is to be found in Christ, and is announced in 7:24. It takes the form of life 'in the Spirit', which is the subject of chapter 8, and the destructive dialogue is thereby replaced by the constructive dialogue of 8:31–39.[89] The transformation is understood by Theissen in psychological terms, in which he takes in a broader view of chapters 7 and 8, understood according to learning theory, psychodynamic processes and cognitive restructuring.[90]

### Addiction as divided self

At first sight, there would appear to be a very significant problem to be encountered by any application of Christian commentary on Romans 7:14–25 to providing a theological account of the subjective experience of addiction. Namely, how can the conflict between pre-Christian and Christian interpretations be accommodated if this passage is taken to be descriptive of the subjective experience of addiction? Whichever interpretation is accepted, addiction is clearly not confined exclusively either to those who are not Christians or to those who are.[91] It is encountered among people of every religious tradition, as well as among atheists and agnostics.[92] Therefore, if Cranfield and Dunn are correct in asserting that the experience described by Paul in Romans 7:14–25 is a result of the work of the Holy Spirit in specifically Christian experience, or that it is initiated by entry of the Christian at conversion into the new epoch of Christ, how can it be descriptive of the experience of the Buddhist, atheist or agnostic alcoholic? Conversely, if Ziesler and Theissen are correct in their assertion that this passage describes a human predicament to which Christ is the solution, a predicament which Christians have therefore left behind, how can it be

---

[88]  Ibid., pp. 260–261.      [89]  Ibid., p. 261.

[90]  See ibid., pp. 222–265. A full discussion of this psychological analysis is beyond the scope of this book. However, Theissen portrays Christ as a 'learning model for overcoming normatively conditioned anxieties' (p. 226), a 'symbol of an integration of originally antagonistic tribunals' (p. 249), and a means of making possible a 'new interpretation of the human situation' (p. 263). He does not explore adequately, so far as this reader is concerned, the extent to which Christ may be understood as fulfilling these roles in a unique way, although to some extent this could be taken as implicit. The danger would appear to be that redemption is understood in a purely psychological sense, addressed primarily to the resolution of the inner conflict between willing and action. Theological discourse could thereby be understood as reduced entirely to the terms of secular discourse, and as adding nothing to it. I do not think that this is Theissen's intention, but the question remains of how this model of understanding Romans 7–8 may be seen to have unequivocally avoided such a conclusion.

[91]  See, for example, Fichter, 1982.

[92]  Although there are differences of prevalence between these groups (G. Edwards, Marshall and Cook, 2003, p. 19).

descriptive of the experience of the Christian alcoholic? Surely, according to either interpretation, we must conclude that Paul is describing a different kind of experience altogether? The divided self of Romans 7:14–15 is therefore not a description of the experience of addiction; it is a description of another kind of experience – perhaps similar or analogous to addiction in some way – but actually confined either to Christian or non-Christian experience, according to one's assessment of the arguments presented by different commentators.

While this argument may appear compelling in some ways, it does not withstand closer scrutiny. In particular, it might be argued that Cranfield, Dunn, Ziesler and Theissen are all somewhat too preoccupied with making a decision between the pre-Christian and Christian interpretations of the passage. Surely, the passage could be descriptive of both Christian and non-Christian experience? According to Paul, both Christians and non-Christians are caught up in the human experience of both positive and negative aspects of createdness in this world. Both have σωμα and σαρξ, body and 'flesh', with all the good things and all the problems that this entails. Those who are outside Christ are not necessarily viewed by Paul as being without any moral awareness or sense of inner conflict.[93] Similarly, he has no illusions that Christians have automatically become sinless,[94] and indeed the continuing struggle with sin is inherent in the eschatological tension between the old and new epochs, within which Paul understands Christians as being involved.

But is there a valid parallel between this passage and the subjective experience of addiction?

Dunn, Ziesler and Theissen all draw specific attention to the way in which the passage is concerned with the conflict between will and action. As far as will is concerned, Paul indicates that he can 'will what is right' (v. 18), or 'want' to do something (vv. 15, 19), and then finds that he does not do it. Conversely, he can *not* want to do something (vv. 16, 19, 20), or even 'hate' something (v. 15), and then finds that he nevertheless does it. As far as action is concerned, Paul finds that he does not understand his own

---

[93] See, for example, the conflict alluded to in Romans 2:14–15. Unfortunately, there is further debate here also! As far as our present commentators are concerned, Dunn clearly understands this passage as referring to non-Christian Gentiles (Dunn, 1988a, pp. 98–99, 105–106) whereas Cranfield concludes that the reference is to Gentile Christians (Cranfield, 1995, p. 50).

[94] See, for example, Romans 6:12. Although for Ziesler (1989, p. 164) this is an anomaly, for according to his understanding we might expect Christians to be sinless and therefore to need no such advice, he clearly recognises that Paul actually does not expect this. He sees, rather, that the Christian now has the 'possibility' of defeating sin. How he might reconcile this with his interpretation of 7:14–25 as applying only to pre-Christian experience is not entirely clear. If he sees Christians as no longer being under the 'power' of sin (p. 165), why do they sin at all?

actions (v. 15), that he does what he does not want (vv. 15, 16, 19, 20), and even does what he hates (v. 15). Conversely, he does not do what he wills to do (v. 18) and wants to do (vv. 15, 19). All of this would certainly appear to be very similar indeed to the subjective experience of drinkers who want to stop drinking, but then find themselves drinking again, and who want to abstain, but find that they do not.

The subjective compulsion of the alcohol dependence syndrome, however, also incorporates the experience of craving or desire for alcohol. Is this also to be found in Romans 7:14–25? At first, it would seem that the answer is clearly 'no'. Whereas the alcohol-dependent person desires both to stop drinking, and also to resume or continue drinking, Paul speaks clearly of a desire to do what is right, but does not admit to a desire to do that which is evil. Perhaps, then, the subjective experience of Romans 7 is qualitatively different from that of alcohol dependence? Whereas Paul (assuming for a moment that he does write autobiographically) finds himself willing and wanting only one thing, the addict finds that he or she is torn between competing desires, which engender correspondingly competing wills to do different and opposite things. However, this cannot be a complete contrast with Romans 7, for verses 1–13 are concerned with desire (in the form of 'sinful passions' in v. 5, and covetousness in vv. 7–13), and it will be recalled that Ziesler considered the possibility that Paul was in fact still talking about conflicting desires in verses 14–25. Similarly, Theissen considered that Paul's account of the divided self in verses 14–25 was influenced by the Greek tradition of conflict between affect and reason, or between conflicting affective states. His 'three tribunal' model further postulates that the self stands between the antagonistic tribunals of the law of God and the law of sin, drawn in opposite directions by each. Furthermore, Cranfield and Dunn each portray Christians as being caught in a conflict or tension created by their experience of the power of sin. How is this power experienced, if not as an affective state or desire?

The competing desires of the person caught up in the subjective experience of alcohol dependence must actually be of different qualitative kinds. The rational desire to stop drinking is presumably based upon a recognition of the harm that drinking has caused (especially over a longer chronological perspective), a desire to be free of this harm, and a sense of what is recognised as 'right' or necessary in the circumstances. The desire to continue drinking is presumably much more affective, or appetitive, and perhaps therefore more biological, in nature. It almost certainly includes a variety of components, such as the desire to relieve withdrawal symptoms, a desire to experience the short-term relief of anxiety or dysphoria, and a desire for the positive subjective effects of alcohol intoxication. The discourse in Romans 7:14–25 can similarly be understood as recognising competing desires of contrasting kinds. On the one hand is the more rational and explicit desire, expressed in the will to do that which is spiritual (v. 14), good (vv. 16, 19, 21), and according to the law of God (v. 22) or the 'law of my mind' (v. 23). On the other hand is a more implicit desire, induced by the power of sin, and variously experienced as 'slavery under sin' (v. 14), 'sin that dwells within me' (vv. 17, 20), evil that 'lies close at hand' (v. 21), and 'another law' which makes one 'captive to the law of sin that dwells in my members' (v. 23).

Understood in this way, Paul's theology of sin, and the subjective experience of the divided self described in Romans 7:14–25, would together appear to describe subjective phenomena very similar to those experienced as a part of the alcohol dependence syndrome. In other words, Paul's account of the struggle with sin would appear to be of a very similar nature to the subjective experiences of desire and compulsion which are associated with alcohol dependence. Both are concerned with the relationship between will and behaviour. Both acknowledge a tension within the self between that which is recognised as good, rational and delightful, on the one hand, and that which is recognised as 'evil', contrary to reason and enslaving, on the other. Both acknowledge competing 'desires' of different kinds: the one a more rational desire, and the other more affective, or perhaps even biological in nature.

The strong similarities evident in this parallel between the subjective experience described in Romans 7 and the subjective experience of the alcohol dependence syndrome do not necessarily demonstrate that addiction can be reduced without remainder to a Pauline understanding of the inner conflict generated by the power of sin. (It almost certainly cannot.)[95] Neither do they necessarily mean that all human beings suffer from a 'sin dependence syndrome'. However, they do clearly suggest that the relationship between sin and addiction is worthy of further exploration. They also suggest some important possible implications for a theological understanding of addiction.

First, addiction may be concerned not so much with sins as with sin. It may be concerned not so much with freely made moral decisions as with a struggle against the power of sin. This power has a tendency to enslave, and to corrupt the attitudes, values and actions of individuals and of society. It is

---

[95] A cursory consideration of the seven elements of the alcohol dependence syndrome would immediately suggest that tolerance, withdrawal symptoms, relief drinking and reinstatement, at the least, are without any direct or obvious parallel in the Pauline understanding.

not a power which affects only the addict or alcoholic. It has influence in the lives of all human beings. The plight of the alcoholic is at least very similar to the plight which we all share and in which we are all involved. This idea of a 'power' of sin as implicated in the nature and origins of addiction offers a level of understanding of the experience of addiction which is not to be found in moral, disease or purely scientific models. Addiction is not concerned simply with freely made moral choices, and neither is it concerned purely with deterministic forces that act upon a helpless victim. It is concerned with an interplay of agent and environment in such a way that subjects experience themselves as 'drawn into' an addictive pattern of behaviour for which they are neither entirely responsible, nor entirely without responsibility. This pattern of behaviour involves the whole person, in interaction with his or her social context.

Secondly, addiction may be understood, like sin, as being essentially concerned with a personal attitude or orientation towards God. Because this assertion is based here upon a fundamental prior assumption of Pauline theology, at least insofar as sin is concerned, it is in no sense offered as evidence that the phenomenon of addiction can be understood only within a theistic framework. However, it does show that a context of relationship with God can offer an informative approach to understanding addiction. The inner conflict of addiction can be understood as concerned with a division of the self between openness to the grace and power of God in Christ, on the one hand, and openness to the power of sin, on the other hand. The former offers the possibility of freedom, whereas the latter offers only further entrapment in the addictive process. Self-reliance does not offer a solution, for it is the powerlessness of the self in the face of the power of sin that is at the root of the problem.[96]

Thirdly, because the power of sin cannot be conquered by the mind or will alone, we all stand in need of the grace of God if we are to be set free from our enslavement or captivity to it. What this means for the treatment of addiction will be discussed further, below. However, the danger of pursuing a heavily psychological understanding, such as that followed by Theissen, is that freedom from sin becomes ultimately a matter of psychological health, and redemption is to be found in psychotherapy (whether in the guise of Christian faith or in some other form). The danger of pursuing too

---

[96] It is of note that this is at the heart of the philosophy of the Twelve Step programme of AA, which emphasises both the need to recognise powerlessness over alcohol, and also the need to orientate life towards a Higher Power, or God. (See the Twelve Steps of AA, and especially the first three steps; for example, as quoted and discussed in G. Edwards, Marshall and Cook, 2003, pp. 300–303, 306–307).

enthusiastically a heavily Christological understanding, such as that offered by Pauline theology, is that it might appear that freedom from addiction can be found only through Christian faith, whereas it is clear that psychological and other approaches are effective.[97] The nature of this tension is not dissimilar to the tension between pre-Christian and Christian understandings of Romans 7. The one understanding, if over-emphasised, denies ongoing inner conflict in the Christian life, which is clearly not true to Christian experience. The other, if over-emphasised, fails to acknowledge the reality and similarity of the inner conflict experienced by non-Christians, and the uniqueness of the solution to this conflict that is offered by the grace of God in Christ.

## AN AUGUSTINIAN THEOLOGY OF SIN AND ADDICTION

Augustine of Hippo understood a yearning (*desiderium*) for God as being at the heart of Christian faith. He wrote an extensive work on the Trinity, placed a high value on his understanding of the Christian community as the body of Christ, and was increasingly concerned during his lifetime with the proper interpretation of scripture. He was engaged in various religious controversies of his time and argued strongly in various writings against the Manichaeans, the Donatists and the Pelagians.[98]

Augustine understood that all things have been created by God from nothing (*ex nihilo*) and that, as God is good, all things must therefore be good:

Because, therefore, no good things whether great or small, through whatever gradations of things, can exist except from God; but since every nature, so far as it is nature, is good, it follows that no nature can exist save from the most high and true God: because all things even not in the highest degree good, but related to the highest good, and again, because all good things, even those of most recent origin, which are far from the highest good, can have their existence only from the highest good.[99]

Sin, therefore, cannot be a desire for evil things as such, for no things which are evil by nature exist. Sin is, rather, concerned with the misuse of that which is good:

---

[97] G. Edwards, Marshall and Cook, 2003, especially pp. 333–336.

[98] Cross and Livingstone, 1997, pp. 128–130. Brief biographical details have already been provided in Chapter 4, and will not be repeated here.

[99] *Concerning the Nature of Good, Against the Manichaeans*, 1. This, and other quotations here from Augustine's works, are (unless specified otherwise) taken from the Christian Classics Ethereal Library CD-ROM, version 4, Calvin College, Grand Rapids.

Sin is not the striving after an evil nature, but the desertion of a better, and so the deed itself is evil, not the nature which the sinner uses amiss. For it is evil to use amiss that which is good. Whence the apostle reproves certain ones as condemned by divine judgment, 'Who have worshipped and served the creature more than the Creator.'[100] He does not reprove the creature, which he who should do would act injuriously towards the Creator, but those who, deserting the better, have used amiss the good.[101]

Exactly when, in practice, the striving or desire for a lesser good constitutes sin is not entirely clear. The distinction may be concerned with justice, itself derived in turn from the edicts or laws of God; ultimately it is concerned with a turning away from God himself, a failure to love God.[102] The problem is thus not with the existence of evil things – for evil things as such do not 'exist' – but with the inordinate desire of human beings for good but inferior things; in other words, a perversion of desire and will.[103]

For Augustine, sin could be traced back to the rebellion against God of the Devil, and the disobedience of Adam and Eve in the garden of Eden, both acts representing freely made, sinful, choices motivated by pride.[104] The latter act, in particular, was understood by Augustine as being the means by which humans acquired 'original sin'. Original sin was in turn understood as a fundamental change in the human condition imposed by God as a punishment for the sin of Adam. This condition included mortality, pain, fatigability, disease, degeneration with age, and lust. It is a biological condition, genetically transmitted and innate to all human beings.[105] Although it is not fundamentally an impairment of reasoning or will,[106] it is reflected in bad judgements that human beings make, in habits that they develop, and in a disposition to misuse their free will. However, it is also a secondarily acquired condition. It is not fundamentally the way that God created things to be.[107] If sin has become our second nature, it is not our primary nature – which is still good.[108]

McFadyen[109] suggests that there are four corollaries of the doctrine of original sin. First, sin is a contingent but non-necessary consequence of free will. Secondly, sin is more concerned with an enduring human 'condition' or 'situation' than it is with individual sinful acts. Thirdly, sin is

---

[100] Romans 1:25.     [101] *Concerning the Nature of Good, Against the Manichaeans*, 36.

[102] Mann, 2002, pp. 45–46.     [103] Mathewes, 2001, pp. 73, 80; Burnaby, 1991, p. 185.

[104] Mann, 2002, pp. 46–47. Pride is thus the ultimate origin of sin. See also Burnaby, 1991, p. 189.

[105] Mann, 2002, p. 47; McFadyen, 2000, pp. 16, 189–190. However, it has been pointed out that the imposition of modern views of biology upon the thinking of Augustine is an anachronism (Mathewes, 2001, pp. 83–84).

[106] Mann, 2002, p. 47.     [107] Mathewes, 2001, pp. 74–75.     [108] Ibid., p. 81.

[109] McFadyen, 2000, pp. 16–18.

communicated to human beings such that it is present from the very earliest stages of biological being, even before they are capable of self-determining (morally culpable) acts. It is an inheritance of a distortion of personhood and of alienation from God which incurs guilt. Fourthly, sin is a universal human condition and experience. The last three of these corollaries in turn suggest that sin has ontological substance and that it is not primarily concerned with the exercise of human will, but is an inescapable aspect of human being. For many critics, both Christians and others, this renders it unacceptable on both scientific and ethical grounds: on scientific grounds, because the fall is understood as mythological, and on moral grounds, because of a consensus that ethics are concerned with free choices made by responsible, autonomous, personal agents.

For Augustine, sin was identical neither with actions nor with will. Sinful actions were understood as willed.[110] But willing was not to be understood as the neutral selection from available choices – actions are willed under the influence of affection and desire, and a motivation to pursue the good.[111] Furthermore, willing does not depend upon choice. It is possible to will an action, even where there is no choice.[112] For Augustine, freedom was not to be found in withholding oneself from God – for that would be to display pride and to demonstrate bondage to sin in the process of pursuing an inferior representation of the good. Freedom is to be found, therefore, only under the influence of the grace of God, the source of all goodness, where persons are so orientated towards God that their desire, volition and actions are brought into harmony.[113]

Original sin is associated in the work of Augustine with concupiscence. Concupiscence is a loss of control of the spirit over the flesh.[114] Concupiscence is concerned with the overpowering of the rational will by desire, and thus leads to the situation in which the will is 'divided' in the face of competing desires.[115] McFadyen writes: 'Sins of concupiscence are consequently failures in willing actually to pursue that which one would; failures coherently and consistently to instantiate in practice the life-orientation consented to in faith.'[116] In Augustine's understanding, the divided will is the result of concupiscence. Concupiscence is a disorder of desire which is partly biological and partly socially conferred. Even for those who are baptised, their personal history of habit and practice in relation to this disorder of desire will ensure a continuing power and influence of it. But the grace of God, received through baptism, brings a person under the effects

---

[110] Ibid., p. 187.   [111] Ibid., p. 179.   [112] Ibid., pp. 180–184.   [113] Ibid., pp. 184–187.
[114] Burnaby, 1991, p. 208.   [115] McFadyen, 2000, pp. 190–194.   [116] Ibid., p. 192.

of a new power and influence – the grace of God – which disempowers concupiscence. The power of sin can no longer rule unchallenged, and thus the Christian is drawn in two directions.[117]

His interpretation of Paul's theology of grace was in fact fundamental to Augustine's understanding of sin and willing. He understood the necessity of God's grace for human salvation as implying that human beings were fundamentally flawed – that they could not desire or will that which is good without God's action upon them from outside themselves. Nonetheless, he still saw that goodness of the individual as being, in some sense, their own.[118] For Augustine, the grace of God provided both a representation of perfect goodness and also the desire for it.[119] The grace of God thus brings about an orientation towards God such that desire and volition are integrated. Competing attractions are denied their capacity to motivate towards action. Only in this way, according to Augustine, can a person be truly said to be free.[120]

### CONFESSIONS, BOOK VIII: THE DIVIDED WILL

The text which has been selected for special attention here is book VIII of Augustine's *Confessions*. When Augustine wrote his *Confessions*, in about 397 CE, he was both relating an autobiography of his conversion to Christian faith from Manichaeism some eleven years earlier and also rebutting the arguments of the Manichees, whose radical dualism understood there to be not so much a divided will as two minds or substances at work within human experience.[121] He did this in a literary form which was almost without precedent, providing a compelling and inspiring account of the inner subjective experience of a man who strove relentlessly to find philosophical truth.[122]

In *Confessions*, Augustine presents himself as having lived a sinful life until the age of thirty-two years, at which time he was converted to Christianity. However, given his purpose in writing the book, and given his theology of grace and sin, it is quite possible that he tended to exaggerate his own sinfulness prior to conversion. He was clearly keen to persuade his readers that any sanctity he might have, and for which he had in fact gained quite a reputation, was attributable only to the grace of God.[123]

Book VIII of *Confessions* is concerned with Augustine's conversion to Christianity. The book opens with Augustine on the brink of conversion.

[117] Ibid., pp. 192–193.    [118] Ibid., pp. 173–176. See also Bernasconi, 1992, pp. 62–63.
[119] Ibid., pp. 179–180.    [120] Ibid., pp. 184–187.    [121] *Confessions*, VIII, v, 22–24.
[122] O'Donnell, 2002, p. 20.    [123] Pine-Coffin, 1961, pp. 11–18.

It is his reluctance to embrace sexual continence which seems to hold him back. He relates how he was told the story of the conversion of the philosopher Victorinus, and how he was inspired to emulate him, but then found himself prevented:

> I was eager to imitate [Victorinus] . . . for he had found a reason for giving his time wholly to thee. For this was what I was longing to do; but as yet I was bound by the iron chain of my own will. The enemy held fast my will, and had made of it a chain, and had bound me tight with it. For out of the perverse will came lust, and the service of lust ended in habit, and habit, not resisted, became necessity. By these links, as it were, forged together – which is why I called it 'a chain' – a hard bondage held me in slavery. But that new will which had begun to spring up in me freely to worship thee and to enjoy thee, O my God, the only certain Joy, was not able as yet to overcome my former wilfulness, made strong by long indulgence. Thus my two wills – the old and the new, the carnal and the spiritual – were in conflict within me; and by their discord they tore my soul apart.[124]

The obviously autobiographical nature and context of Augustine's account allows more clarity concerning the development of the divided will than does Paul's account of the divided self. Augustine tells us that he developed a new will, which was eager to imitate Victorinus. He perceived this as a joyful experience of freedom to worship God. But this new will came into conflict with an older will – initially described as 'my own will'. This old will he perceived as 'bondage' and 'slavery', and as having been made strong by 'habit' and 'long indulgence'. The two wills are described as being in conflict: a conflict which Augustine portrays as the tearing apart of his soul.

There need be no uncertainty here, as there was in interpreting Romans 7. Augustine was reflecting on a time when he was almost, but not yet, a Christian. He was reflecting upon a new subjective experience – but one which was the outcome of a clash between new experiences, notably his hearing of the conversion of Victorinus, and long-established habits, which he now desired to change.

The relationship between will and desire (or 'lust') is also clear in this passage. Interestingly here, it is desire which arises from will in Augustine's understanding, rather than the other way around. However, it is also clear that it is the 'service of lust' which leads to habit, and the failure to resist habit which leads to 'necessity'. The sequence seems to be: will – desire – behaviour. Where actions are repeated, they lead to habit and a sense of compulsion. Where habit is resisted (implicitly by the will) that sense of compulsion may be broken.

---

[124] *Confessions*, VIII, v, 10.

Augustine interpreted his experience in the light of scripture, quoting specifically from two of Paul's letters.[125] First, he refers to Galatians (5:17), as a basis for interpreting his experience in terms of conflicting desires:

Thus I came to understand from my own experience what I had read, how 'the flesh lusts against the Spirit, and the Spirit against the flesh.'[126] I truly lusted both ways, yet more in that which I approved in myself than in that which I disapproved in myself. For in the latter it was not now really I that was involved, because here I was rather an unwilling sufferer than a willing actor. And yet it was through me that habit had become an armed enemy against me, because I had willingly come to be what I unwillingly found myself to be.[127]

Augustine thus recognised that he desired both to imitate Victorinus and also to remain in his old way of life. He approved of the former desire, which he estimated to be the stronger, but disapproved of the latter. He is now ready to identify the latter desire as 'not now really I', on the basis that he was an 'unwilling sufferer' of that desire, although he recognised that he had played a willing role in bringing it to be. However, the desire to imitate Victorinus is identified with the desire of 'the Spirit' in Galatians 5:17, and the desire to remain in his old way of life is identified with 'the flesh'. In the present context, it is important to note that in Galatians 5:19–21 Paul lists a number of works of the flesh, and that they include drunkenness. For Augustine, the Pauline concept of 'the flesh' was concerned with living for self rather than for God.[128]

Secondly, Augustine refers to Paul's letter to the Romans (7:22–25) as a basis for interpreting his experience as one of captivity of the will:

In vain did I 'delight in thy law in the inner man' while 'another law in my members warred against the law of my mind and brought me into captivity to the law of sin which is in my members.' For the law of sin is the tyranny of habit, by which the mind is drawn and held, even against its will. Yet it deserves to be so held because it so willingly falls into the habit. 'O wretched man that I am! Who shall deliver me from the body of this death' but thy grace alone, through Jesus Christ our Lord?[129]

---

[125]  Augustine also quotes (in VIII, v, 12) from Ephesians 5:14: 'Awake, you who sleep, and arise from the dead, and Christ shall give you light.' This quotation appears to reflect his understanding of the challenge to 'awake' and 'arise' and receive 'light' that was presented by his hearing of the conversion of Victorinus. Our concern here, however, is more with Augustine's interpretation of the inner conflict in which he found himself involved as a result of this challenge.

[126]  In the NRSV, Galatians 5:17 reads: 'For what the flesh desires is opposed to the Spirit, and what the Spirit desires is opposed to the flesh; for these are opposed to each other, to prevent you from doing what you want.'

[127]  *Confessions*, VIII, v, 11.      [128]  This is discussed further in Chapter 4.

[129]  *Confessions*, VIII, v, 12.

Augustine particularly draws here on Paul's tension between the law of God in the inner man (or mind), and the law of sin in his 'members'. He explicitly understands the latter law as the 'tyranny of habit' which brings the mind into captivity against its own will. It is easy to assume here that he conceives of the law of sin as operating at the level of purely bodily desire (in the 'members'), but things cannot be this simple, for he clearly recognises that this 'tyranny' was *willingly* entered into. In other words, the will is brought into captivity by means of its own complicity with, and failure to resist, the formation of habit.

Augustine goes on to relate how he was told of the conversion of two agents of the Emperor,[130] and how this threw him into a state of turmoil and self-loathing.[131] This led him eventually to a further description of the inner conflict that he experienced:

The mind commands the mind to will, and yet though it be itself it does not obey itself. Whence this strange anomaly and why should it be? I repeat: The will commands itself to will, and could not give the command unless it wills; yet what is commanded is not done. But actually the will does not will entirely; therefore it does not command entirely. For as far as it wills, it commands. And as far as it does not will, the thing commanded is not done. For the will commands that there be an act of will – not another, but itself. But it does not command entirely. Therefore, what is commanded does not happen; for if the will were whole and entire, it would not even command it to be, because it would already be. It is, therefore, no strange anomaly partly to will and partly to be unwilling. This is actually an infirmity of mind, which cannot wholly rise, while pressed down by habit, even though it is supported by the truth. And so there are two wills, because one of them is not whole, and what is present in this one is lacking in the other.[132]

It becomes clear here that Augustine understood himself as possessing two wills in opposition to each other. The one will commanded that his mind should will that he follow the example of Victorinus. This was evident in his consciousness of 'commanding' himself to do the same. The other will was his unwillingness to follow Victorinus. This was evident in the fact that the 'command' was not actually obeyed. He understands this state of affairs as reflecting an 'infirmity of mind' in which there are two partial wills, neither of which is 'entire' or 'whole'.

However, this interpretation does not seem to do full justice to the subjective state that Augustine describes here, for he also puts most of the emphasis on one of these wills, in such a way that only one is referred to here as a will as such, and the other is an *un*willingness to implement it.

---

[130] *Confessions*, VIII, vi, 15.  [131] *Confessions*, VIII, vii, 16–18.  [132] *Confessions*, VIII, ix, 21.

It is really the one will with which Augustine is most concerned, which is 'supported by the truth' but 'pressed down by habit'. It is true that, owing to the latter influence, it is only a 'partial' will, which commands something that does not happen. If it were a complete will, the command to follow Victorinus would be implemented, and there would be only one will, where will and action were one and the same. The will would then not 'command' itself at all – for what was willed would simply happen. However, because it is only a partial will, the will finds itself commanding itself to do something, which does not happen. This understanding has close parallels with Harry Frankfurt's[133] distinction between first- and second-order volitions (or desires), where Augustine's will to follow Victorinus might be understood as a second-order volition, and his unwillingness to do so as a first-order volition to remain in his old way of life. This model will be discussed further below.

Augustine continued to describe his state of inner conflict as both partial willingness and partial unwillingness. He recognised, on the one hand, that willingness and unwillingness were both aspects of his own mind and self, such that he was 'at war' with himself and 'torn apart'. But, on the other hand, and with further allusions to Romans 7 (this time to v. 17), he understood the unwillingness as being no longer himself, but rather the 'sin that dwelt in [him]':

While I was deliberating whether I would serve the Lord my God now, as I had long purposed to do, it was I who willed and it was also I who was unwilling. In either case, it was I. I neither willed with my whole will nor was I wholly unwilling. And so I was at war with myself and torn apart by myself. And this strife was against my will; yet it did not show the presence of another mind, but the punishment of my own. Thus it was no more I who did it, but the sin that dwelt in me – the punishment of a sin freely committed by Adam, and I was a son of Adam.[134]

There is a clear implication here of the effects of original sin – the 'punishment of a sin freely committed by Adam' – which now exerted its influence upon Augustine, such that he did not do that which he wanted to do.

With further echoes of the Pauline understanding of the Christian as caught in a tension between two epochs, or powers, Augustine summarised his own state of conflict in more general terms:

When eternity attracts us from above, and the pleasure of earthly delight pulls us down from below, the soul does not will either the one or the other with all its force, but still it is the same soul that does not will this or that with a united will,

---

[133] Stump, 2002, pp. 126–127.    [134] *Confessions*, VIII, x, 22.

and is therefore pulled apart with grievous perplexities, because for truth's sake it prefers this, but for custom's sake it does not lay that aside.[135]

Augustine therefore saw himself, along with all human beings who are attracted by 'eternity . . . from above', as being drawn into a state of inner conflict generated by a tension between that force of heavenly attraction and an opposing force 'from below'. The force from above was represented for Augustine by the life that Victorinus had adopted – a life given wholly to God. The force from below seems to have much in common with Paul's understanding of 'the flesh', but it is concerned also with Augustine's doctrine of original sin, and further with the influence of a lifetime of 'habit' which binds people to ways of life that they might (at least partially) wish to break away from.

It may be argued that Augustine saw the will as not so much divided as 'partial', or incomplete, or held captive. Or again, it may be argued that he saw the inner conflict generated within people as a result of the competing attractions of 'eternity' and 'earthly delight' as being concerned with two conflicting wills, or perhaps between willingness and unwillingness. However, overall, Augustine's understanding of the will in the state of inner conflict associated with his desire to give his life wholly to God, as Victorinus had done, would seem to be well described as being a 'divided will', and it is this term which will be used here.

Whatever terminology one may wish to use, it is clear that this state of inner conflict was associated, at least in Augustine's experience, with a strong affective component. Distraught, he went aside to weep, alone, beneath a fig tree in a garden. It was then that he heard a child playing, and chanting: 'Pick it up, read it; pick it up, read it.'[136] Interpreting this as a divine command to read scripture, he picked up a Bible and read Romans 13:13:

I snatched it up, opened it, and in silence read the paragraph on which my eyes first fell: 'Not in rioting and drunkenness, not in chambering and wantonness, not in strife and envying, but put on the Lord Jesus Christ, and make no provision for the flesh to fulfil the lusts thereof.' I wanted to read no further, nor did I need to. For instantly, as the sentence ended, there was infused in my heart something like the light of full certainty and all the gloom of doubt vanished away.[137]

Thus, book VIII of *Confessions* concludes with Augustine's conversion to faith in Christ.

---

[135] *Confessions*, VIII, x, 24.    [136] *Confessions*, VIII, xii, 29.    [137] Ibid.

### Addiction as divided will

Eleonore Stump,[138] and others, have interpreted Augustine's understanding of the divided will in terms of Frankfurt's distinction between first- and second-order desires and volitions. First-order desires are simply 'desires to do or not to do one thing or another'. Second-order desires are concerned with wanting 'to have (or not to have) certain desires and motives'. Second-order desires thus require a capacity for 'reflective self-evaluation'.[139] For Frankfurt, the will is understood as *effective* desire', and is thus a desire expressed in motivation for action.[140] A first-order volition is an action or intention to action motivated by a first-order desire. A second-order volition is concerned, however, with wanting a particular first-order desire to be the will, whether or not it actually is, and it is this which, for Frankfurt, is essential to the concept of personhood.[141] According to this understanding, Augustine's awareness of the will commanding itself[142] was a description of a second-order volition. According to this understanding also, the will may variously be divided against itself – at first or second-order levels, or between first- and second-order levels.[143]

Both Stump and Frankfurt provide examples concerned with addiction, and indeed addiction appears to provide the almost quintessential example of conflict between first- and second-order volitions.

For Frankfurt,[144] the narcotic addict may have first-order desires both to take the drug, and not to take it. The former is in both cases, more or less, generated by physiological dependency upon the drug. The 'unwilling addict', however, also has a second-order volition to stop taking the drug, and therefore identifies self with this first-order desire, while withdrawing from the first-order desire to continue using the drug:

It is in virtue of this identification and withdrawal, accomplished through the formation of a second order volition, that the unwilling addict may meaningfully make the analytically puzzling statements that the force moving him to take the drug is a force other than his own, and that it is not of his own free will but rather against his will that this force moves him to take it.[145]

Frankfurt contrasts the 'unwilling addict' with the 'wanton addict'. The latter lacks either the capacity or interest for evaluating desires self-reflectively. In the case of the wanton addict, whichever first-order desire is stronger will win but, whichever desire does win, this addict will have no personal sense of winning or losing a struggle at all. Indeed, according to Frankfurt,

---

[138] Stump, 2002, pp. 126–127.  [139] Frankfurt, 1971, p. 7.  [140] Ibid., p. 8.
[141] Ibid., p. 10.  [142] *Confessions*, VIII, ix.  [143] Stump, 2002, p. 126.
[144] Frankfurt, 1971, pp. 12–14.  [145] Ibid., p. 13.

the wanton addict does not have the characteristics of a *person* at all. However, Frankfurt also considers the possibility of a third type of addict: the 'willing addict'. The willing addict has both a second-order volition and a first-order volition to take the drug. According to Frankfurt, it is therefore possible to understand a personal state of addiction in which first- and second-order desires do not come into conflict, and in which the will is therefore not divided.

Frankfurt's proposition of the willing addict is actually put forward in the course of an argument concerning freedom of the will, and it presupposes that there are no first-order volitions to discontinue drug use which might provide a source of conflict with the second-order volition to continue drug use. In fact, research on the alcohol dependence syndrome makes clear that such first-order volitions almost certainly will arise, since psychological, social and biological harm associated with the dependent pattern of use is likely to motivate cessation of drug use, or at least reduction of use. However, the phenomenon of salience (as an element of the dependence syndrome) reflects the observation that all types of addicts (willing, unwilling or wanton) do in fact tend to implement first-order volitions to continue drug use despite first-order volitions to discontinue. It would therefore appear likely in practice that established addiction will be associated with at least a degree of division of the will, both at the level of competing first-order volitions, and between the levels of first- and second-order volitions, whether an addict is willing or unwilling. However, it remains possible that the willing addict may experience no such internal conflict. Such a possibility may in fact be realised relatively frequently in the early stages of development of the dependence syndrome, when first-order volitions to reduce or discontinue drug use may be less frequently encountered. But, as Frankfurt suggests, this is in fact a state of 'overdetermination' of the first-order desire for drug use.[146] This would seem likely to reinforce the dependent pattern of drug use, and thus pave the way for a later conflict between first- and second-order volitions if and when the second-order volition should change from that of a 'willing' to that of an 'unwilling' addict. It is also highly consonant with Augustine's understanding, both of the willingness of the self in generation of the internal conflict, and of the part played by habit. Recall, for example, his statement that

the law of sin is the tyranny of habit, by which the mind is drawn and held, even against its will. Yet it deserves to be so held because it so willingly falls into the habit.[147]

---

[146] Ibid., pp. 19–20.    [147] *Confessions*, VIII, v, 12.

Stump provides a very similar example of addiction, concerned with a smoker who wants to give up smoking.[148] Again, there is a powerful first-order volition, this time to continue smoking, in conflict with a second-order volition to stop. However, Stump's purpose in analysing this example is different from Frankfurt's. In particular, she is concerned primarily with resolving the tension between grace and free will in Augustine's thought. The question here is about where the second-order volition of faith might arise from. Is it implanted as an act of God, by grace, and therefore not ultimately an act of will of the individual at all, or is it an act of free will of the individual? This is a fundamental problem in Augustine's work, where it would seem that he wishes to insist both that the grace of God is the sole source of human goodness and faith, and also that human beings have free will and thus responsibility for the evil that they commit.

Stump considers the imaginative possibilities of a technical device which might be operated by the smoker, so as to bring about a first-order volition not to smoke, or a neurosurgeon who might be able to perform an operation with the same effect. In either case, where the device is active at the smoker's behest, or the operation is undertaken only with the smoker's consent, it may be argued that the ultimate determinant of the outcome is the free will of the individual concerned.[149] The device is arguably not dissimilar to the action of certain 'anti-craving' drugs which are currently the subject of research in the field of alcohol dependence.[150]

Stump argues that Augustine understands God as willing to give grace to those who ask in such a way that God is analogous to the technical device or the neurosurgeon.[151] In this way, Augustine's understanding of the necessity of the grace of God might appear to have been retained along with an understanding of the free will of the individual in asking for that grace. However, the problem simply recurs at the level of the second-order volition. If the second-order volition is also given by God, human free will would appear to be only illusory.

A full analysis of this problem is not directly relevant to the purpose of this book. However, the question still arises of an appropriate

---

[148] Stump, 2002, pp. 127–130.

[149] This assumes, of course, that causal determinism is rejected, and that the possibility of indeterminate actions resulting from the exercise of free will is accepted.

[150] E.g. Acamprosate and naltrexone (G. Edwards, Marshall and Cook, 2003, pp. 328–331). The device is also not dissimilar to another pharmacological treatment for alcohol dependence, namely disulfiram. Disulfiram confers an aversive response when alcohol is consumed, and thus assists patients in maintaining abstinence. A decision to take disulfiram is thus a second-order volition, but the drug does not reduce craving and therefore does not actually remove the first-order desire to drink. (See review: Hughes and Cook, 1997.)

[151] Stump, 2002, p. 133.

understanding of the nature of the relationship between grace and free will in any theological response to the problem of addiction. If the divided will of Augustine's experience in coming to Christian faith is in principle the same as the divided will of the addicted person, what does this mean for our understanding of the latter? More specifically, is the addict, ultimately, dependent only upon the grace of God for freedom from this state of conflict or captivity, or does personal choice and free will also play a part?

First, it is surely now clear that a second-order volition to stop drinking, smoking, drug use, or any other addictive pattern of behaviour, would appear to be essential if a pattern of addictive behaviour is to be broken. The 'willing addict' that Frankfurt envisaged would seem very unlikely indeed ever to change his or her addictive behaviour. One could perhaps imagine strong first-order volitions which might develop, perhaps as a result of the biological, psychological and social harms of drinking, which might set up a division of the will between a second-order volition to continue drinking and a first-order volition to stop. Indeed, such cases are sometimes encountered in clinical practice. However, the prognosis in such cases (from the perspective of abstinence as a 'good' outcome) is, in my experience, usually poor. The will is divided not only between first- and second-order volitions, but also at the level of opposing first-order divisions. The addictive behaviour is strongly over-determined and is unlikely to change, except perhaps on a temporary basis.

Secondly, any solution to the problem of addiction must take account of the seriousness of the internal conflict which the divided will represents. If it were easy, of one's own volition, to break free from this experience of conflict, incompleteness and captivity of the will, it would not represent the source of turmoil that it clearly presented to Augustine and which it similarly presents to the addict. As Augustine so vividly portrays, and as Frankfurt so logically argues, the will to adhere to familiar patterns of behaviour, reinforced by habit, and made all the more compelling by physiological processes that strengthen desire, can be a formidable obstacle to behavioural change. But is this the only obstacle, or is this obstacle adequately understood in this way alone?

Thirdly, then, the analysis of Frankfurt, orientated as it is towards a concern with philosophical issues of personhood and free will, surely neglects important aspects of Augustine's theology. In book VIII of *Confessions*, Augustine is preoccupied with a Pauline tension between the 'flesh' and the 'Spirit', the competing powers of the 'law of sin' and God's law, and the competing attractions of 'eternity' and 'earthly delight'. He understands human beings as suffering the consequences of original sin, such that without the grace of God they are caught in a subjective experience of being unable to break free from the power of sin, habit and earthly delight. Or – for our present purposes – individuals caught in a pattern of addictive behaviour find that they need more than just their own willpower if they are to break free.

Fourthly, Stump proposes a possible solution to Augustine's dilemma concerning libertarianism and grace, which is understood in terms of an analysis of the options available to human beings in response to the grace that God offers.[152] She suggests that refusal and assent are only two possibilities, and that it is also open to human beings to adopt a neutral position of non-refusal and non-assent. If we understand human beings as being normally in a state of continuous refusal of grace, by virtue of original sin, then they might still be able to cease refusing grace, and thus receive it, even though they are otherwise unable to actively request it or assent to it. Thus, the second-order volition of faith might be understood as entirely the gift of God, but also dependent upon the free will of an individual to cease refusing it. Perhaps a similar understanding might be helpful in the specific case of addiction?

If we imagine that the addict is positively held, or attracted in some way, not just by a neutral choice between first-order desires, but by a nature which is in some way biased against the very thing that a second-order volition ought to choose – both for the longer-term benefit of the self, and for the benefit of others who suffer as a result of the addiction – we come closer both to the experience of addiction and to Augustine's account of the divided will. For Augustine, this division, captivity or incompleteness of the will could be mended only by the grace of God. For many alcoholics who follow the Twelve Step programme of Alcoholics Anonymous (AA), experience has suggested that it can be mended only by a 'Power greater than [them]selves'.[153] In either case, it was not so much that a first-order volition was suddenly made in favour of freedom, as that the individual (Augustine or the alcoholic respectively) ceased making a second-order volition to continue in their existing way of life. Thus, Augustine became open to a second-order volition of faith, conferred by the grace of God. Thus the alcoholic becomes open to a second-order volition for abstinence, conferred (using the language of AA) by a Power greater than self.[154]

---

[152] Ibid., pp. 139–142.

[153] The second step of the Twelve Steps of AA (G. Edwards, Marshall and Cook, 2003, p. 302).

[154] The third of the Twelve Steps of AA refers to the making of 'a decision to turn our will and our lives over to the care of God' (G. Edwards, Marshall and Cook, 2003, p. 302).

It would therefore appear to be the case that Augustine's experience of the divided (or captive or incomplete) will shows strong parallels with the subjective experience of addiction. Indeed, if we accept the analyses of Frankfurt and Stump, both Augustine's experience of struggling with the decision to adopt sexual continence in order to give his life wholly to God, and the experience of the alcoholic struggling to stop drinking, are identical experiences of inner conflict between first- and second-order volitions. Furthermore, in his understanding of the significance of the words of Romans 13:13, Augustine himself seems implicitly to have recognised that his struggle with sexual desire was similar to a desire for drunkenness, although the latter was not a desire with which he struggled. But is there not also an important difference? Augustine was concerned primarily with a spiritual and religious decision (whether or not to become a Christian), which had behavioural and psycho-social implications (celibacy). The alcoholic is concerned primarily with a behavioural decision (whether or not to abstain), which has bio-psycho-social implications (withdrawal symptoms, craving, stigma, etc.). These decisions are of a qualitatively different kind, and present different challenges.

For a decision to convert to Christianity, a theology of grace might well be an essential part of the healing of a divided will. But is it equally necessary in the case of alcoholism? Are pharmacological and psychological treatments, informed by the natural, behavioural and social sciences, not sufficient?

For Augustine, the distinction here would be quite unrecognisable. The initial psychological barrier to his conversion seems to have been primarily concerned with his desire for sexual fulfilment. But, for him, this was little different from other desires of the flesh, including drunkenness, which might equally have held him back from giving his life wholly to God. Similarly, all such desires ultimately present the same challenge. Will life be fulfilled by striving for the highest good, or will it be subject to concupiscence, and thus characterised by a divided, captive, will? For Augustine, the solution to this dilemma was to be found in the grace of God, which alone provided a route to freedom.

For contemporary clinicians, social scientists, neuroscientists, counsellors and psychotherapists in western society, however, the distinction is very recognisable indeed. Religion has been relegated to the private domain, and theology is not admitted to participation in secular discourse on such matters. Conversion to Christianity and therapy for alcohol dependence are either completely unrelated matters, or at least should be addressed in different conversations, according to different rules. The former is the province of those who constitute a community of faith, and the latter the province of those who constitute the community of science. The latter can be addressed without addressing the former, and *vice versa*. Scientific outcome studies would appear to support this contention. Therapies of various kinds are apparently equally successful as treatments for alcohol dependence, and Christian faith does not appear to be an essential prerequisite for a good outcome.

However, the distinction that Augustine fails to recognise, and that post-Enlightenment western society insists upon, is perhaps more real than the former could have realised, and more illusory than the latter cares to allow.

For embodied persons such as human beings, the neurochemistry of craving, lust and other biological drives is a very significant consideration indeed, about which Augustine can have suspected little and known nothing. Where 'anti-craving' drugs offer a therapeutic opportunity to modify or eliminate such drives, they offer an opportunity for at least partial freedom for a captive will. Similarly, psychological treatments such as motivational interviewing might be understood to be offering support for fragile first- or second-order volitions for abstinence or moderation. In this sense, we might wish to reverse Stump's analogy, and suggest that such treatments are analogous to the part played by God in Augustine's conversion, rather than the other way around. They are certainly, however, at least in a limited sense, a means of grace. They offer an opportunity of freedom which individuals could not have achieved for themselves, which is based upon the intervention of an external (therapeutic) power. But all such interventions are focussed only on the solution to a particular problem – that of alcohol dependence. They do not offer any broader understanding of what it means to be a creature with a 'divided will' – or (in Frankfurt's terms) what it means to be a 'person'.

But, on the other hand, the phenomenon of addiction may be much more closely related to a broader human experience of division of the will and thus (if Frankfurt is correct) personhood than many contemporary scientists and therapists might readily admit. From this perspective, a focus upon addiction as somehow apart from 'normal' human experience may be very unhelpful. Perhaps addiction is, after all, simply one example of the many and varied ways in which different human beings struggle with a sense of wishing to be something other (or rather better) than that which they actually find themselves to be. And if this struggle is, after all, as Augustine suggested in relation to his own experience, ultimately therefore a personal struggle for the highest good, it is necessarily also a religious, or at least spiritual, matter and not a purely scientific one. In this case, the nature of the struggle itself, the very recognition of the division, captivity and limitations of the human will, would appear to beg the assistance of all that is ultimately good in achieving that which is personally the highest achievable good. In other words, the nature of the struggle implicitly recognises the need for grace as the means of finding freedom and wholeness.

## DEPENDENCE AND SIN: TOWARDS A THEOLOGICAL MODEL OF ADDICTION

Having, in Chapter 2, briefly reviewed the alcohol dependence syndrome as a scientific interpretation of the concept of addiction, and having in this chapter considered the ways in which Pauline and Augustinian theologies (as exemplified in two selected texts) might shed light upon the subjective experience of addiction, what may we now say about the possibilities for a Christian theological model of addiction?

### *A theological model is not a resurrection of the moral model!*

Although drunkenness has always been understood as an ethical concern of the Christian tradition, the moral model of addiction has suffered from unhelpful emphases and diverse interpretations. The most unhelpful perceived emphasis would appear to be in placing the blame mostly or entirely upon the individual drinker, as though it were a simple matter of 'telling [other] people not to do it'. This approach does not do justice to the complexity of this bio-psycho-social problem, and neither does it show understanding of, or sympathy for, the subjective plight of the drinker who suffers from the alcohol dependence syndrome. However, it is also extremely unfortunate that the notion of a 'moral model' has become so unpopular in relation to a contemporary social problem which has enormous ethical implications – not merely on the part of the individual drinker, but in terms of the whole context of the production, sale and consumption of alcohol, and the consequences of the same, within society as a whole. A more sophisticated ethical analysis of this complex system is, in the view of the present author, urgently needed.

This chapter does not provide that analysis, at least not comprehensively, and it is not an attempt to reintroduce the old moral model. Indeed, it suggests that a model which conceives of either morality or addiction as being concerned simply with freely made choices on the part of an impartial moral agent is simply unrealistic. However, it does seek to explore some of the possibilities for constructing a Christian theological model of addiction. This in turn is of potentially great importance for a Christian ethical analysis of this serious contemporary problem. A theological model of addiction is not at all the same thing as the old moral model – but it certainly does offer an important contribution to moral and ethical debate.

### Recognition of the contribution of theology to discourse on addiction

Over a period of almost eighteen centuries, Christian theology came to provide one of the main foundations for understanding the problem of drunkenness in western society. Over the last century, theology has been largely excluded from public discourse on alcohol-related matters, but it is argued here that theology still has a significant contribution to make to discourse about addiction. Addiction is concerned with some fundamental aspects of human experience with which Christian theology is also concerned. As with McFadyen's analysis of the Holocaust and the sexual abuse of children, theology also offers both descriptive and explanatory power. This is particularly evident in terms of the Pauline account of the divided self, and the Augustinian account of the divided will, both of which show significant parallels with the subjective experience of addiction. The Pauline and Augustinian accounts emphasise aspects of the experience of addiction that have been neglected, or only partially explained, in secular discourse. In particular, theology draws attention to aspects of addiction which relate to universal human experiences of self-reflection, internal conflict and choice. It sets these considerations in a broader, theistic, context and shows how such experiences are not properly understood in terms either of causal determinism or of completely free human agents who make completely free, self-determined choices.

### Recognition of addiction as one manifestation of the human condition

While the alcohol-dependent person may have experienced cravings, withdrawal symptoms, affective states or other 'pathological' experiences, the model that is suggested by the present exploration of Pauline and Augustinian theology is not that of the uniqueness of the subjective experience of addiction so much as that of its universality. In other words, there are aspects of the subjective experience of addiction which are common to the human experience of personhood. In particular, human persons have a capacity to be self-reflective and to will to change, but also experience a power of resistance to that change which appears as though contrary to their own will.

Does this mean that addiction does not constitute any kind of disorder or disease at all? It is certainly difficult to see how, in theological terms, it can be construed as qualitatively different from the normal range of human experience. However, that is not to say that there are not important scientific discriminators. Just as personality disorders are understood as matters of clinical concern, representing as they do the statistical extremes of normal human personality traits, even though they may not strictly be diseases or illnesses at all,[155] perhaps addictive disorders are at least *disorders* in some statistical and scientific sense. However, the danger in this argument lies in Frankfurt's contention that secondary volitions are distinctive to personhood. This argument might, therefore, make it appear as though some people are more fully *people* than others (as indeed Frankfurt's discussion of the wanton addict does appear to be in danger of implying).

Perhaps the difference, therefore, lies not so much in fundamental qualitative or quantitative differences between the subjective inner conflict of addiction as compared with the similar inner conflicts experienced by Paul, Augustine and others, but rather in the focus and scope of the conflict(s). As discussed briefly above, individual differences in the ways in which subjective desires such as lust or craving for alcohol are mediated at the neurochemical level may be more important in determining the nature and range of subjective human experience than Augustine or Paul ever could have imagined. However, both Paul and Augustine do appear to have recognised a range of difference vices as being essentially manifestations of the same underlying weakness of the flesh (e.g. the 'revelling and drunkenness . . . debauchery and licentiousness. . . quarrelling and jealousy' of Romans 13:13). This leaves much scope to understand environmental and genetic differences which might make different individuals more or less vulnerable to internal conflict in some areas than in others (e.g. to alcohol dependence rather than quarrelling, or to nicotine dependence rather than sexual licentiousness).

It may therefore be the case, not so much that addiction is the universal human condition (as, for example, Lenters[156] would have us believe), as that the subjective experience of division of will and self is universal, and is experienced in different ways by different people. For one person it may be experienced in the domain of a struggle with alcohol dependence, and for another (as, perhaps, with Augustine) in the domain of grappling with sexual desire. For one person, the struggle may in some sense be identified as 'addiction' (traditionally this would have been by virtue of drug

---

[155] P. Hill, Murray and Thorley, 1987, pp. 197–198.    [156] See Chapter 2, pp. 18–19.

dependence) and in another it might not be (e.g. the habitual quarreller). In some cases, biological predisposition might be strong, and biological features of tolerance and withdrawal might be predominant (e.g. in alcohol dependence) and in other cases, the pattern of behaviour might appear much more psychological in both aetiology and presentation (e.g. in forms of behaviour such as 'pathological shopping').[157] In other cases (e.g. sexual behaviour) it might be much more debatable whether to construe the struggle as a behavioural 'addiction' or simply as habitual behaviour.

Perhaps the key lesson here is that we may all identify with the essential subjective experience of addiction in one area of our lives or another, but that this does not mean to say that we are all 'addicted' in any scientific or sociological sense. The universality of the human experience is such that none of us should feel able to look down on the addict, as though we were morally superior. On the other hand, this understanding does not construe addiction (in any scientific or sociological sense) as being a universal human disorder. Not everyone suffers from the alcohol dependence syndrome – or indeed any dependence syndrome at all.

## *Pauline and Augustinian understandings of the power of sin*

One of the features of the theological understandings of both Paul and Augustine which may be considered most objectionable in secular discourse about addiction is that of the power of sin. And yet, it is also this theology of sin which seems to provide a better account of the experience of addiction than do purely scientific theses. Both Paul and Augustine understood sin as exerting a power over people such that their moral choices are distorted and impaired. At the same time, the weakness of the flesh, and concupiscence, tend to make human beings vulnerable to this power, such that they make morally wrong judgements and misuse their free will. In short, sin tends to enslave and to bring people into captivity to self-indulgence. Original sin and concupiscence, according to Augustine, are biologically acquired. But sin also affects social relationships and is socially effected. As McFadyen eloquently shows in the context of the Holocaust and child sexual abuse, sin can so permeate the social environment that it engages as willing participants those who are its victims. Those who are not morally culpable in the usual secular sense become engaged as active participants in the very processes of injustice and immorality of which they are themselves victims.

---

[157] Glatt and Cook, 1987.

This would seem to offer a very good description of the way in which biological, psychological and social processes contribute to the pathology of addiction. Inherited predispositions to alcohol dependence combine with social pressures to conform to a heavy drinking culture, and with the psychological power of habit in such a way that people are innocently drawn into dependent patterns of drinking which they then actively seek to continue, even to their own detriment and that of those around them. In this sense there is an apparent 'power' of addictive behaviour which seems to enslave and to bring people into captivity. Thus dependent drinkers find that they hide their drinking, and sacrifice those people and things which they hold as valuable at the altar of that which has enslaved them.

The present argument is intended to imply neither the objective reality of evil powers nor their demythologisation. What is inherent to the present discussion is that sin is experienced as a power which adversely influences human choice and decision-making, and which engages people in the very processes which bring about their own enslavement. This would indeed also appear to provide a good account of the processes of addiction.

## *The internal struggle: divisions of self and will*

The exploration of the parallels between addiction and sin which has been undertaken here has focussed especially upon subjective experience. It has been argued that the experience of the divided self in Romans 7, and the experience of the divided will in book VIII of Augustine's *Confessions*, both provide accounts of subjective experiences which have many features in common with the subjective experience of addiction. While these accounts are both primarily theological, the philosophical analysis and contemporary language and terminology of Frankfurt are also helpful in clarifying the nature of the division of the will which is experienced in addictive disorders such as alcohol dependence, and which is also to be found in Augustine's account of his personal journey to conversion to Christianity. Frankfurt further argues that this capacity to self-reflect and to make second-order volitions is at the heart of what it means to be a person. Perhaps, then, the possibility of addiction is inherent in the human experience of personhood.

Theologically, this internal conflict is made possible by the meeting of concupiscence and original sin with the grace of God in the experience of individual human beings. Human beings do not make decisions about life with full knowledge of their consequences, and neither do they do so in a completely neutral and rational way. The weakness of human beings (in their *flesh*) is easily drawn by the power of sin towards self-indulgence and a form of religion which is self-serving, but also radically self-enslaving. On the other hand, at least according to Augustine and Paul, they have the opportunity to serve God, and in so doing to experience freedom. Only in this way may desire, volition and action be brought into harmony and the divisions of the will be healed. Human beings thus face a choice between two competing powers, or (to use the language of Theissen) tribunals. We are not neutral agents (perhaps most especially we are not when we imagine that we are) – we will be drawn into the sphere of influence of one or the other. The one will enslave, and the other will bring freedom.

McFadyen has developed this theme in terms of worship and idolatry. Worship of God, which might appear at first to be a form of slavery, is actually characterised in Augustinian theology as life-enriching and as a state of 'loving joy'. Idolatry, as worship of anything that is not God, acts to block and disorientate joy. Alcohol dependence, with its narrowing of the repertoire of enjoyment of alcohol, its salience of alcohol over other (more highly valued) people and things, and its subjective compulsion towards harmful behaviour is just such an orientation of life under the power of sin. For the willing addict, this may initially not offer a source of conflict. However, for the unwilling addict who is attracted (to use Pauline and Augustinian terminology) by the grace of God, an experience of division of the will must arise. The pattern of behaviour which has been the object of willing consent then becomes understood as a habit which enslaves. The will which was identified as 'self' becomes understood as 'now not really I' and the 'true' self is understood as an unwilling sufferer, held captive by the power of sin.

### The search for the highest good

Augustine's search for the highest good is the essential context to an understanding of the turmoil of his divided will in Book VIII of *Confessions*. For Augustine, perfect freedom was to be found only in a proper orientation towards God. For Paul also, Christ was everything, to be sought above all other things which (in comparison) he regarded as 'rubbish'.[158] It is in this context that these two men have left us with their accounts of the divided self and the divided will. Can such a single-minded existential quest be expected of those who merely seek to be free from the life-restricting influence of alcohol dependence?

---

[158] Philippians 3:8.

It is of importance to note that the Twelve Step programme of AA does indeed require that life be turned over to God (Step 3) and that conscious contact be sought with him through prayer and meditation (Step 11). In his history of AA, Ernest Kurtz emphasises the importance to alcoholics in AA of recognising that they are 'not God'.[159] Something beyond the self, something transcendent of the self, seems to have been recognised by the founders of AA as being necessary for recovery from alcoholism. However, it is clear that the treatment of alcohol dependence is not always associated with this transcendent goal. Perhaps, for those who recover through other means, it is merely necessary to acknowledge pursuit of a *higher* good than the state of alcohol dependence in which they have found themselves entrapped. However, the second-order volition that would seem to be necessary to any kind of recovery would appear to require acknowledgement at least of this – that individuals desire something better, something other, than that they remain dependent upon alcohol.

## The need for grace

We thus come, at last, to the acknowledgement of both Paul and Augustine that only the grace of God provides a way out of the inner conflict of the division of self and will. It would seem inherent to the experience of Paul, Augustine, and the founders of AA that they each faced an awareness that they could not 'will' themselves out of the captivity in which they found themselves held.

For Paul, the solution was to be found in an assertion of eschatological hope, founded upon faith in the uniqueness of the gracious act of God in Jesus Christ. For Augustine, it was only by an act of the grace of God that he was able to 'put on the Lord Jesus Christ' at last. For the founders of AA, it was a recognition that they had to turn over their lives to God, as they understood him.

For Augustine, a lifetime of struggling to understand what had happened failed to address the paradox presented by his conviction that faith in Christ was both a matter of free choice and also wholly the grace of God. Perhaps Stump's analysis of this problem provides at least a partial answer in terms of the need for the person with a divided will to stop resisting the grace of God, so that God may then graciously confer a second-order volition of faith. Similarly, for the alcohol-dependent person, at least an end to the second-order volition to continue drinking would seem to be a necessary prelude

[159] Kurtz, 1991, pp. 3–4.

to finding a second-order volition to stop drinking. But is something more than this required?

It is suggested here that a theological model of addiction must follow Paul and Augustine in recognising the need for the grace of God in recovery from addiction. Perhaps there are those who find recovery without recognising this need. But the whole dynamic of the division of self and will is concerned with human weakness in the face of the power of sin. The sense of powerlessness of will that is inherent in the experience of a divided will is such that it requires an individual at least to look towards something higher than self as offering a way out. Even if this is not the *highest* good, it must needs be a *Higher* Power. The nature of the struggle implicitly recognises the need for grace – or at least something which looks very much like it – as the means of finding freedom and wholeness.

# CHAPTER 7

# *Alcohol, addiction and Christian ethics*

I hope that the previous six chapters will not have left the reader in any doubt concerning the serious nature of the actual and potential harms that alcohol has presented, and continues to present, to individuals and society. These harms, especially in recent years, have often been presented primarily and pragmatically as a challenge to health care and public policy, and there is no doubt that they do indeed offer a very major challenge to clinicians, researchers and policy-makers. But what is the ethical and theological nature of this challenge? And do the Christian resources of scripture, tradition and theological reason that have been explored in the earlier chapters of this book offer us a valuable resource for a contemporary response to this challenge?

In this chapter, I will attempt to employ the conclusions and implications of previous chapters in order that they might inform a theological model of alcohol use and addiction which is both scientifically informed and ethically informative. In support of this endeavour, a number of considerations arising from the earlier chapters of the book might helpfully be identified at the outset:

1. Social and scientific constructions of addiction have historically been subject to change. While modern scientific understandings of addiction might with good reason be considered better, and more objectively evidence-based, than those that have gone before, we do not know what future scientific research will reveal. Furthermore, a plurality of concepts of addiction is in operation in the world today.

2. It is clear that alcohol 'misuse', addiction and other alcohol-related harms cannot be treated completely separately from social and (apparently) harm-free alcohol use by individuals and groups. A theological and ethical analysis must address both the individual and population perspectives of alcohol use and alcohol-related harm.

3. A Christian theological and ethical analysis of the subjective experience of addiction must recognise both human freedom to choose and also

the apparent impairments, restrictions and limitations of that freedom. A soteriological understanding of the grace of Christ as a solution to the latter must also recognise the reality and efficacy of the forms of 'salvation' that are also offered by secular alcohol treatment and policy.

4. The proper goals of contemporary alcohol treatment and policy are commonly viewed as harm reduction and the public good. But, in a Christian analysis, consideration must also be given to better understanding the goals of treatment and policy in the context of the *summum bonum*, or the supreme good.

### ALCOHOL AS DESIRABLE COMMODITY

The title of a recent World Health Organization Report on alcohol research and public policy makes clear that alcohol is 'no ordinary commodity'.[1] It is *no ordinary* commodity most notably because of the human harm with which it is associated. But it is still a *commodity*. It is manufactured, distributed, taxed, purchased and consumed. It is associated with a vast multinational economy. And, most importantly, it is in demand.

The demand for alcohol, given the harm and cost with which it is associated, could be seen as absurd – and indeed perhaps it is. But alcohol is associated with considerable ambiguity.[2] Its use is deeply embedded in many of the world's cultures and traditions. It is enjoyed as a beverage, its effects are perceived as both pleasurable and stress-relieving, its use is widely socially encouraged, and it has been understood as having medicinal benefits. The desirability of alcohol thus has a biological, social and psychological basis – concerned with its consistent pharmacological effects, the variable vulnerability of the human constitution, and the complex and variable psycho-social context of its consumption. To use psychological terminology, its use is strongly reinforced.

Within the Judeo-Christian tradition alcohol also has important religious significance by virtue of its use at the Passover and in the Eucharist. Scripture contains positive references to alcohol use, as well as warnings against alcohol-related harm. Perhaps most importantly for Christians, a straightforward reading of the New Testament would appear to make it quite clear that Jesus himself drank wine.[3] Not only this, but in the fourth

---

[1] Babor et al., 2003.

[2] My acknowledgements here to Griffith Edwards, who entitled one of his many books on the subject *Alcohol: The Ambiguous Molecule* (G. Edwards, 2000).

[3] I will not re-engage here with the issues already covered in Chapter 5. Notwithstanding the continued influence of arguments such as those employed by Dawson Burns and others in the nineteenth

gospel we are provided with an account of a miracle in which the evangelist tells us that Jesus converted 120 gallons or more of water into wine for the benefit of wedding guests who had already been drinking.[4] It is perhaps not surprising, then, that Christians have generally seen alcohol as Increase Mather did, as the 'good creature of God', to be received with thankfulness.

Alcohol is, then, a commodity which is in demand – a desirable commodity – if also an extraordinary and somewhat ambiguous one. Already, the use of such language as that of 'commodity' is rather different from that used by Increase Mather. Perhaps, for Christians, Mather's terminology and Whitefield's emphasis on the need for responsibility in the proper use of created things offer a better emphasis than that of understanding alcohol as the object of commerce. However, it is important to be aware that alcohol is an object of commerce, and it would be foolish indeed to deny this reality. In any case, all objects of commerce are in some sense also 'creatures of God' and Christians have not generally eschewed the buying and selling of goods. Alcohol is a very desirable commodity, and this should not in principle conflict with an understanding of it as a creature which Christians may use responsibly, and for which they can give thanks to God.

Problems arise because of the combination of desirability and harm which constitute the extraordinariness of alcohol as commodity and the ambiguity of alcohol as substance. The desirability of alcohol acts as a force which motivates personal use despite awareness of possible or likely harm, and continued use despite experience of ongoing harm. Of course, all other things being equal, this situation need not get out of hand. Individuals might be expected to make balanced judgements about the extent to which they enjoy, or benefit from, alcohol use and to weigh these carefully against the extent to which they suffer harm. Where harm outweighs benefit, people might then be expected to discontinue or reduce their consumption of alcohol, and the problem would be abated. But all other things are not equal.

Importantly, things are not at all equal in the case of the alcohol dependence syndrome, and we shall consider this situation more carefully in a moment. However, even where alcohol dependence is not instituted, individuals vary in their biological and psychological vulnerability to the ill

---

century, the great weight of scholarship today would not appear to me to support the view that Jesus only drank non-alcoholic wine. Continued arguments to the contrary appear to me to be generally unconvincing (but see, for example, Bacchiocchi, 1989) and appear to introduce debatable hermeneutical principles which simply allow scriptural passages that are negative to be interpreted as referring to alcoholic wine, while others are positively interpreted as referring to non-alcoholic wine.

[4] John 2:1–11.

effects of alcohol. Judgement about drinking behaviour is influenced by drinking itself, such that wrong decisions are made about the amount, context and timing of consumption. Drinking that is safe in one context may be highly dangerous in another (as most notably when drinking and driving). Sometimes, family, friends and others may suffer the harms, while the individual drinker perceives only benefit to himself. In other cases, the drinker may be unaware of the harm that she is causing to herself or others. And almost always, the perceived benefits of alcohol consumption are short-term, whereas the harms that it causes have long-term significance. There is thus a variety of reasons why people might misjudge their drinking, or otherwise make wrong decisions about their drinking which allow harm, or risk of harm, to arise or continue out of all proportion to any arguable benefit.

Because its personal use is thus motivated, trade in alcohol as commodity may be economically desirable to some members of society even in circumstances where its sale and consumption might cause harm to others. In such circumstances harm and benefit are distributed unequally in the community. Some individuals may indeed drink responsibly and safely, and shareholders in the beverage alcohol industry may benefit financially, while others suffer harm. And those who suffer harm may be in another country, or in another section of society, such that the harm that they experience is easily hidden or ignored. Furthermore, advertising allows a commodity to be promoted to a population in such a way as might be expected to influence demand. Vulnerable drinkers may thus come under the influence of psychological and social forces likely to encourage further their purchase and consumption of alcohol despite its harmful effects upon them.

The variously expressed concerns of Robin Room, Richard Holloway and Pekka Sulkunen in respect of the conflict between personal ethical responsibility on the one hand and the public good on the other[5] would therefore appear to be well founded. So, what should individuals and populations do about their drinking? The 'mean of virtues', as espoused by Thomas Aquinas, might be good in theory, but, given all that we now know about the complexities of this ambiguous commodity, is it achievable in practice? And is it equally suitable to offer as moral advice to individuals and populations alike?

Doubtless the reader will form his or her own views on this question. If it is concluded that a mean of virtues is in this case either unachievable or undesirable, it would seem that total abstinence must present the only

---

[5] See Chapter 1, pp. 5, 7.

alternative ethical position. It might well still be argued, now as in the nineteenth century, that the world would be a better place without the 'drink curse'. However, the political reality is that prohibition is unlikely to be accepted on a widespread basis in any non-Islamic country in the world today. In any case, it is debatable whether or not it would be a good thing if it were. The experience of prohibition in the United States in the twentieth century is variously interpreted. While it might not have been the complete failure that it is sometimes portrayed as being, it was certainly repealed, and the act as legislated had mixed, and sometimes unintended, outcomes.[6] The legislatively enforced abstinence of whole populations would not appear to be an attractive, realistic or even completely effective policy option today.[7]

A personal commitment to abstinence is, of course, another matter. Even if widespread prohibition is politically unachievable, it might still be argued that a personal commitment to total abstinence from all alcoholic beverages offers the best personal protection against alcohol-related harm, and is the most responsible stance in relation to wider society. *Pace* Thomas Aquinas, it would seem difficult to argue in this context that abstinence might be understood as a vice opposed to drunkenness. In theory, perhaps, abstinence could sometimes be associated with harm, and might influence others adversely. Thus, for example, it might be argued that it sets a model of extreme behaviour, and that whereas those who emulate it will do well, those who react against it may simply be repelled to the opposite extreme – namely, drunkenness. Alternatively, it might be argued that there are benefits for health associated with low to moderate consumption of alcohol.[8] However, as the nineteenth-century temperance campaigners were keen to argue, abstinence has always been espoused by some within the Judeo-Christian tradition and there would not seem to be any serious evidence that this causes anyone any harm. Abstinence would appear to be a responsible and ethically acceptable option for those who choose it.

Accepting for a moment that not everyone will be willing to adopt total abstinence, perhaps there should still be more of a place than there currently is among Christians today for temporary periods of complete abstinence from alcohol as an act of spiritual devotion or self-discipline. Seen as a form of partial fasting, this might be understood as an act of self-sacrifice, an aid to prayer, an expression of desire for God above other things, or a

---

[6] G. Edwards, 2000, pp. 73–92.    [7] Babor et al., 2003, pp. 118–119.

[8] Ibid., pp. 67–69. However, it is generally suggested that this is not a sufficient reason to advocate encouraging the total abstainer to begin drinking. More importantly, at the population level, methods have not yet been identified by which only the number of light drinkers in a population can be increased.

penitential act. It might also be an aid to preventing drinking of alcohol from becoming excessive, while also being understandable as an act of thanksgiving for a good gift of God's creation.[9] But this begs the ethical question about moderate alcohol consumption, to which we must now turn.

Notwithstanding the commendability of complete abstinence for those who choose it, the application of Aquinas' mean of virtues as an ethical framework to govern moderate drinking behaviour also has much to commend it. As a general rule, it would certainly seem that it is 'excessive' or heavy consumption that is associated with the greatest risk of harm, although there is a need to remember that the prevention paradox suggests that a moderate level of consumption alone will not solve all alcohol-related problems at the population level.[10] A scientifically determined mean of the virtue of alcohol consumption would have to be set personally, taking into account the current state of generally available knowledge about sensible levels of alcohol consumption, but taking into account also a personal knowledge of one's own vulnerability, and the effects that given levels of consumption in different and particular contexts have had in one's own experience. Thus, an adult would be expected to have developed a responsible self-awareness concerning the virtue of drinking, avoiding any excess which might impair personal ability to act responsibly or which might put self or others at risk of harm.

Aquinas' approach provides a helpful, indeed prophetic, reminder of the need to avoid drunkenness, as well as the other vices and harms to which excessive drinking may lead, and not to allow alcohol critically to impair reason. While moderate alcohol consumption may be understood as virtuous, there is no basis in Christian scripture or tradition for understanding drunkenness as anything other than a vice, or in other words as sin. Of course, we now know that there is no clear demarcation between 'drunkenness' and lesser levels of intoxication, and so a personal awareness of alcohol-induced impairment of reason and psychomotor skills, and the likely implications of this for any given social context, become important. Scientific evidence suggests that total abstinence from alcohol is the only safe course of action when driving, operating machinery, swimming or exercising safety-critical occupational responsibilities. On the other hand, the effects of three or four drinks in the company of friends at home would not seem to pose any significant risk of harm or be likely to lead to vice or wrongdoing.

---

[9] Cf. fasting in general (see Wakefield, 1988, p. 148).      [10] See Chapter 2.

Aquinas' approach is also a helpful reminder that Christians who drink should not do so as though indulging in an acceptable level of vice, but rather with thanksgiving for alcohol as a good gift of God which is to be used responsibly and thoughtfully. If alcohol is the good creature of God, then it brings with it a responsibility that human beings, who are also creatures of God, should use it wisely and thoughtfully, with an awareness of both its advantages and its associated dangers.

However, if this is a helpful approach at the individual level and in the context of personal ethical reflection, it does not seem to have had much support as a policy measure at the population level. Education, including the use of 'sensible drinking' messages which recommend particular levels of consumption, as well as warning labels and school-based programmes, has not generally been found to be effective in reducing alcohol consumption, alcohol-related problems or economic costs to society.[11] This is not to say that people should be left uninformed about the nature of alcohol-related problems, or that there is no value in education, or that an ethical approach informed by Aquinas' mean of virtues is invalidated. However, it does suggest that education and recommendations on moderate or safe drinking levels, if offered without the support of other policy measures, should not be expected to be effective policies at the population level.

If we over-simplify matters somewhat, it might therefore be said that both complete abstinence and moderation can provide an ethical basis for personal lifestyle, but that neither appears to provide a satisfactory basis for alcohol policy at the population level. Fortunately, reports such as *Alcohol: No Ordinary Commodity* do provide a scientific analysis to guide policy-makers in effective ways of reducing alcohol-related harm at the population level. Not to take effective action, when evidence exists to indicate the kind of action that is likely to be effective to reduce the harms experienced by a population, would appear to be a *prima facie* unethical act of omission. However, before considering more carefully the proper goals of alcohol policy, in support of which research evidence should be put to service, we must turn to the ethical and theological issues raised by the phenomenon of alcohol dependence.

## ADDICTION AS THEOLOGICAL DISORDER

In the alcohol dependence syndrome the desire for alcohol becomes salient over other desires, goals and objectives in life. If alcohol is an 'ambiguous

---

[11] Babor et al., 2003, pp. 189–207, 270.

molecule', its ambiguities are here placed in even greater contrast and tension. On the one hand is the desirability of alcohol, now appearing to be magnified by the subjective compulsion to drink which is so characteristic of the syndrome in its fully developed form,[12] and this is reinforced by the relief that alcohol provides in relation to the withdrawal symptoms that are experienced if even brief periods of abstinence are unavoidably encountered. Because of tolerance, a greater dose of alcohol is also required in order to achieve the same effects as before. On the other hand are the harms and complications of heavy and unremitting alcohol consumption, which are likely to increase in proportion to the degree of dependence. Health is impaired, social and personal obligations are unfulfilled, constructive interests and occupations are neglected, and life comes to revolve more and more around the demand for alcohol. Life becomes focussed on alcohol; alcohol is the bio-psycho-social goal in life which increasingly assumes priority over other goals.

To the casual observer, there might now appear to be no ambiguity at all. Alcohol dependence, especially in its more severe form, is most unambiguously a very bad state of affairs indeed. And the pleasant desirability of alcohol taken in moderation is now lost to the dependent person, whose subjective compulsion is more cruelly motivated: positively by inner craving and negatively by the relief of withdrawal symptoms. But, to dependent drinkers, the internal ambiguity is heightened by their relationship with a commodity which they can no longer live happily with, but which nonetheless they cannot live without.

Perhaps this depiction is a little stereotypical and extreme. But, depending upon the degree of dependence encountered, there will be a degree of truth about it for each person for whom a diagnosis of alcohol dependence may correctly be made. And in extreme cases, the reality is if anything worse, rather than less, than this brief description might convey.

As discussed in Chapter 6, the state of dependence is characterised by a division of the will, such that conflicting desires to continue drinking and to stop drinking are in tension with each other. However, this division of the will is not qualitatively different from the division of the will that all individuals experience when they find themselves doing things that they know they should not do, or when they fail to do that which they know they must do. Phenomenologically, the state of dependence closely resembles the experiences described by Augustine of Hippo, in *Confessions*, and by Paul

---

[12] See Chapter 2.

the apostle, in his letter to the Romans. And the ethical and theological implications are also similar.

Perhaps addiction, therefore, is best understood, not so much as a medical disorder (although alcohol dependence must certainly be classified as such), and not so much as a 'disease of the will' (although it is certainly a division of the will), but more as a facet of the human capacity for a self-reflectiveness which desires to be different in the face of the experience of personal imperfection and sinfulness.

Understood in this way, addiction is not really a disorder at all, but rather an aspect of what it is to be human. Or at least, addiction is one way in which this human capacity to want to be other than we are presents itself. To the extent that it is a disorder, it is a disorder from which we all suffer in one form or another, and it is a disorder in our relationship with that which is most desirable. It is a theological disorder.

From a Christian theological perspective, nothing is more desirable than God. The Psalms affirm that there is nothing on earth to be desired other than God,[13] and that God himself is the proper satisfaction and fulfilment of the desires of human creatures.[14] It is God who is supremely able to satisfy the desires of the human heart.[15] In the Song of Songs, traditionally allegorised by Christians as being concerned with the love of Christ and the Church, the woman refers to her beloved as 'altogether desirable'.[16]

Much could be said about Christian writing on the desirability of God. For example, Julian of Norwich describes the longing of the soul for God thus: 'God, of your goodness give me yourself, for you are sufficient for me. I cannot properly ask anything less, to be worthy of you. If I were to ask less, I should always be in want. In you alone do I have all.'[17]

Many other examples could be given.[18] But the argument to be made here is that God is *by definition* that which is ultimately desirable. In support of this contention, it is perhaps therefore helpful to consider one example to be found in the writing of Anselm of Canterbury, who was famous for his ontological argument concerning the existence and nature of God. In the *Proslogion*, in which he also presents the ontological argument, Anselm prays: 'Lord my God, You who have formed and reformed me, tell my desiring soul what You are besides what it has seen so that it may see clearly that which it desires.'[19] And a little later he asks: 'What are You, Lord, what

---

[13] Psalm 73:25.  [14] Psalm 145:16, 19.  [15] Psalm 37:4.

[16] Song of Solomon 5:16.  [17] Wolters, 1966, pp. 68–69.

[18] See, for example, Philip Sheldrake's *Befriending Our Desires* (Sheldrake, 1998), in which he gives a variety of such examples.

[19] B. Davies and Evans, 1998, p. 95.

are You; what shall my heart understand you to be? You are, assuredly, life, You are wisdom, You are truth, You are goodness, You are blessedness, You are eternity, and You are every true good.'[20] Thus, when Anselm famously states that God is that 'than which a greater cannot be thought',[21] he clearly also believes that nothing is more desirable than God, for in God is every true good: 'Why, then, do you wander about so much, O insignificant man, seeking the goods of your soul and body? Love the one good in which all good things are, and that is sufficient. Desire the simple good which contains every good, and that is enough. For what do you love, O my flesh, what do you desire, O my soul? There it is, there it is, whatever you love, whatever you desire.'[22]

In God is to be found everything that is truly desirable. It might therefore be said that God is actually 'that than which nothing greater can be desired'. It is not that other things are not desirable and attractive, or that in finding them desirable Christians may not properly appreciate them for what they are as creatures of God. Indeed, Paul Janz has argued that attachment to and desire for God's creation, and for our creaturely life as a part of that, is something which the Christian should seek 'truly and passionately'.[23] But the created order is to be desired as penultimate, not ultimate; it is to be desired as that into which the reality of God in Christ has come. It is to be desired in the same way in which Christ himself desired it – at Gethsemane as well as at Cana.

An appreciation of all that is beautiful and desirable may, then, properly be an appreciation of God himself. The problem is that human beings have a tendency to desire the creature for its own sake, and thus to set it as an alternative object of desire, in conflict with desire for God, or in place of desire for God, rather than as a channel of expression of desire for God. Fulfilment or satiation of that desire then becomes a priority in itself, assuming greater salience than it should in the wider context of life's other priorities and desires, and especially assuming salience over desire for God as the proper ultimate focus of all desire. Holding on to the desire for a creature in this way is unfulfilling, and likely to be at least disappointing, if not eventually destructive. It is disordering of the harmony that is to be found when all desires focus ultimately on God himself. That we all do find ourselves desiring other things in preference to God is a reflection of the influence and power of sin – it is evidence of a disordered relationship

---

[20] Ibid., p. 98.   [21] Ibid., p. 87.   [22] Ibid., p. 101.
[23] Janz, 2004, p. 219; but see also the whole of his chapter 8 (pp. 191–221), in which his understanding of penultimacy as creaturely human being is elaborated.

with God.[24] It is a desiring of that which, once removed from its proper context, is actually undesirable.

Augustine of Hippo, in *The City of God*, thus says:

> For there is pleasure in eating and drinking, pleasure also in sexual intercourse. But when it is preferred to virtue, it is desired for its own sake, and virtue is chosen only for its sake, and to effect nothing else than the attainment or preservation of bodily pleasure. And this, indeed, is to make life hideous; for where virtue is the slave of pleasure it no longer deserves the name of virtue.[25]

But this does not mean that the experience of a multiplicity of desires is entirely a bad thing. Philip Sheldrake, in his book *Befriending our Desires*, points out that desire is also a metaphor for change and for a journey towards God.[26] To find that we have many desires, and even that these desires are in conflict with one another is to be expected, and the process of choosing between them can be a positive one, which leads to personal growth and integration.[27] Recognition of the reality, force and nature of our desires can thus be therapeutic.

Jean Porter has argued that Aquinas should be understood as arguing that true temperance is to be seen, not so much in the person who struggles with his or her desires as in the person whose desires are appropriate to the situation and to his or her aims in life.[28] Thus, we might admire more greatly the person who always drinks moderately and appropriately than the one who struggles with an overwhelming desire to drink. Porter suggests, therefore, that 'the truly virtuous person is one who has succeeded in integrating the multitude of desires and aversions into a unified character, who is able, therefore, to perceive the world clearly from the standpoint of her central commitments, and to act accordingly'.[29] However, she recognises that Aquinas is somewhat ambivalent about this himself, and that the underlying principle applies more readily to a virtue such as temperance than to one such as courage. Thus, we do not so readily admire the person who struggles with a desire to drink too much (or eat too much, or be promiscuous, etc.) as we do the person who struggles with fear of death and danger. Porter does not question as much as perhaps she might have done whether or not we are right to esteem so much more the person who struggles to be brave than the one who struggles to be temperate. Neither

---

[24] This might be considered as a disorientation of desire, as for example McFadyen argues (McFadyen, 2000, pp. 189–192, 213–214, 225), or else perhaps as a reflection of the fact that human beings easily become engrossed in desires which are more superficial, or less 'authentic' (Sheldrake, 1998, pp. 12–14).

[25] Book XIX, chapter 1.  [26] Sheldrake, 1998, pp. 17, 29.

[27] Ibid., pp. 73–92.  [28] Porter, 2002, pp. 170–179.  [29] Ibid., p. 173.

does she examine the implications of her own statement that it is 'not all that difficult' for most people to develop 'appropriate attitudes' in respect of physical desires.[30] Surely, if it is not difficult for most people, that still might leave some for whom it is very difficult indeed? And are not some of these struggles actually quite difficult for almost all of us at some point in our lives?

As people progress through the process of learning and internalising of virtue, their struggle with desire – either through no fault of their own or else at least partly through factors beyond their control – might at times be very great indeed. The desires with which the addict struggles are complex and attributable to life experiences, biology, social pressures, culture and other factors. They are also subjective. Who can know whether or not they are stronger for one person than for another? But, in any case, the integrated ideal of the truly virtuous person that Porter describes is the destination rather than the starting point of virtue. If the truly virtuous person is one whose integration of self has taken him or her beyond struggles with desires which represent divisions of the self, then this is clearly the point of healing towards which – if we will allow it – grace draws us all. And, if Romans 7 is indeed a description of Paul's Christian (rather than non-Christian or pre-Christian) experience, then complete integration would seem to be a destination that is not reached easily – indeed perhaps not even commonly – by Christian saints.

Alcohol, as a desirable commodity, as the good creature of God, is therefore not in itself bad. Whatever partisan or denominational reasons Professor Edgar, Cardinal Manning, Thomas Bridgett and others may have had for making their arguments, they were right to emphasise that any evil principle there may be concerning drunkenness lies not in alcohol itself.[31] But the salience of drink-seeking behaviour observed as an element of the alcohol dependence syndrome reflects a disordering of relationship with that which is desirable. Paradoxically, this disordering is such that the desired object becomes, at least to the objective observer, something which is most undesirable indeed.

Of course, alcohol is not completely unique in its desirability or in its propensity to become the focus of disordered relationships. The concept of the dependence syndrome has been applied to patterns of addiction to other drugs and to a variety of different addictive behaviours in which no substance at all is involved. While rather different conceptual models are sometimes applied to understanding these behaviours, it is of interest to

---

[30] Ibid.    [31] See Chapter 5.

note that spirituality has emerged as a theme of increasing interest among those concerned with understanding and treating addictive disorders. While spirituality is a concept susceptible to various understandings, and while many of those working in this field would not understand it in a specifically Christian sense, nonetheless it is often held to be concerned with relationships with other persons, with the wider universe and especially with the transcendent.[32] Perhaps, in rather different language, this literature reflects a recognition among clinicians and researchers that addiction is concerned with the way in which relationships are disordered by making a particular substance or behaviour an object of desire for its own sake. Similarly, the Twelve Steps of Alcoholics Anonymous, which have been one of the prime sources of inspiration for the literature on addiction and spirituality, focus on the importance of making amends in relationships that have been damaged by addiction to alcohol, and on the need to reorientate life around a Higher Power, or God.[33]

Addictive disorders are perhaps especially obvious examples of the 'theological disorder' that has been described here. But the theological disorder that has been described here does not afflict only those who suffer from alcohol dependence, or from some other form of the dependence syndrome. It is universal to human experience, with the sole exception to be found in the life of Christ himself.

Thus, when Paul exhorts the readers of his letter to the Romans to 'live honourably as in the day, not in revelling and drunkenness, not in debauchery and licentiousness, not in quarrelling and jealousy',[34] his words apply as well to those who are argumentative or self-protectively suspicious and envying of others as to those who are prone to drunkenness. They apply as well to those who have been guilty of only two or three episodes of drunkenness as they do to those who display all elements of the alcohol dependence syndrome to their fullest possible degree of severity. Paul clearly does not intend his list to be exhaustively comprehensive. We thus find that elsewhere he refers in a similar vein to other vices, such as fornication, impurity, idolatry, sorcery, and 'things like these'.[35] Addiction, or specifically the dependence syndrome, is not qualitatively different from human sinfulness in general. The social stigma with which people who suffer from addictive disorders are associated is therefore particularly inappropriate from a Christian perspective, unless of course it is seen as a stigma to be borne by us all. But to discriminate against the alcoholic or drug addict as being

---

[32] Cook, 2004.    [33] G. Edwards, Marshall and Cook, 2003, pp. 300–312.
[34] Romans 13:13.    [35] Galatians 5:19–21.

especially evil, or unusually immoral, is fundamentally contrary to the Christian gospel. The old 'moral model' of alcoholism is not a Christian model, unless its scope is broadened to include us all.

### THE SUPREME GOOD AS GOAL OF ADDICTION TREATMENT

Consequentialist arguments have been encountered again and again during the course of our survey of Christian ethical thinking about drunkenness. Thomas Aquinas was concerned with the impairment of reason brought about by alcohol. His underlying ethical concern was of a teleological nature – being concerned with the ultimate human end which he understood as being the *ratio boni*. But, most notably, Dawson Burns's arguments in support of 'temperance' (understood by him as being complete abstinence) were built almost entirely upon consequentialist argument. Hermeneutics and doctrinal considerations were not ignored by him, and indeed he argued strongly for scriptural support of his position, and clearly had soteriological concerns at heart. However, it is difficult to avoid the conclusions that the bulk of his argument was designed to be of equal appeal to those who did not share his Christian faith, and that his hermeneutical principles were in any case derived from his temperance principles, rather than the other way around.

The contemporary secular concern with harm minimization, as a goal of treatment and policy, reflects a particular form of consequentialism, that of utilitarianism. It might be argued that it is in fact an almost definitive example of negative utilitarianism, focussed exclusively upon the minimisation of harm. However, in practice, treatment programmes do emphasise positive aspects of lifestyle,[36] and (as has been discussed in Chapter 2) alcohol policy is usually directed explicitly towards the public good. There is thus also a positive teleological basis to contemporary alcohol policy and treatment, even if this is not stressed as much as it might be.

The minimisation of harm (although there will be debates about how it is best achieved) and the public good (although there will be debates about exactly what it is) are not objectives with which Christians should take issue. But, from a Christian perspective, they will always remain intermediate and temporal objectives rather than the ultimate goal or *telos*. This is not to suggest that they are unimportant, but rather that they must be set in

---

[36] See, for example, Wanigaratne et al., 1990, pp. 137–150; G. Edwards, Marshall and Cook, 2003, pp. 287–288.

a broader theological context – a context in which all things have their beginning and end in God.[37]

For Augustine of Hippo, the proper concern of ethics was thus the *summum bonum*, or supreme good, which he understood as being located in God himself, and in which alone he understood true happiness is to be found. Ultimately, this was an eschatological concept, which would bring an end to the divided will:

> But, in that final peace to which all our righteousness has reference, and for the sake of which it is maintained, as our nature shall enjoy a sound immortality and incorruption, and shall have no more vices, and as we shall experience no resistance either from ourselves or from others, it will not be necessary that reason should rule vices which no longer exist, but God shall rule the man, and the soul shall rule the body, with a sweetness and facility suitable to the felicity of a life which is done with bondage. And this condition shall there be eternal, and we shall be assured of its eternity; and thus the peace of this blessedness and the blessedness of this peace shall be the supreme good.[38]

For Paul the apostle also, there was an eschatological *telos* which provided context to ethical questions, and to his understanding of the divided self. But neither Augustine nor Paul understood this eschatological good as merely a distant future goal, something to be experienced only after death. It was understood to have deep implications for the present:

> For salvation is nearer to us now than when we became believers; the night is far gone, the day is near. Let us then lay aside the works of darkness and put on the armour of light; let us live honourably as in the day, not in revelling and drunkenness, not in debauchery and licentiousness, not in quarrelling and jealousy. Instead, put on the Lord Jesus Christ, and make no provision for the flesh, to gratify its desires.[39]

For Paul, the supreme good, the eschatological *telos*, was to be found in Christ himself. Salvation, in the sense of a final end to the division of self, lay in the future. But the process of salvation involved a 'putting on' of Christ in the present moment, and in Christ Paul located the grace that could provide freedom from the captivity to sin that was the root cause of the divided self.

In this theological context may be found a motivation and a goal for Christians concerned about alcohol policy and addiction.

---

[37] Thus, for example, the Roman Catholic Bishops of England and Wales, in their statement on *The Common Good and the Catholic Church's Social Teaching*, set the 'common good' firmly in the context of the incarnation of Christ, the Trinity and the ultimate purposes of God (Catholic Bishops' Conference of England and Wales, 1996, paras. 12–18).

[38] *The City of God*, book XIX, chapter 27.     [39] Romans 13:11–14.

Frances Makower, a Roman Catholic nun who has written about her experiences of working with drug addicts in the Kaleidoscope project, based in a Baptist church in Kingston-upon-Thames, provides just one example of the way in which Christ provides the motivation for such work:

Working with our deprived youngsters has enabled me to gain a deeper understanding of the anguish of sordid surroundings, a future without hope and the effects of loneliness, rejection and ensuing bitterness. I am convinced that all these concerns are the key to my peace and happiness. It goes without saying that this positive outlook is sheer grace, for while on the more superficial level I fight both pain and dependence, deep down I find myself grateful for my situation which draws me ever deeper to the pierced heart of Christ, to him to whom I am consecrated and who continues to be reflected in the lives of the powerless, the suffering and the outcast.[40]

It is important to note, in passing, that this motivation betrays the lie of the so-called moral model. Sister Makower did not see the young people with whom she worked as morally inferior to herself, but rather she identified with them and encountered Christ among them.

The supreme good, understood as the grace of God in Christ, is thus also the proper goal of treatment. Some evangelical Christian groups have sought to give expression to this in an explicit way, by means of programmes in which treatment is more or less explicitly equated with conversion to Christianity,[41] but this is not the only theological model for treatment, as Sister Makower's account of the Kaleidoscope project illustrates. Perhaps more challenging is the proper Christian theological understanding of what takes place in the secular context.

However many excellent Christian programmes there may be for people with addictive disorders, there are clearly other treatment programmes in which there may be absolutely no spiritual component to treatment, and where perhaps there may not even be a single Christian member of staff, and where those addicted to alcohol may yet find a pathway to recovery which includes no discernable spiritual or religious experience. Viewed from the perspective of the prevailing pragmatic atheism of our age, this may well be an extremely unsurprising observation. Indeed, I can well imagine that the reader who is an atheist or agnostic may consider the question itself to be either arrogant or incoherent. Why indeed should not anyone recover from alcohol dependence without any spiritual experience at all, let alone without any specifically Christian experience of the grace of Christ?

---

[40] Makower, 1989, pp. III–II2. A paragraph break has been removed from the quotation.
[41] E.g. Teen Challenge (National Institute on Drug Abuse, 1977; Thompson, 1994).

I respectfully beg patience from any reader who feels this way, and return to the intentions expressed in Chapter 1. First, I feel that there is a need for Christians to understand clearly what it is that they believe is happening in such occurrences. To this extent, this question is simply not directed at the atheist or agnostic. Secondly, however, I do continue to believe that theology has something useful to contribute to secular discourse on the subject of alcohol. With these two objectives in view, what kind of answer may be given to the question posed at the end of the last paragraph?

Chapter 6 concluded with various pertinent observations. I suggested there that theology reminds us that questions of choice in recovery from addiction are not made either as though we were totally constrained within a deterministic universe, or as though we exercised complete freedom of will. I further suggested that addiction confronts us with important aspects of what it means to be human – capable of self-reflection and of forming a desire to be other than we are. Within this understanding, addiction has an enslaving quality which, from a Christian perspective, is understandable as an effect of the power of sin. It is this which leads to the division of the will which is characteristic of both addiction and wider human experience. I further commented that the Pauline and Augustinian conclusion is that freedom is to be found only through the grace of Christ, but that the Higher Power of the Twelve Step programmes at least provides something which looks very much like this.

These observations take us just so far. I hope that they are helpful in themselves in drawing attention to the nature of the addictive experience, and that they remind us of the extent to which addiction is reflective of an experience of enslavement which affects us all in some way or another. But my comments on the similarities between the Christian understanding of grace in Christ and the Higher Power of Alcoholics Anonymous leave ample room for diverse interpretations. At one end of a spectrum, the Higher Power may be conceived of in an explicitly and exclusively Christian sense, and at the other end of the spectrum grace might be understood merely as one example of how the Higher Power may be construed. And this construal need not be theistic at all.

For the Christian seeking to understand theologically what happens in secular addiction treatment, I think that there must be a recognition that the common grace that pervades creation allows at least a limited form of salvation which is available to all in addiction treatment. An 'anti-craving' drug[42] may indeed enable an addict to break out of the enslavement

---

[42] For example, acamprosate, if indeed this drug does work by reducing craving.

that their desire for abstinence encounters in the face of a continuing craving for alcohol. Similarly, relapse prevention techniques may enable the previously dependent person to learn ways of resisting social pressures to resume alcohol consumption. These and other therapeutic techniques are grace of a kind, and do produce a form of salvation. But this is a form of salvation which is not expressed in relation to God. It is oriented towards human freedom and fulfilment.[43] If we over-emphasise the extent to which this is *salvation*, rather than merely therapy, then the question might be raised regarding whether or not theology actually has anything distinctive to say which is not already being said by the natural and social sciences.[44] On the other hand, it would seem odd if the soteriology of an incarnational faith such as Christianity did not connect at all with such realities. This in turn raises the question of what Christian salvation is in its broadest sense.

The problem is not that Christian theology has no idea of what salvation might mean, but rather that it has a multiplicity of ideas. There is a diversity of biblical images, including (among many others) metaphors of release, transformation, identification with Christ, sacrifice and restored relationship.[45] Most importantly, there is the Christian understanding of the uniqueness of the life, death and resurrection of Christ as a salvific event.[46] All of these portray salvation in relation to God and, unsurprisingly, this is what is distinctive about Christian salvation:

Salvation – in the Christian sense – is what people seek when they know that God is the reality to be reckoned with from first to last. For people who seek salvation, whatever else they may think they can know about God, it is self-evident that God is the source and goal of all things, never a means to an end. God is the source and goal of my freedom, never its function. I do not know what Christians mean by salvation until I realise I can be fully myself only in receiving myself from God and in giving myself utterly to God. Salvation is to experience as the source and the goal of my own living and being the one who is the source and the goal of all things.[47]

What Paul and Augustine discovered was that the grace of God transformed their whole lives, not just specific instances of one or two things with which they struggled. Such a transformation inevitably addresses itself to the captivity of addictive behaviour, because it addresses the all-encompassing

43 Doctrine Commission of the General Synod of the Church of England, 1997, pp. 31–40.
44 Wiederkehr, 1979, p. 49.
45 Hart, 1997; Doctrine Commission of the General Synod of the Church of England, 1997, pp. 120–143.
46 Wiederkehr, 1979, pp. 15–35; Doctrine Commission of the General Synod of the Church of England, 1997, p. 101.
47 Doctrine Commission of the General Synod of the Church of England, 1997, p. 35.

captivity of which addiction is but a part. But it is not primarily a release from addictive behaviour – it is a process of salvation from the all-encompassing power of sin. And, because it is a process which is not complete until it reaches its eschatological *telos* in Christ, and because it is not primarily concerned with addictive disorder, it may or may not result in immediate release from addictive behaviour. Thus, while there are accounts of conversion experiences that mark a dramatic end to an addictive desire for alcohol,[48] there are also individual Christians who continue to struggle with the desire to drink. The supreme good, the grace of Christ, is an eschatological and soteriological goal. It is the ultimate answer to the divided self, but it is not primarily therapy for addiction.

On the other hand, addictive disorder is very much a part of the wider theological problem of the divided will. It is therefore set in the context of further-reaching goals and desires than simply those concerned with drug use. Abstinence from alcohol is unlikely to be a satisfactory treatment goal when more profound and widely-reaching issues are not addressed. It is therefore not surprising that secular treatment programmes have incorporated concepts such as spirituality, and broader concerns with lifestyle, in an attempt to address these broader and more ultimate goals. The trend towards doing so would appear to reflect a need that is perceived by service users and by those who seek to help people suffering from addictive disorders. Even outside a Christian context, it may therefore be helpful for addiction treatment to incorporate client reflection on what constitutes the supreme good as treatment goal. But, in terms of Christian theology, it must be argued that the grace of God in Christ offers the only proper goal and context of treatment.

### THE COMMON GOOD AS AIM OF ALCOHOL POLICY

If the supreme good is proposed as the proper goal of addiction treatment, then clearly it is also to be considered as the proper aim of alcohol policy. This proposal is again made in awareness that it will not be seen as relevant in secular debate. However, limitations of policy aims such as the public good, or the improvement of public health and social well-being, are apparent.

First, if public health is concerned only with harm minimisation, then this is a very negative take on utilitarianism. In theory at least, it could be argued that harm could be minimised simply by restricting the size of a population. Limitations of research evidence further restrict the value

---

[48] See, for example, James, 1985, pp. 201–203.

of harm minimisation as aim of alcohol policy, for it is not always clear what course of action will actually reduce harm to the lowest possible level. There are also problems concerning the way in which small amounts of harm experienced by large numbers of people compare with great harm experienced by a few. And finally, it is very restrictive to consider only alcohol- or drug-related harm in isolation. Alcohol and drug policy must always be considered in the context of their impact on the population as a whole. Aims such as the public good or social well-being are therefore appropriately more positive and widely reaching.

But what constitutes public good or social well-being? A public good might be described as 'a good that is present for all members of a relevant community if it is there for any of them'.[49] It is perhaps the closest contemporary equivalent to the 'common good', which was understood by Aristotle as the fitting goal of a good human life. For Aquinas, the common good and the supreme good were equivalent, since 'the good of all things depends on God'.[50] But, as David Hollenbach has pointed out,[51] there is an important difference between public goods and the common good. The former tend to be understood as external to the relationships that bind members of a community together. The latter includes the immanent good of being a community, which is located within the community itself and involves the bonds of love and mutual affection that bind the community together.

In a pluralistic and individualistic society such as that of the contemporary western world, the common good is arguably no longer a politically feasible aim. Rather, tolerance must allow disagreement about, and diversity of opinion concerning, what exactly constitutes the good life. And the Reformation has left a deep-seated distrust concerning any possibility of locating a vision of the good life in any form of religion. Hollenbach thus argues that the *summum bonum* in America today is, at least according to consensus, tolerance rather than the common good.

The authors of the latest WHO-sponsored report on alcohol, *Alcohol: No Ordinary Commodity*, while locating alcohol policy firmly within the arena of public health, refer to the pursuit of health as 'one of modern society's most highly cherished values'.[52] But, if public health is to be viewed as a public good (and the previous WHO report on alcohol was entitled *Alcohol Policy and the Public Good*), health is still rather individualistically defined in this report, so as to include the maximisation of biological, psychological and social functioning of persons rather than of communities. The authors

---

[49] Hollenbach, 2002, p. 8.　　[50] Ibid., p. 4.　　[51] Ibid., pp. 8–31.　　[52] Babor et al., 2003, p. 9.

note also that health – this highly cherished value – comes into conflict with other values, such as free trade, open markets and individual freedom.[53] So it would appear that, in the alcohol policy arena, health as a public good and policy objective comes into conflict with other valued tenets of western society. How can a pluralistic and individualistic society effectively address such conflicting objectives?

Hollenbach suggests that the common good is 'an idea whose time has once again come'.[54] The common good, of being a community of persons in relationship, on a global level, is undoubtedly an ambitious goal of social policy, but it would seem that subsidiary goals, where health is but one of a series of public goods, are unlikely to adequately address the conflicts of interest that occur in the alcohol policy arena.

Examples of the conflicts of interest that arise in practice have already been described in Chapter 2, as for example in the form of allegations involving the influence of the alcohol industry on debate and policy. There is reason to believe that governments also are not unconflicted on such matters, when revenue from taxation and popularity with drinking voters conflict with particular public goods such as that of health. A point of reference is needed which transcends particular public goods, and yet this is just what contemporary secular discourse vehemently disallows. The profit of shareholders, while a necessary factor of a market economy, can all too easily become a distraction from the supreme good or the common good, or might even idolatrously be perceived as being such a good. But the balancing of health concerns against the benefits of alcohol in society will never be an easy matter while health is merely set against the pleasures which some associate with alcohol. A point of reference is required which lies beyond profit, and even beyond health and pleasure.

Hollenbach suggests that 'intellectual solidarity' is the key to a renewed vision for the common good in contemporary society.[55] His understanding of intellectual solidarity requires respectful communication, which will engage across boundaries and despite differences of perspective, even where this leads at times to argument. In the political sphere, he understands this as requiring that reasoned arguments be presented in support of institutions or policies, in such a way that they might demonstrate how a vision of the common good might be achieved in some particular aspect of life. Such debate, he suggests, should be conducted in an atmosphere of civility, and it requires that governments defend the basic

---

[53] Ibid.    [54] Hollenbach, 2002, p. 243.    [55] Hollenbach, 2002, and especially see his chapter 6.

rights and freedoms which make it possible. Intellectual solidarity is both a means to achieving the common good and is also itself an aspect of that good.

Intellectual solidarity is threatened by coercion and manipulation in support of the interests of narrowly defined groups of people, particularly when this occurs in the context of an imbalance of power that allows people to become marginalized and excluded from the common good. In the debate about alcohol policy, it is exactly such an imbalance and abuse of power that threatens the common good. Most tangibly, the imbalance arises from the enormous economic advantage which the industry holds. Academic communities, and even the World Health Organization, simply cannot compete with the resources which the beverage alcohol industry is able to devote to the promotion of its position. In the western world, this is compensated for to some extent by the freedoms which allow academics and others to engage in public debate. These freedoms are compromised and subverted, however, if hidden payments are made so as to influence in some way the contributions that are made to the debate. An even greater imbalance of economic power exists when an industry wealthy even by western standards engages with the business of promoting its product in poorer countries. And an even more fundamental cause for concern arises when governments give an appearance of being partially deaf to respected academic debate but attentive to an industry from which they derive economic wealth through taxation.

However, a superficial representation of the problem would be allowed if the argument were left there. Governments should properly receive revenue from an industry whose product generates considerable health-care and social costs.[56] They are understandably loath to risk alienating voters who are strongly attached to their freedom to exercise their own judgements about drinking alcohol, and if they do they will not be able to effect any kind of policy once they lose an election. And the alcohol industry is economically wealthy only because alcohol is such a desirable commodity, which is in great demand. The imbalance of power that threatens the common good in alcohol policy debate is thus ultimately contributed to by voters and by consumers, by free trade and by the individualism beloved of western society. It is an imbalance of power in which we are all personally and collectively involved. Demonisation of alcohol, or of the beverage alcohol industry, or of government, did not solve the problem in the nineteenth century and would not appear to be a satisfactory twenty-first-century response to that

---

[56] According to the AHRSE, the cost to England is around £20 billion per year.

same problem, although robust criticism of industry and government may well be required as a part of an effective response.

The ambiguities associated with alcohol thus affect us all, and the division of the self, which is characteristic of both the addict and all human persons, is unsurprisingly reflected in wider society as a collective ambivalence towards this desirable commodity. The concerns about alcohol policy debated within communities thus strikingly resemble the concerns of treatment for addicted individuals. Just as addiction might be understood as an expression of the divided self, treatment of which (or salvation from which) requires a 'Higher Power' (or divine grace), so communities afflicted by the ravages of alcohol misuse are divided within themselves. This division might equally be understood as requiring healing and integration which can come only graciously from without. But while human communities, at least in the western world, continue to hang on to their cherished values of free trade and individualism, can there be any healing? Perhaps the problems of alcohol misuse that afflict our society require us to look beyond individualism, and even beyond particular public goods, in order that we may acknowledge the need for the grace of a Higher Power at work within our communities. And even if the pluralistic nature of our communities makes it unlikely that we will agree on the Christian understanding of that Higher Power as necessarily dwelling within Christ himself, perhaps at least the recognition that we are in need of such a transcendent point of reference will open up possibilities which are currently denied.

What does this mean in practice? I can immediately imagine representatives of both industry and government arguing that their preference for partnership and co-operation represents exactly the kind of way in which intellectual solidarity, and thus the common good, might best be achieved. And perhaps they are partly right. Exclusion of any party from the debate is inherently undesirable, as it is by definition contrary to solidarity. However, just as an addict who denies that he or she has a problem is in need of confrontation, not collusion, so true solidarity in debate about alcohol policy cannot be achieved unless or until governments and industries publicly admit the conflict of interest that is inherent in their position in respect of alcohol. This conflict is a dynamic for which we all share responsibility, and in which we all participate, in some way or another, and it is the denial rather than the existence of it which is most contrary to the common good. Sadly, true partnership and co-operation would seem unrealistic and unachievable unless this admission is made. Pretences at the same would seem likely only to become fertile ground for further coercion and manipulation which are actually contrary to the common good.

If partnership and co-operation of the kind proposed by the beverage alcohol industry would therefore appear more likely to work contrary to the common good, rather than in support of it, other ways of achieving intellectual solidarity must be found. Where dialogue with industry, or government, or other parties with a conflict of interest, is concerned, the party experiencing the conflict of interests should declare it. Where such declarations are refused, and assuming that there are good grounds for believing that a conflict of interests does in fact exist, then such refusals should be firmly, politely and consistently challenged. It would seem unlikely that true intellectual solidarity can be achieved until at least the debate focusses on the true and fundamental level of disagreement – which would appear to be the existence of the conflict of interest itself. In general, a 'hermeneutic of suspicion' would appear appropriate. The greater onus for justifying policy options should rest with powerful bodies that stand to gain – financially or otherwise – from promoting those particular policy options. Evaluations of research evidence conducted by disinterested parties, for example under the auspices of the World Health Organization, should be given more weight than those conducted by bodies that might stand to gain financially by supporting one possible interpretation in favour of another.

Co-operation and partnership which do not proceed from this foundation would appear more likely to work contrary to the common good than in support of it, as for example in the case of the licensing of Moo Joose in Queensland.[57] Or, at the very least, they would appear unlikely to be effective in realising the common good, as for example in the case of the working together with industry proposed in *AHRSE*. Advocacy by a government of working with an industry that experiences a conflict of interest which might operate contrary to the common good should be exceptional, and should be expected to require especially strong justification in the form, for example, of strong research evidence or lack of realistic alternative effective options.

On the basis of the foregoing analysis, the politics and realities of alcohol policy would therefore appear to require the following:

1. Much more debate about the aims of alcohol policy. It is proposed here that this should be conceived of as the common good. Given that a pluralistic society is likely to experience difficulty in agreeing exactly

[57] See Chapter 2.

what this might mean in practice, intellectual solidarity should at least be aspired to. Where the debate continues to be concerned with public goods, the interactions and conflicts between these goods are in need of careful analysis.

2. Conflicts of interest should be declared not only in academic publications, but in advertising, educational materials, political discourse and other public debate about matters of alcohol policy. Such conflicts should not be seen in themselves as a matter for shame, as they are inevitable both now and for the foreseeable future – but rather, denial of their existence where they are clearly identifiable should be treated as a matter of opprobrium.

3. The freedoms that are necessary to intellectual solidarity and the common good must be defended vigorously by governments.

4. Consideration needs to be given to whether and how the beverage alcohol industry might genuinely and actually demonstrate a commitment to the common good, and how the industry might ethically handle the conflicts of interests that occur when this commitment runs contrary to maximisation of its financial profits.

5. Where an imbalance of economic or other power threatens intellectual solidarity in respect of alcohol policy debate, steps should be taken to address this. Thus, for example, the economic power of the beverage alcohol industry might be diverted into research on alcohol-related problems, treatment programmes for people afflicted by these problems, and alcohol policy, through channels which are governed by independent bodies whose autonomy is both protected and assured. For its economic power to be diverted into these channels without independent mediation and protection would, however, appear likely only to create an opportunity for the abuse of power.

By way of summary, it might be suggested that, while health and pleasure, and even alcohol, are good things, and properly desirable, there is danger when they are allowed to become an end in themselves. Ultimately, only 'that than which nothing greater can be desired' is capable of putting other desirable things into their proper context. Anything less is likely in turn to become its own supreme goal and to enslave. While this principle has been developed here primarily in terms of the individual dynamics of addiction, it would seem also to apply at the social level of analysis. While it has been developed at the level of Christian theology – conceiving of that which is transcendently desirable as God in Christ – it is capable of alternative exegesis. It is also fully compatible with an understanding of the common good as the proper goal of alcohol policy. Intellectual solidarity, an important means towards, and component of, the common good of all human beings, is not served by denial of theological contribution to the debate. Rather, all people of goodwill should be allowed to contribute to the conversation, and the nature of the common good in which we all wish to share should be a concern to us all.

CHAPTER 8

# *Conclusions*

It has been proposed here that the Christian concepts of sin and grace provide a theological framework within which alcohol, drunkenness and addiction might be understood without reverting to what is popularly thought of as being the outmoded 'moral model'. The latter model singled out the drunkard as being sinful because morally weak. But Christian theology has never, properly, singled out drunkenness in such a fashion. Rather, it has understood drunkenness as being only one kind of moral failing, and humanity as universally afflicted by a sinful nature, albeit also enjoying a nature which reflects the image of its divine creator. This, divided, human condition is thus prone both to a desire for the grace which is offered by its creator, who is ultimately good, and also a desire for created objects for their own sake, and for selfish ends, which, thus idolised, become evil. These desires are experienced in different ways by different people, according to the unique biological and psychological makeup of each individual, and the varying physical and social environments in which people find themselves.

Alcohol is but one desirable commodity that human beings may encounter in this context. However, its biological, social and psychological ambiguities perhaps especially predispose it to becoming a very visible and challenging example of the ways in which human beings may become divided within themselves between a desire for that which they recognise as good and a desire for that which is recognised as bad. In the case of addiction, an especially clear example is provided of the way in which human beings may find themselves struggling within, as though drawn in different directions by almost equally powerful magnetic fields of opposite spiritual polarity. It is not that the rest of us are never in this position, and surely all human beings can identify with the qualitative experience that is described here. A man advised by his doctor to eat less finds himself eating more. A woman who knows she should tell her friend the truth about her adultery ends up lying to avoid the shame. Money that should be given to charity is used to buy more things that we do not need. And so the examples go on. But many of them are not conspicuous, and are so ubiquitous that we consider ourselves entitled to indulge them – at least to some extent. In contrast, the man or woman who is alcohol dependent is denied this luxury and, in any case, the stakes are too high. We all understand something of the quality of the dilemma that such people face, but we find ourselves emphasising the differences between their experiences and ours.

If we emphasise the moral differences between the experience of addiction and our own experience, we enter the territory of the discredited moral model. If we emphasise the differences as being between disease and 'normality', we enter the territory of the disease concept. In either case, we protect ourselves from the implications of admitting the divisions of self that we experience and yet deny. Instead, we label the addict as either sinful or sick, projecting on to them the pathology that we disown within ourselves. This is not to say that dependence is not a medical disorder, or that it does not have moral implications. Neither is it being suggested here that everyone is 'addicted' in the sense that we all suffer from some kind of dependence syndrome. However, it is being argued here that the experience of addiction is not completely alien to any human being. Divisions of the will are characteristic of our experience of ourselves.

The theological model that has been described here, relying as it does especially upon the insights of Paul and Augustine, also recognises the need for grace as an essential component of any adequate response to addictive disorders. The reader who does not share my Christian faith will perhaps find comfort in my recognition that this grace may take many forms, and that it might include relapse prevention therapy, treatment with pharmacological 'anti-craving' agents, or a fairly liberal interpretation of the need for the 'Higher Power' of Alcoholics Anonymous. However, my theology is unashamedly Christocentric, and I therefore also argue, in sympathy with Paul and Augustine, that Christ alone provides that grace which is able to set people free from the broader experience of captivity that the divided self represents. It is therefore no surprise to find that there are many accounts in the literature of spiritual and religious experience associated with recovery from addiction. Admittedly, some of these are not explicitly Christian, and it is not my purpose here to enter into theological debate over how a Buddhist or Islamic religious experience should be interpreted. However, I would humbly suggest that the Spirit of God shows a willingness to cross more boundaries than do some of his creatures.

Does this model add anything to, or in any way improve upon, the models offered by the social and natural sciences? Does it offer additional explanatory power? I will leave the reader finally to judge the answers to these questions. It has not been the purpose of this book to show that a theological model provides new insights into the nature and treatment of addiction which were previously unknown. Given 2,000 years of Christian reflection on drunkenness, which has profoundly influenced western culture in diverse ways, it would be surprising if I were to suggest something completely new. In any case, the model proposed is constructed from a position of theological realism which wishes to engage with all the good things that the social and natural sciences have to offer. However, the pragmatic atheism of contemporary discourse, and the unnecessary scientific tendency at times towards reductionism and determinism, do suggest to me that theology has an important corrective to offer to some of the imbalances that are to be found in the field at present. Furthermore, the contemporary ethical dilemmas associated with addiction are not, in my opinion, adequately addressed by any bio-psycho-social scientific model which is understood to have rejected as outmoded its own distorted image of the moral model. Theology certainly appears to me to offer a more positive ethical framework than either this moral model or the harm reduction philosophy of the prevailing clinical and policy culture.

The theological model that is presented here also takes seriously the experienced 'power' of addiction to hold people captive, and the need for an experience of a gracious 'Higher Power' as the basis for finding freedom. That people neither take seriously the power of addiction to hold other people captive nor recognise the extent to which they themselves are held captive by similar powers is at the basis of much of the stigma encountered by those who are addicted to alcohol or other drugs. Such stigma is totally contrary to Christian theology. People who are addicted are fundamentally 'like me' and are in need of the grace of God like me. They are not to be despised or excluded. Neither are they merely to be understood as suitable material for fundamentalist attempts to proselytise and convert. They are people who share the experience of what it is to be the bio-psycho-social creatures that human beings are, who need both the challenge and comfort of a Higher Power – in whatever form that power might reveal itself to be.

A theological model is thus able to address the subjective compulsion of the dependence syndrome in such a way that it neither unhelpfully reinforces any perception of the total inability of addicts to choose the path to recovery nor becomes over-optimistic about their ability to recover through their own efforts. It is further capable of reminding us that we are all involved in this choice insofar as we are responsible for allowing conflicts of interest to remain unchallenged in our society where they set corporate profit or political gain against alcohol-related harm in the population as a whole. Financial profit and political power are all too easily transformed into ultimate objectives of their own, which have the power to enslave as surely as does alcohol. The objective of the common good must be understood as the positive basis for all alcohol policy. Only the grace that is thus offered to us will allow governments, communities and organisations to find freedom from the captivity that alcohol related harm represents at the population level.

The development of a theological model of addiction is represented here as arising out of a kind of dialogue between science and theology. In this dialogue, each party must show respect for the truth conveyed by the other. Therefore, if a theological model of addiction may be of value to science, a scientific understanding of addiction may also be informative to theology. This is not to deny the value of special revelation, but is rather a reminder to Christian theology of its incarnational context. Thus, if addiction might be understood as the division of a self drawn both towards sin and grace, it must also be understandable as a bio-psycho-social dependence syndrome which arises when human beings are subjected to particular environmental conditions. This is not to reduce sin and grace to considerations of neurochemistry and social conditioning, or to imagine that Christian theology should always and entirely be explicable in scientific terms. But it does remind theology that the 'power' of sin must be, at least partly, understandable in terms of a neurochemical or psychological account of what lies beneath the subjective compulsion for something that is not God. Similarly, biological accounts of mystical experience[1] should not appear theologically surprising or somehow contradictory of what theology has to say about the human condition.

John Robinson, in his book *The Human Face of God*, raised the question of whether or not Christ might have suffered from a mental disorder.[2] His conclusion, that such a possibility should be understood as consonant with the humanity of Christ, must also be considered applicable in the focus of this work upon the desirability of alcohol, and the nature of addictive disorder. Not that Christ in his humanity necessarily experienced addiction, but that the core experience of addiction, that of the divided self, would appear to be so intimately connected with what it means to be human that a fully human Christ must have entered into the subjective experience of what it means to be addicted. Indeed, another theological resource that could have been chosen alongside chapter 7 of Paul's letter to the Romans, and Augustine's *Confessions*, might have been the synoptic accounts of the

---

[1] D'Aquili and Newberg, 1999.　　　[2] Robinson, 1973, p. 7.

temptation of Christ in the wilderness.³ Anchoring our discussion in these texts might well have served to illustrate that addiction is not about *being* sinful or immoral so much as about being potentially vulnerable to the powers of sin and grace. And, indeed, a focus on Christ's conquest of the former power in this way, and his total submission to the latter, might well have further illuminated the importance of grace as the fundamental alternative to, or therapy for, addiction.

It was noted in Chapter 3 that there is an eschatological context to the ethics and theology of drunkenness, and this would seem to be the most appropriate place in which to conclude a Christian theological consideration of alcohol and addiction. Drunkenness and addiction are not necessarily actual harms or actual sins, but both of them certainly predispose to harm and to sin. Whereas addiction is presented here as a special case of the general condition of the divided self, and thus a particular temporal manifestation of the general human condition, drunkenness is a transient state of altered perception and judgement in which aspects of human vulnerability are enhanced or exaggerated, and over which rational control is impaired. Whereas human beings in this world are always likely to reflect a degree of division of self, which will be resolved finally only in union with Christ in an eschatological context, it is not necessarily the case that human beings should always be drunk or intoxicated. Indeed, it is a matter of social consensus that they should not be. Sobriety is properly expected as a condition for fulfilment of obligations towards self, family, employers or clients, and the wider community. Occasional drunkenness might not impair the ability to fulfil such obligations, but chronic or frequent drunkenness certainly will. Similarly, drunkenness might be understood as a state of impaired readiness for participation in the kingdom of God, both as it is to be experienced in the here and now, and as it is expected in the Christian eschatological context. The Christian who seriously desires the coming of that kingdom will not wish to be found, when it at last unexpectedly arrives, in a state of complete unreadiness for it.⁴

More importantly, drunkenness and addiction are both aspects of life in this world which are inconceivable in the eschatological context of the gathering together of all things in Christ himself.⁵ In Christ, perception and judgement will ultimately be illuminated by God himself. In Christ, all divisions of the self will finally be healed in perfect and eternal submission to the power of grace.

³ Matthew 4:1–11; Mark 1:12–13; Luke 4:1–13.  ⁴ Matthew 25:1–13; Luke 12:35–40; 1 Peter 4:3–5.
⁵ Ephesians 1:10.

# Bibliography

Ali, A. Y. (ed.). 2000. *The Holy Qur'an: Translation and Commentary.* Birmingham: IPCI: Islamic Vision.

American Psychiatric Association. 1994. *Diagnostic and Statistical Manual of Mental Disorders: DSM-IV.* 4th edn. Washington DC: American Psychiatric Association.

Anderson, P. 2002. *The Beverage Alcohol Industry's Social Aspects Organizations: A Public Health Warning.* St Ives: Eurocare.

Anonymous. 1995. 'Row over drinks industry attempt to "rubbish" alcohol report', *The Globe* 1: pp. 4–6.

Babor, T., Caetano, R., Casswell, S., Edwards, G., Giesbrecht, N., Graham, K., Grube, J., Gruenewald, P., Hill, L., Holder, H., Homel, R., Österberg, E., Rehm, J., Room, R., Rossow, I. 2003. *Alcohol: No Ordinary Commodity.* Oxford: Oxford University Press.

Bacchiocchi, S. 1989. *Wine in the Bible: A Biblical Study on the Use of Alcoholic Beverages.* Berrien Springs: Biblical Perspectives.

Barbour, I. G. 1998. *Religion and Science.* London: SCM Press.

Barrett, C. K. 1978. *The Gospel According to St John.* 2nd edn. London: SPCK.

1994. *Paul: An Introduction to His Thought.* London: Geoffrey Chapman (Davies, B., ed., Outstanding Christian Thinkers).

Beauchamp, D. E. 1976. 'Exploring new ethics for public policy: developing a fair alcohol policy', *Journal of Health Politics, Policy and Law* 1: pp. 338–354.

Beecher, L. 1845. *Six Sermons On the Nature, Occasions, Signs, Evils and Remedy of Intemperance.* 10th edn. New York: American Tract Society.

Bernasconi, R. 1992. 'At war within oneself: Augustine's phenomenology of the will in the *Confessions*', in Van Tongeren, P., Sars, P., Bremmers, C., Boey, K. (eds.), *Eros and Eris: Contributions to a Hermeneutical Phenomenology.* Dordrecht: Kluwer, pp. 57–65.

Berridge, V. 1990. 'The Society for the Study of Addiction 1884–1988', *British Journal of Addiction* 85: pp. 983–1087.

Best, E. 1982. *1 Peter.* Grand Rapids: Eerdmans (Clements, R. E., Black, M., eds., The New Century Bible Commentary).

Betz, H. D. 1979. *Galatians.* Philadelphia: Fortress (Koester, H., Epp, E. J., Funk, R. W., MacRae, G. W., Robinson, J. M., eds., Hermeneia).

Bridgett, T. E. 1876. *The Discipline of Drink: An Historical Enquiry into the Principles and Practice of the Catholic Church Regarding the Use, Abuse, and Disuse of Alcoholic Liquors, Especially in England, Ireland, and Scotland, from the 6th to the 16th Century.* London: Burns and Oates.

Briggs, J. H. Y. 1994. *The English Baptists of the Nineteenth Century,* III. Didcot: The Baptist Historical Society (Hayden, R., ed., A History of the English Baptists).

Brown, R. E. 1966. *The Gospel According to John: I–XII.* 2nd edn. New York: Doubleday (The Anchor Bible, 29).

Bruce, F. F. 1998. *The Epistle to the Galatians.* Grand Rapids: Eerdmans.

Burnaby, J. 1991. *Amor Dei: A Study of the Religion of St Augustine.* Norwich: Canterbury Press.

Burns, D. 1875. *Christendom and the Drink Curse: An Appeal to the Christian World for Efficient Action Against the Causes of Intemperance.* London: Partridge and Co.

Caetano, R. 1985. 'Alcohol dependence and the need to drink: a compulsion?', *Psychological Medicine* 15: pp. 463–469.

Carpenter, E. 1997. *Cantuar: The Archbishops in Their Office.* 3rd edn. London: Mowbray.

Carr, W., Capps, D., Gill, R., Obholzer, A., Page, R., van Deusen Hunsinger, D., Williams, R. (eds.). 2002. *The New Dictionary of Pastoral Studies.* London: SPCK.

Catholic Bishops' Conference of England and Wales. 1996. *The Common Good and the Catholic Church's Social Teaching.* London: Catholic Bishops' Conference of England and Wales.

Colson, F. H., Whitaker, G. H. (eds.). 1958. *Philo,* II. London: Heinemann (Warmington, E. H., ed., Loeb Classical Library).

 (eds.). 1968. *Philo,* III. London: Heinemann (Warmington, E. H., ed., Loeb Classical Library).

Committee on Intemperance, Convocation of the Province of Canterbury. 1869. *Report On Intemperance.* London: Longman, Green, Reader, and Dyer.

Conzelmann, H. 1981. *1 Corinthians.* Philadelphia: Fortress (Koester, H., Epp, E. J., Funk, R. W., MacRae, G. W., Robinson, J. M., eds., Hermeneia).

Cook, C. C. H. 1994. 'Aetiology of alcohol misuse', in Chick, J., Cantwell, R. (eds.), *Seminars in Psychiatry: Alcohol and Drug Misuse.* London: Royal College of Psychiatrists, pp. 94–125.

 2004. 'Addiction and spirituality', *Addiction* 99: pp. 539–551.

Cook, C. C. H., Gurling, H. M. D. 2001. 'Genetic predisposition to alcohol dependence and problems', in Heather, N., Peters, T. J., Stockwell, T. (eds.), *International Handbook of Alcohol Dependence and Problems.* Chichester: Wiley, pp. 257–279.

Coverley Veale, D. M. W. de. 1987. 'Exercise dependence', *British Journal of Addiction* 82: pp. 735–740.

Cranfield, C. E. B. 1995. *Romans: A Shorter Commentary.* Edinburgh: T. and T. Clark.

Cross, F. L., Livingstone, E. A. (eds.). 1997. *The Oxford Dictionary of the Christian Church.* 3rd edn. Oxford: Oxford University Press.

Cunningham, J. A., Sobell, L. C., Freedman, J. L., Sobell, M. B. 1994. 'Beliefs about the causes of substance abuse: a comparison of three drugs', *Journal of Substance Abuse* 6: pp. 219–226.

Dant, C. H. 1903. *Archbishop Temple.* London: Walter Scott.

D'Aquili, E., Newberg, A. B. 1999. *The Mystical Mind: Probing the Biology of Religious Experience.* Minneapolis: Fortress.

Davies, B., Evans, G. R. (eds.). 1998. *Anselm of Canterbury: The Major Works.* Oxford: Oxford University Press.

Davies, J. B. 2000. *The Myth of Addiction.* 2nd edn. Amsterdam: Harwood.

Dawson, D. A., Archer, L. D. 1993. 'Relative frequency of heavy drinking and the risk of alcohol dependence', *Addiction* 88: pp. 1509–1518.

Doctrine Commission of the General Synod of the Church of England 1997. *The Mystery of Salvation.* London: Church House Publishing. GS1155.

Dodd, C. H. 1967. *New Testament Studies.* Manchester: Manchester University Press.

Drummond, D. C. 1990. 'The relationship between alcohol dependence and alcohol related problems in a clinical population', *British Journal of Addiction* 85: pp. 357–366.

    2001. 'Theories of drug craving, ancient and modern', *Addiction* 96: pp. 33–46.

Dunn, J. D. G. 1988a. *Romans 1–8.* Dallas: Word (Hubbard, D. A., Barker, G. W., Martin, R. P., eds., Word Biblical Commentaries, 38a).

    1988b. *Romans 9–16.* Dallas: Word (Hubbard, D. A., Barker, G. W., Martin, R. P., eds., Word Biblical Commentaries, 38b).

    1993. *The Epistle to the Galatians.* London: A. and C. Black (Black's New Testament Commentaries).

    1998. *The Theology of Paul the Apostle.* Edinburgh: T. and T. Clark.

Edwards, G. 1977. 'The alcohol dependence syndrome: usefulness of an idea', in Edwards, G., Grant, M. (eds.), *Alcoholism: New Knowledge and New Responses.* London: Croom Helm, pp. 136–156.

    2000. *Alcohol: The Ambiguous Molecule.* Harmondsworth: Penguin.

Edwards, G., Anderson, P., Babor, T. F., Casswell, S., Ferrence, R., Giesbrecht, N., Godfrey, C., Holder, H. D., Lemmens, P., Mäkelä, K., Midanik, L. T., Norström, T., Österberg, E., Romelsjö, A., Room, R., Simpura, J., Skog, O.-J. 1994. *Alcohol Policy and the Public Good.* Oxford: Oxford University Press.

Edwards, G., Gross, M. 1976. 'Alcohol dependence: provisional description of a clinical syndrome', *British Medical Journal* 1: pp. 1058–1061.

Edwards, G., Gross, M. M., Keller, M., Moser, J., Room, R. 1977. *Alcohol Related Disabilities.* Geneva: World Health Organization.

Edwards, G., Marshall, E. J., Cook, C. C. H. 2003. *The Treatment of Drinking Problems: A Guide for the Helping Professions.* 4th edn. Cambridge: Cambridge University Press.

Edwards, J. [1754] 1969. *Freedom of the Will.* Indianapolis: Bobbs-Merrill.

Erens, B., Laiho, J. 2001. 'Alcohol consumption', in Erens, B., Primatesta, P., Prior, G. (eds.), *Health Survey for England: The Health of Minority Ethnic Groups '99*, 1. London: The Stationery Office, pp. 121–141.

Fee, G. D. 1987. *The First Epistle to the Corinthians.* Grand Rapids: Eerdmans (Stonehouse, N. B., Bruce, F. F., eds., The New International Commentary on the New Testament).

Felscher, H., Koenigsberg, R. (eds.). 1993. *Stedman's Pocket Medical Dictionary.* London: Williams and Wilkins.

Ferguson, E., McHugh, M. P., Norris, F. W. (eds.) 1999. *Encyclopedia of Early Christianity.* 2nd edn. New York: Garland.

Ferguson, S. B., Wright, D. F., Packer, J. I. (eds.). 1988. *New Dictionary of Theology.* Leicester: Inter-Varsity Press.

Fichter, J. H. 1982. *The Rehabilitation of Clergy Alcoholics: Ardent Spirits Subdued.* New York: Human Sciences Press.

Fingarette, H. 1989. *Heavy Drinking: The Myth of Alcoholism as a Disease.* Berkeley: University of California Press.

Francis, F. O., Sampley, J. P. 1984. *Pauline Parallels.* 2nd edn. Philadelphia: Fortress.

Frankfurt, H. G. 1971. 'Freedom of the will and the concept of a person', *The Journal of Philosophy* 68: pp. 5–20.

Freedman, D. N. (ed.). 1997. *The Anchor Bible Dictionary.* New York: Doubleday. CD-ROM.

Gelder, M., Gath, D., Mayou, R., Cowen, P. 1996. *Oxford Textbook of Psychiatry.* 3rd edn. Oxford: Oxford University Press.

Gill, R. 1997. *A Textbook of Christian Ethics.* 2nd edn. Edinburgh: T. and T. Clark.
    2004. 'Theological purity versus theological realism', *Crucible*: pp. 37–42.

Glatt, M. M., Cook, C. C. H. 1987. 'Pathological spending as a form of psychological dependence', *British Journal of Addiction* 82: pp. 1257–1258.

Goodwin, D. W., Johnson, J., Maher, C., Rappaport, A., Guze, S. B. 1969. 'Why people do not drink: a study of teetotalers', *Comprehensive Psychiatry* 10: pp. 209–214.

Groves, P., Farmer, R. 1994. 'Buddhism and addictions', *Addiction Research* 2: pp. 183–194.

Gusfield, J. R. 1962. 'Status conflicts and the changing ideologies of the American temperance movement', in Pittman, D. J., Snyder, C. R. (eds.), *Society, Culture and Drinking Patterns.* New York: Wiley, pp. 101–120.

Hannum, H. 1997a. 'The Dublin principles of cooperation among the beverage alcohol industry, governments, scientific researchers, and the public health community', *Alcohol and Alcoholism* 32: pp. 639–640.
    1997b. 'The Dublin principles of cooperation among the beverage alcohol industry, governments, scientific researchers, and the public health community', *Alcohol and Alcoholism* 32: pp. 641–648.

Harmon, A. M. (ed.). 1960. *Lucian*, 11. London: Heinemann (Page, T. E., Capps, E., Rouse, W. H. D., Post, L. A., Warmington, E. H., eds., The Loeb Classical Library).

Harrison, B. 1971. *Drink and the Victorians: The Temperance Question in England 1815–1872.* Pittsburgh: University of Pittsburgh Press.

Hart, T. 1997. 'Redemption and fall', in Gunton, C. E. (ed.), *The Cambridge Companion to Christian Doctrine.* Cambridge: Cambridge University Press, pp. 189–206.

Hasin, D., Paykin, A. 1999. 'Alcohol dependence and abuse diagnoses: concurrent validity in a nationally representative sample', *Alcoholism, Clinical and Experimental Research* 23: pp. 144–150.

Heather, N., Rollnick, S., Winton, M. 1983. 'A comparison of objective and subjective measures of alcohol dependence as predictors of relapse following treatment', *British Journal of Clinical Psychology* 22: pp. 11–17.

Herbermann, C. G., Pace, E. A., Pallen, C. B., Shahon, T. J., Wynne, J. J. (eds.). 1907. *The Catholic Encyclopedia,* 11. London: Caxton.

Hill, P., Murray, R., Thorley, A. 1987. *Essentials of Postgraduate Psychiatry.* London: Grune and Stratton.

Hill, S. Y. 1985. 'The disease concept of alcoholism: a review', *Drug and Alcohol Dependence* 16: 193–214.

Hollenbach, D. 2002. *The Common Good and Christian Ethics.* Cambridge: Cambridge University Press (Gill, R., ed., New Studies in Christian Ethics, 22).

Holloway, R. 2000. *Godless Morality.* Edinburgh: Canongate.

Houlden, J. L. 1989. *The Pastoral Epistles.* London: SCM Press.

Hughes, J., Cook, C. C. H. 1997. 'Disulfiram in the management of alcohol misuse: a review', *Addiction* 92: pp. 381–395.

Hyslop, R. M. 1931. *The Centenary of the Temperance Movement 1832–1932.* London: Independent Press.

International Center for Alcohol Policies. 2000a. *The Geneva Partnership On Alcohol: Towards a Global Charter.* Washington DC: International Center for Alcohol Policies.

2000b. *A New Force for Health.* Washington DC: International Center for Alcohol Policies.

James, W. 1985. *The Varieties of Religious Experience.* Harmondsworth: Penguin.

Janz, P. D. 2004. *God, the Mind's Desire.* Cambridge: Cambridge University Press.

Jordan, M. D. 1993. 'Theology and philosophy', in Kretzmann, N., Stump, E. (eds.), *The Cambridge Companion to Aquinas.* Cambridge: Cambridge University Press, pp. 232–251.

Kahler, C. W., Epstein, E. E., McCrady, B. S. 1995. 'Loss of control and inability to abstain: the measurement of and the relationship between two constructs in male alcoholics', *Addiction* 90: pp. 1025–1036.

Kalivas, P. W. 2004. 'Choose to study choice in addiction', *American Journal of Psychiatry* 161: pp. 193–194.

Kelly, J. N. D. 1990. *A Commentary on the Epistles of Peter and of Jude.* London: A. and C. Black (Chadwick, H., ed., Black's New Testament Commentaries).

Kent, B. 2002. 'Augustine's ethics', in Stump, E., Kretzmann, N. (eds.), *The Cambridge Companion to Augustine.* Cambridge: Cambridge University Press, pp. 205–233.

Kerr, N. 1888. *Inebriety.* London: Lewis.

Kreitman, N. 1986. 'Alcohol consumption and the prevention paradox', *British Journal of Addiction* 81: pp. 353–363.

Kroeger, R., Kroeger, C. 1978a. 'An inquiry into evidence of Maenadism in the Corinthian congregation', in Achtemeier, P. J. (ed.), *Society of Biblical Literature 1978 Seminar Papers*. Society of Biblical Literature, pp. 331–338.

Kroeger, R., Kroeger, C. C. 1978b. 'Pandemonium and silence at Corinth', *The Reformed Journal*: pp. 6–11.

Kurtz, E. 1991. *Not-God: A History of Alcoholics Anonymous*. Center City: Hazelden.

Lader, D., Meltzer, H. 2002. *Drinking: Adults' Behaviour and Knowledge in 2002*. London: Office for National Statistics.

Lee, S. (ed.). 1920. *Dictionary of National Biography*. 2nd supplement, 1901–1911. London: Oxford University Press.

Lees, F. R., Burns, D. 1880. *The Temperance Bible-Commentary*. London: Partridge.

Lender, M. 1973. 'Drunkenness as an offense in early New England', *Quarterly Journal of Studies on Alcohol* 34: pp. 353–366.

Lenters, W. 1985. *The Freedom We Crave*. Grand Rapids: Eerdmans.

Leverton, M., Buckingham, J., Naclerio, S., Crutcher, M. B., Alexander, B., Willersdorf, G., Montijn, S., Simpson, R., Jones, M., MacDonald, J. P., Botha, A. 2000. 'Drinks industry response', *Addiction* 95: pp. 1430–1431.

Levine, H. G. 1978. 'The discovery of addiction: changing conceptions of habitual drunkenness in America', *Journal of Studies on Alcohol* 39: pp. 143–174.

    1984. 'The alcohol problem in America: from temperance to alcoholism', *British Journal of Addiction* 79: pp. 109–119.

Little, H. 2000. 'Alcohol as a stimulant drug', *Addiction* 95: pp. 1751–1753.

Longenecker, R. N. 1990. *Galatians*. Dallas: Word (Metzger, B. M., Martin, R. P., Losie, L. A., eds., Word Biblical Commentary, 41).

Macdonald, A. M. (ed.). 1982. *Chambers Twentieth Century Dictionary*. Revised edn. Edinburgh: Chambers.

Macquarrie, J., Childress, J. (eds.). 1986. *A New Dictionary of Christian Ethics*. London: SCM.

McCormick, P. 1989. *Sin as Addiction*. New York: Paulist Press.

McCreanor, T., Casswell, S., Hill, L. 2000. 'ICAP and the perils of partnership', *Addiction* 95: pp. 179–185.

McDonald, W. J., Magner, J. A., McGuire, M. R. P., Whalen, J. P. (eds.). 1967. *New Catholic Encyclopedia*, 11. New York: McGraw-Hill.

McFadyen, A. 2000. *Bound to Sin: Abuse, Holocaust and the Christian Doctrine of Sin*. Cambridge: Cambridge University Press.

McInerny, R. 1993. 'Ethic', in Kretzmann, N., Stump, E. (eds.), *The Cambridge Companion to Aquinas*. Cambridge: Cambridge University Press, pp. 196–216.

Makower, F. 1989. *Faith or Folly?* London: Darton, Longman and Todd.

Malcolm, E. 1986. *'Ireland Sober, Ireland Free': Drink and Temperance in Nineteenth-Century Ireland*. Syracuse: Syracuse University Press.

Mann, W. E. 2002. 'Augustine on evil and original sin', in Stump, E., Kretzmann, N. (eds.), *The Cambridge Companion to Augustine*. Cambridge: Cambridge University Press, pp. 40–48.

Mathewes, C. T. 2001. *Evil and the Augustinian Tradition.* Cambridge: Cambridge University Press.

Maxwell, M. A. 1950. 'The Washingtonian movement', *Quarterly Journal of Studies on Alcohol* 11: pp. 410–451.

May, G. G. 1988. *Addiction and Grace.* San Francisco: HarperCollins.

Mercadante, L. A. 1996. *Victims and Sinners.* Louisville: Westminster John Knox Press.

Meyer, R. E. 1996. 'The disease called addiction: emerging evidence in a 200-year debate', *Lancet* 347: pp. 162–166.

Midanik, L. T. 1999. 'Drunkenness, feeling the effects and 5+ measures', *Addiction* 94: pp. 887–897.

Miller, W. R., C'de Baca, J. 2001. *Quantum Change.* New York: Guilford.

Mounce, W. D. 2000. *The Pastoral Epistles.* Nashville: Nelson (Metzger, B. M., Martin, R. P., Losie, L. A., eds., Word Biblical Commentary, 46).

National Institute on Drug Abuse. 1977. *An Evaluation of the Teen Challenge Treatment Program.* Rockville: National Institute on Drug Abuse.

Newman, J. H. [1852] 1996. *The Idea of a University.* New Haven: Yale.

O'Donnell, J. J. 2002. 'Augustine: his time and lives', in Stump, E., Kretzmann, N. (eds.), *The Cambridge Companion to Augustine.* Cambridge: Cambridge University Press, pp. 8–25.

Orford, J. 2001. 'Addiction as excessive appetite', *Addiction* 96: pp. 15–31.

Parry, C. D. H. 2000. 'ICAP's agenda of concern to developing countries', *Addiction* 95: pp. 192–193.

Paulus, M. P. 2005. 'Neurobiology of decision-making: quo vadis?', *Cognitive Brain Research* 23: pp. 2–10.

Pine-Coffin, R. S. (ed.). 1961. *Saint Augustine: Confessions.* Harmondsworth: Penguin.

Plantinga, C. 1996. *Not the Way It's Supposed to Be: A Breviary of Sin.* Grand Rapids: Eerdmans.

Playfair, W. L. 1991. *The Useful Lie.* Wheaton: Crossway.

Porter, J. 2002. *Moral Action and Christian Ethics.* Cambridge: Cambridge University Press (Gill, R., ed., New Studies in Christian Ethics).

Prime Minister's Strategy Unit 2004. *Alcohol Harm Reduction Strategy for England.* London: Strategy Unit.

Raw, M. 1994. 'News and notes', *Addiction* 89: pp. 1333–1337.

Reich, T., Edenberg, H. J., Goate, A., Williams, J. T., Rice, J. P., Van Eerdewegh, P., Foroud, T., Hesselbrock, V., Schuckit, M. A., Bucholz, K., Porjesz, B., Li, T.-K., Conneally, M., Nurnberger, J. I., Tischfield, J. A., Crowe, R., Cloninger, C. R., Wu, W., Shears, S., Carr, K., Crose, C., Willig, C., Begleiter, H. 1998. 'A genome-wide search for genes affecting the risk for alcohol dependence', *American Journal of Medical Genetics* 81: pp. 207–215.

Reicke, B. 1980. *The Epistles of James, Peter, and Jude.* 2nd edn. Garden City: Doubleday (Albright, W. F., Freedman, D. N., eds., The Anchor Bible, 37).

Ridderbos, H. N. 1977. *Paul: An Outline of His Theology.* London: SPCK.

Rix, K. J. B. 1989. '"Alcohol intoxication" or "drunkenness": is there a difference?', *Medicine, Science and Law* 29: pp. 100–106.

Robinson, J. A. T. 1973. *The Human Face of God.* London: SCM Press.

Rolleston, J. D. 1927. 'Alcoholism in classical antiquity', *The British Journal of Inebriety* 24: pp. 101–120.

Room, R. 1997. 'Alcohol, the individual and society: what history teaches us', *Addiction* 92 (Suppl. 1): 7–11.

    2004. 'Disabling the public interest: alcohol strategies and policies for England', *Addiction* 99: pp. 1083–1089.

Royal College of Psychiatrists. 1986. *Alcohol: Our Favourite Drug.* London: Tavistock.

Rush, B. 1943–4. 'An inquiry into the effects of ardent spirits upon the human body and mind with an account of the means of preventing and of the remedies for curing them', *Quarterly Journal of Studies on Alcohol* 4: pp. 325–341.

Ryder, C. 1906. *Life of Thomas Edward Bridgett C. SS. R.* London: Burns and Oates.

Schaler, J. A. 2002. *Addiction Is a Choice.* Chicago: Open Court.

Seevers, M. H. 1962. 'Medical perspectives on habituation and addiction', *Journal of the American Medical Association* 181: pp. 92–98.

Seller, S. C. 1985. 'Alcohol abuse in the Old Testament', *Alcohol and Alcoholism* 20: pp. 69–76.

Sheldrake, P. 1998. *Befriending Our Desires.* London: Darton, Longman and Todd.

Siegler, M. 1968. 'Models of alcoholism', *Quarterly Journal of Studies on Alcohol* 29: pp. 571–591.

Skehan, P. W., Di Lella, A. A. 1987. *The Wisdom of Ben Sira.* New York: Doubleday (Albright, W. F., Freedman, D. N., eds., The Anchor Bible, 39).

Smith, R. 1994. 'Questioning academic integrity', *British Medical Journal* 309: pp. 1597–1598.

Stark, R., Bainbridge, W. S. 1996. *Religion, Deviance and Social Control.* New York: Routledge.

Stephen, L., Lee, S. (eds.). 1908. *Dictionary of National Biography*, III. London: Smith, Elder and Co.

Stump, E. 2002. 'Augustine on free will', in Stump, E., Kretzmann, N. (eds.), *The Cambridge Companion to Augustine.* Cambridge: Cambridge University Press, pp. 124–147.

Suliman, H. 1983. 'Alcohol and Islamic faith', *Drug and Alcohol Dependence* 11: pp. 63–65.

Sulkunen, P. 1997. 'Ethics of alcohol policy in a saturated society', *Addiction* 92: pp. 1117–1122.

Sullivan, J. (ed.). 1965. *Petronius: The Satyricon and the Fragments.* Harmondsworth: Penguin.

Theissen, G. 1987. *Psychological Aspects of Pauline Theology.* Edinburgh: T. and T. Clark.

Thomas, C. E. 1996. 'Sports', in Van Ness, P. H. (ed.), *Spirituality and the Secular Quest.* London: SCM Press, pp. 498–519 (Cousins, E., ed., World Spirituality).

Thompson, R. D. 1994. *Teen Challenge of Chattanooga, TN: Survey of Alumni.* Springfield: Teen Challenge.

Tomasino, A. J. 1992. 'History repeats itself: the 'fall' and Noah's drunkenness', *Vetus Testamentum* 42: pp. 128–130.

Trotter, T. 1988. *An Essay, Medical, Philosophical, and Chemical, On Drunkenness and Its Effects on the Human Body.* London: Routledge.

Vaillant, G. E. 1983. *The Natural History of Alcoholism: Causes, Patterns, and Paths to Recovery.* Cambridge, MA: Harvard University Press.

Vardy, P., Grosch, P. 1994. *The Puzzle of Ethics.* London: Fount.

Vellacott, P. (ed.). 1971. *Euripides: The Bacchae and Other Plays* Harmondsworth: Penguin (Radice, B., Baldick, R., eds., Penguin Classics).

Victor, M., Adams, R. D. 1977. 'Alcohol', in Thorn, G. W., Adams, R. D., Braunwald, E., Isselbacher, K. J., Petersdorf, R. G. (eds.), *Harrison's Principles of Internal Medicine.* 8th edn. Tokyo: McGraw-Hill Kogakusha, pp. 707–716.

Wakefield, G. S. (ed.). 1988. *A Dictionary of Christian Spirituality.* London: SCM Press.

Wanigaratne, S., Wallace, W., Pullin, J., Keaney, F., Farmer, R. 1990. *Relapse Prevention for Addictive Behaviours.* Oxford: Blackwell Scientific Publications.

West, R. 2001. 'Theories of addiction', *Addiction* 96: pp. 3–13.

Wiederkehr, D. 1979. *Belief in Redemption.* London: SPCK.

Winskill, P. T. 1892a. *The Temperance Movement and Its Workers: A Record of the Social, Moral, Religious, and Political Progress,* I. London: Blackie and Son.

    1892b. *The Temperance Movement and Its Workers: A Record of the Social, Moral, Religious, and Political Progress,* II. London: Blackie and Son.

    1892c. *The Temperance Movement and Its Workers: A Record of the Social, Moral, Religious, and Political Progress,* III. London: Blackie and Son.

    1892d. *The Temperance Movement and Its Workers: A Record of the Social, Moral, Religious, and Political Progress,* IV. London: Blackie and Son.

Winstanley, G. 1995. 'Comments on the European Alcohol Action Plan', *Addiction* 90: pp. 583. Letter.

Wolters, C. (ed.). 1966. *Julian of Norwich: Revelations of Divine Love.* London: Penguin.

World Health Organization 1992. *The ICD-10 Classification of Mental and Behavioural Disorders: Clinical Descriptions and Diagnostic Guidelines.* Geneva: World Health Organization.

World Health Organization 1999. *Global Status Report on Alcohol.* Geneva: World Health Organization.

World Health Organization 2004. *Global Status Report: Alcohol Policy.* Geneva: World Health Organization.

World Health Organization Regional Office for Europe 1995. *European Charter on Alcohol.* Copenhagen: World Health Organization Regional Office for Europe.

Ziesler, J. 1989. *Paul's Letter to the Romans.* London: SCM Press.

    1990. *Pauline Christianity.* Oxford: Oxford University Press.

# Index of Bible references

# Index of names and subjects

1001806

Printed in Great Britain by
Amazon.co.uk, Ltd.,
Marston Gate.